Table of Contents

Acknowledgements   vii

An Introduction to Murder in Canada   1

Chapter One   Killings: Our History   11

Chapter Two   Killing Family   72

Chapter Three   Killing Acquaintances   123

Chapter Four   Killing for Money   161

Chapter Five   Killing for Sex   201

Chapter Six   Emotionally Disturbed and   243
                  Mentally Handicapped Killing

THE LAST DANCE:

MURDER IN CANADA

THE LAST DANCE:
MURDER IN CANADA

by Neil Boyd

Prentice-Hall Canada Inc., Scarborough, Ontario

Excerpt from Audrey Thomas, ''Real Mothers'', reprinted by permission of Audrey Thomas.
Excerpt from Bryan Adams and Jim Vallance, ''Native Son'', reprinted by permission of Bryan Adams and Jim Vallance.
Excerpt from Leonard Cohen, ''There Ain't No Cure for Love'', reprinted by permission. ©1986 Leonard Cohen.

Canadian Cataloguing in Publication Data

Boyd, Neil, 1951-
  The last dance: murder in Canada

ISBN 0-13-523887-0

1. Murder — Canada. 2. Crime and criminals —
Canada. I. Title.

HV6535.C3B69 1988   364.1'523'0971   C88-094465-X

©1988 by Prentice Hall Canada Inc., Scarborough, Ontario

Prentice-Hall Inc., Englewood Cliffs, *New Jersey*
Prentice-Hall International, Inc., *London*
Prentice-Hall of Australia, Pty., *Sydney*
Prentice-Hall of India Pvt., Ltd., *New Delhi*
Prentice-Hall of Japan, Inc., *Toyko*
Prentice-Hall of Southeast Asia (Pte.) Ltd., *Singapore*
Editora Prentice-Hall do Brasil Ltda., *Rio de Janeiro*
Prentice-Hall Hispanoamericana, S.A., *Mexico*

Production Editor: Sharyn Rosart
Design: Dave Peden
Manufacturing Buyer: Don Blair
Composition: Jay Tee Graphics
ISBN: 0-13-523887-0
Printed and bound in Canada by Gagné Printing Ltd.
1 2 3 4 5 G 92 91 90 89 88

Acknowledgements

This book is an attempt to combine academic analysis with popular culture — to describe killings in a way that will both interest and inform the reader. For the most part, I am telling stories — about people who kill family, about people who kill their friends, and so on.

But this is not only an exercise in description. Murder has always evoked strong emotional responses and the killings presented in this book are no different. These stories are often upsetting and horrifying, and occasionally disgusting. What I am going to tell you about killers is, however, not what you usually hear in the popular media and probably not consistent with your sense of what these people are like.

This study of murder had three major sources of data. The first was the National Archives' Capital Case Files, 1867 to 1962. I randomly selected one murder case from each of these 96 years, and then sifted through each file, xeroxing relevant documents — police files, memoranda to Cabinet, parts or all of the trial transcript, psychiatric reports, letters from the public, and newspaper clippings. The 96 cases produced about 5,000 pages of documentation.

I owe my greatest debt for this research, and generally speaking, to Isabel Otter. In this instance, she helped to streamline collection of the data and shared responsibility for the selection of relevant documents. Her support throughout this project was indispensable, whether as an editor, or as my wife.

The staff of the National Archives were consistently helpful during our time in Ottawa; particular thanks to Jim Whalen for his advice, and to Sylvie Mackenzie and Duncan Roberts of Access Restrictions for their many hours of reviewing files. The Office of the Privy Council was also prompt and cooperative in making available, via the *Access to Information Act*, minutes of Cabinet meetings covering each execution or commutation of death from 1959 to 1962.

The second part of this study involved interviewing 35 men and five women now serving time for either first or second degree murder, and asking them about their lives before the killing, about the killing itself and why it happened, and about their lives after the killing. These interviews were tape-recorded and transcribed, and produced about 1,000 printed pages.

I thought that I should ask people who had significant experience in prison to conduct the interviews, given the sensitive nature of the discussion, and so left most of this work to three women — Liz Elliott, who conducted half of the interviews and then transcribed and printed the contents of all 40 tapes, Chris Bruckert, and Judi Gedye. The transcripts have been a crucial part of this project and I am very thankful for all of this time, effort and skill.

I would particularly like to express my gratitude to the 40 men and women who volunteered for these interviews — with no benefit but the opportunity to tell the stories of their killings to an interested listener. In many ways, their statements form the crucible in which this book is cast.

The third and final source of data collection — the Homicide Return of the Canadian Centre for Justice Statistics — has given us a numerical backdrop against which to place the human or qualitative experience of murder. Thanks to Joanne Lacroix and Sharon Longchamps for their provision of unpublished data. I'd also like to acknowledge the value of one particular publication, *Homicide in Canada: A Statistical Synopsis*. Some 12 years after its release, it remains our most comprehensive empirical analysis of the phenomenon of murder. One of the authors of that report — Bob Gaucher — has greatly facilitated this research, in a number of different ways.

A number of research grants have also made much of this study possible. I would like to acknowledge, in this respect, the assistance of a President's Research Grant, Simon Fraser University, of the Steel Fund, Simon Fraser University, and of the contributions programme of the Solicitor-General, Canada.

Finally, there are a number of other individuals and organizations to be thanked for a number of different kinds of assistance: John Lowman, Bob Menzies, Simon Verdun-Jones, Margaret Jackson, Nola Jones, Robbie Robidoux, Jimmy Chan, Rob and Dave Hocking, Heather Prittie, John Otter, Bob Cooper, Mike Stoian, Ron Cooney, RCMP Superintendent Ari Oosthoek, Correctional Services Canada, Iris Skeoch of Penguin Books, and Tanya Long and Sharyn Rosart of Prentice-Hall Canada.

A few years ago, in the city, she had come home from school and announced, at dinner, that a policeman had come to the school and given a talk about "strangers." Her mother and father glanced quickly at one another. A little girl, her lunchbox beside her, had been found dead in a ditch.

"And what are strangers?" asked her father gently, curious as to what she had been told, yet wanting to keep the story light.

The child's reply was very serious.

"Strangers are usually men."

— Audrey Thomas, "Real Mothers"

An Introduction

to Murder in Canada

Canada is a more violent country in the late 1980s than it was 30 years ago. In the late Fifties and early Sixties we had half as many homicides per capita as today, less reported assault and less robbery; the situation was much the same in the United States. In both countries the period of critical change occurred between 1966 and 1975; the homicide rate more than doubled and convictions for most kinds of violent crime escalated rapidly.

It is tempting to conclude that this happened because we became too lenient. But to understand why we will have more killings per capita in 1988 than we did in 1958, we have to turn our thoughts away from the penalties that we impose and towards the events of the late Sixties and early Seventies. After the key period of growth in homicide rates between 1966 and 1975, the proportional figures have remained relatively constant. In the late 1980s our country experiences the same number and rate of killings as it did during the mid-Seventies — about 650 homicides annually or approximately 2.5 killings per year for every 100,000 Canadians.

Between 1966 and 1975 there were significant changes in the nature and structure of Canadian social life — changes that remain with us today. The divorce rate in Canada exploded after 1966, after a generation of stability. The greatest increase occurred in 1968, after a liberalization of the country's *Divorce Act*. The rate continued to climb from the late Sixties through the mid-Seventies. The dissolution of a marriage in Canada was over four times as likely in 1975 as in 1966.

The technology of birth control, first made available in the early 1960s, gave women the opportunity to treat their sexuality as something other than property for the marriage bed. This new ability to control the risk of pregnancy provided women with some measure of the sexual freedom that men had traditionally enjoyed. The women's liberation movement organized and developed these sentiments and others, providing an ideological framework in which women could place their changing lifestyles.

At the same time, women were entering the labour force in unprecedented numbers; there were 2.3 million women working in Canada in 1966 and 5.5 million working in 1975. In the midst of this increasing sexual and economic autonomy, both men and women were drinking more. Alcohol consumption in Canada rose by over 50% per capita during this decade.[1]

The late Sixties and early Seventies were also a time of expansion for the distribution of illegal drugs. One result was more than a tripling of what Statistics Canada calls "unsolved gangland killings" — deaths usually arising from arguments over territory or violent disagreements over what one might term business ethics. This was an era in which the slogans of youth openly challenged parental mores — the generation under 30 urged its elders to "make love, not war," and, in a somewhat more rash moment, to "tune in, turn on, and drop out." The slogans provoked a backlash in the same way as the increasing emancipation of women provoked a backlash — and the addition of alcohol and other drugs was only more grist for the mill.

This was also the peak of the baby boom. The post-war babies — those born between 1946 and 1955 — created a population bulge when they reached the crime-prone years of young adulthood. Given that 90% of killings are committed by men between the ages of 16 and 40, we can expect more murder and manslaughter if the size of this particular age category increases.

This cluster of difficult social changes was particularly troubling for Canadian men. Males have always been responsible for the overwhelming majority of violent crime — our most recent figures indicate that they are about 10 times more likely to kill than Canadian women. The story of murder, the most serious of all homicide offences, is fairly described as the story of male violence, whether directed at women, or at other males. One recent study indicates that 98% of Canada's convicted murderers are men.

On those rare occasions when women kill, they are proportionately more likely than men to commit the offence of manslaughter. They tend to kill almost exclusively for reasons of passion — in blind rages. Women kill family members and those they know well. Men kill for money and sex — in addition to killing family members and acquaintances. Some will argue that this difference is a matter of biological destiny, but I am far from convinced by this argument. Violence is a learned response and our culture has consistently rewarded men for aggression in a wide range of settings and circumstances.

But what are we to do about this annual toll of 650 killings? The question of appropriate punishment for killing another human being has been with us for as long as we have been a nation. Between 1867 and 1962 Canada hanged 693 men and 13 women who had killed. It is virtually inevitable that, among these, we hanged a number of innocent people. In my own selection of 96 capital cases, I found four in which there was no sound evidence linking the accused with the crime, and in which innocence seemed more likely than guilt — the convictions of Bobby Cook, John Davidoff, Wilbert Coffin, and Abraham Steinberg. Their stories are in this book.

I may be wrong about one or two of these men, but I doubt very much that I am wrong about all of them. And, had I looked at the files of all 693 men that Canada hanged, I suspect, given existing probabilities, that I would have found at least another 10 cases of a similar kind.

It is highly unlikely that Nova Scotia's Donald Marshall is the only Canadian ever to have been wrongfully convicted of a killing. What comes out of rereading old murder files is the realization that we have been fallible in our judgements of guilt and innocence — and that as a consequence of our fallibility, we have hanged innocent people.

Capital punishment is not related in any systematic way to the amount of violent death that we experience annually. Study after study has concluded that we will not lower our homicide rate by imposing the death penalty. The most recent and comprehensive of these empirical reports, analyzing reported data from 110 countries, has demonstrated that this is as true of the global community as it is of Canada.[2]

We must also recognize that most killings are defined by our courts as acts of manslaughter, that is, crimes committed "in the heat of passion caused by sudden provocation." The increase in homicide that we experienced between 1966 and 1975 was primarily an increase in manslaughter — as defined by our courts.

As a consequence, it is more accurate to say that we have experienced a rapid escalation in our *manslaughter* rate than to say that we have experienced an increase in our murder rate. And in this context, the circumstances that underlie crimes of passion — alcohol, sexual betrayal, separation and divorce — become particularly relevant.

The reasons for homicide in Canada haven't really changed much in this century. About 80% of convicted murderers still kill either family or acquaintances. The more frightening killings — for money or sex, or for the most bizarre of reasons — are proportionately about as common in Canada today as they were a generation ago. And the percentage of murders committed by strangers has not changed in over a decade.

But the specific issue of reducing killings, which is part of the larger issue of reducing social violence, remains unresolved. Before we address these points, however, we need to place Canada's killings within a global context. Cross-national comparisons suggest that our country has a relatively low murder rate, compared with other nations. The United States has 20,000 murders annually, in comparison with our 600, a rate of killing that is about four times our own. Britain and Japan both have, however, about half as much murder per capita as we do; Australia and the Netherlands have close to twice as much.

The United States is a less civil society than Canada. With a cult of individualism that makes confrontation almost inevitable, disparities of wealth that significantly exceed Canadian standards of fairness, and a culture that has made the right to bear arms into a national fetish, our good friends to the south have stacked the deck against themselves, at least in the matter of interpersonal violence. Britain and Japan are more civil societies, with less severe sanctions for those who kill. Japan imposes an average term of imprisonment for murder of about five years. As a general rule, countries with the greatest numbers of killings typically impose the most severe penalties for murder. And countries with relatively few killings typically impose less severe penalties.

I have already stated that it is certain changes in Canadian social life that influence the amount of interpersonal violence that we experience. But we also like to think that the punishments we impose are critical. It is somehow comforting to believe that if we treat murderers more harshly, there will be less public interest in committing such a crime.

But the reality is more complex. The amount of murder that we experience doesn't appear to relate to changes in law, and we must remember that the overwhelming majority of murderers will ultimately be released into the community. Fewer than one per cent will kill again.

We have no evidence that long jail terms will make our communities more safe. For the most part, the lengthy minimum terms for first and second degree murder simply make life more difficult both for those who work in our penitentiaries and those who are confined there. A man facing 25 years in jail is a man who has very little to lose. In a maximum security penitentiary like B.C.'s Kent Institution or Ontario's Millhaven, a visitor can feel the tension. For the prisoner, this tension really only recedes after transfer to lower-security prisons — a signal that a man is on his way to the street.

The mandatory minimum sentences that we have for murder — 25 years for first degree and 10 years for second — may seem appropriate, but they will not help us. The person who has lived for 20 or 25 years in an institution will be poorly equipped for independence, and potentially either a threat or, more likely, a liability to the community upon return. As prolonged isolation in a penitentiary only increases our social risks, the goal of our corrections service should be earlier community reintegration of offenders. The 25-year mandatory minimum term for first degree murder could be lowered to 10 years in penitentiary and the current 10-year mandatory minimum for second degree murder could be lowered to five years in penitentiary — without any identifiable loss in community safety.

An alternative reform is that of collapsing the legal definitions of first and second degree murder into a single category of murder. As you will see with the cases that follow, the line between first and second degree murder has not been drawn — and probably cannot be drawn — in a reliable manner. The only reason for creating two kinds of murder in 1961 was to separate those deserving capital punishment from those deserving life sentences — and the difficulties that we encountered in determining which killers should die are no different from the difficulties that we now encounter in determining who should be found guilty of first degree murder and who should be found guilty of second.

There may be cases like Clifford Olson's, in which a judge might want to set a 25-year minimum term before eligibility for parole, but our criminal law should not permit the passing of such an extreme sentence as a matter of course. We can give Canadian judges the discretionary power to sentence murderers like Olson to very lengthy minimum terms without requiring that all those found guilty of murder be similarly treated.

I am not arguing for less social control of killers, but for a realignment of our present practices and priorities. We should, generally speaking, decrease the time murderers spend in prison and correspondingly increase both community support and supervision. If we accept the reality that most of Canada's murderers will ultimately return to their communities

— and current legislation does — then we ought to pursue the objective of release from the point of the killer's initial entry into prison.

This suggestion will require fundamental change in Canada's parole system. Members of our national and provincial Parole Boards are not really any more accurate than the rest of us in their predictions of an individual's readiness for release. The best guesses are based on past criminal record and age, not on any specialized psychiatric or psychological expertise. Beyond such objective measures, the prediction of future criminal behaviour is little more than speculation. It is, as a number of researchers have demonstrated, no better than flipping coins in the courtroom.

But the arbitrariness of the parole system notwithstanding, the support and supervision provided by parole officers to those released early from life terms should not be abandoned. There should be some recognition, however, of the incompatibility of these two roles. We need to provide both support and supervision, at least during the early stages of release, but we should not expect a single person to perform both functions. A parole officer cannot be, in the same instant, a friend and an informer. Ideally our parole service should assign these separate roles to separate individuals.

The decision to grant parole for the men and women convicted of murder is, of course, taken very seriously. And if the conviction is for first degree murder — the most serious criminal charge that an individual in Canada can face, barring treason — there will be even greater caution. Section 214 of our *Criminal Code* defines murder as first degree when it is planned and deliberate, when it is carried out under contract, when the victim is a police officer or prison guard, when it occurs during a hijacking, kidnapping or hostage-taking, or when it occurs during a sexual assault. All other killings, outside of those determined to be manslaughter, are defined as second degree murder.

This book describes a number of first and second degree murders, but it is not organized around these legal themes. I begin with a chapter titled "Killings: Our History," and follow it with five descriptive chapters: "Killing Family," "Killing Acquaintances," "Killing for Money," Killing for Sex," and "Emotionally Disturbed and Mentally Handicapped Killing." I have chosen these categories because they cover the range of murder in Canada — the annual toll of 650 murders can be broken down into these five types. I have chosen to write about more than 40 of the 136 murder cases that I studied in detail. From 96 archival cases, I chose either those with the most complete files available or those that were historically representative. Out of 40 transcribed interviews I chose the ones that yielded the richest description.

You will find common themes as you read. Canadians convicted of murder are, for the most part, socially disadvantaged. They approach life with poorly developed social skills, lacking what we might call social intelligence. In some cases they are miserable, just as likely to kill themselves as they are to kill others. They are typically working class or poorer, and occasionally involved in the business of crime — living off prostitution, distributing illegal drugs or planning armed robberies or contract killings.

Drug abuse is a prominent feature of their lives. There are some killings related to the distribution of heroin, amphetamines, marijuana, and cocaine. In the absence of government regulation, the industry regulates itself with guns and knives. But the drug of choice in the matter of violence is alcohol, a relevant factor in about 30% of all killings.

For the most part, murder in Canada is simply human tragedy. Our killers are usually confused and angry men; they are rarely predators. Over the past 10 years I have spoken with about 50 men convicted of homicide offences. I count a couple of them as friends, and for the most part, I like them.

But I've also met killers I would not want released and killers I don't like. In telling the stories in this book I have tried to keep my own opinions out of my descriptions, preferring that you draw your own conclusions from available evidence. As I indicated in my acknowledgements, my primary objective is to describe the phenomenon of killing in Canada.

My chapter titles reflect the empirical reality of murder in our country: killing for reasons of anger, hatred, quarrel, or revenge constitutes 80% of all murder in Canada, with killings of family and killings of acquaintances each accounting for half of the total. Killing for money represents 10%; killing for sex five per cent, and killing by the emotionally disturbed another five per cent.

This evidence speaks for itself — most murderers are basically ordinary people in socially and economically desperate circumstances. They were fuelled by alcohol or other drugs, and killed family and friends, usually over money or sexual betrayal. With contract killings, killings for sex and killing as a result of emotional disturbance, some of the portraits become a little more frightening. These tend to be the men, and very occasionally, women, who were either predators or close to the edge of what the law calls "insane."

But tendencies are not set in stone. Human beings are too complex to fit comfortably into the categories that we impose on them, and a human being who has killed is really no different. The fact that a man is a murderer tells you something important about him, but it represents only a part, albeit an indelible part, of his life.

[1] For empirical substantiation of these points see Statistics Canada, *Divorce: Law and the Family in Canada*, Ministry of Supply and Services, Ottawa, 1983, 89; *Sales of Alcoholic Beverages by volume and per capita*, Statistics Canada, *CAT: 63-202*, Annual, 1966-1984; and *Labour Force, Canada, Females, 15 years and over*, Statistics Canada *CAT 71-201*

[2] Dane Archer and Rosemary Gartner, *Violence and Crime in Cross-National Perspective*, Yale University Press, New Haven, 1984.

Chapter One

KILLINGS: OUR HISTORY

Gordon Parker was the youngest in a family of three boys. His father was an alcoholic who drifted away from home when Parker was still a child. His mother raised him on her own. "She worked very, very hard all her life.... I probably was mothered and pampered to the point where it did me more harm than good."[1]

Parker quit school when he was in Grade Eight and drifted into religion. "My mother, when I was a young child, had studied with them and I remember going from door to door. The Jehovah's Witnesses call it 'witnessing', or field service."

He was 15 and very unhappy. His brothers had been offered the religion and ultimately rejected it, but to Gordon it seemed a way out of his misery. "I asked my mother why is the world the way it is and how are we having all these problems, what's the future going to hold...all these big questions...and she told me basically the Jehovah's Witness theory and that got me into it. That gave me all the answers to life. So that pretty much guided my life the next 10 years, 'cause I tried to be a good JW."

Parker occasionally lashed out at others in his misery. When he was about 13, seeing a three-year-old playing alone, he used a slingshot to hit her in the back with a stone. "She never knew where it come from but she cried and yelled and went into the house." When his best friend was given a new bicycle, Parker went over to his house and scratched it up. "It gave me pleasure to realize how unhappy somebody else was going to be, like me. I wanted to make somebody as unhappy as I was. That's my indirect way of hurting people."

When he was about 16, Parker dropped out of his religion. He had started masturbating, and felt very guilty about it. He couldn't square his behaviour with life among the Witnesses. He went to work as a disc jockey with a small American radio station. "Little, small stations, working my way up. And that's what I really loved, that was my purpose, my new purpose in life. But all the while, I couldn't forget my religion, so I started going back, attending the meetings again, this time at different congregations."

He had a mission when he returned to the fold of the Witnesses. He wanted to find a wife among "the sisters"; he was impressed by the happy couples who came into meetings with their children, and decided that was what he wanted. "So I went on my search for a sister, visiting different congregations on the pretense of being this spiritually strong brother. So I was being deceptive and pretending to be somebody that I wasn't. And it didn't work. The sisters weren't interested in me."

His life was deteriorating in other ways. He tried to commit suicide by overdosing with pills. He had also stolen an expensive camera, shoplifted food for himself, and earrings and other jewellery for the sisters. The camera theft caught up with him and when the local sheriff started asking questions about it, he decided to leave town, moving to another part of the United States, thousands of miles away.

He was put up by a local Witness family when he arrived, and the next morning he met two sisters visiting from Canada, one of whom he would later marry. He spent three days with her. "Gail just had a very shy, unthreatening way about her, a very soft sort of a voice. I could talk with her and joke around with her. I couldn't do this with the other sisters. And I could tell right away that intellectually...well, I guess morally too...she was superior to me, which intimidated me a little bit, but I didn't know it enough at that time."

Before she returned to Canada, Parker managed to get her to admit that she was interested in him. "I said, I've got two things I can do. Either stay here and save more money or move immediately by you where I can date you. I want to get to know you. And she opened the doors by saying that would be nice, I can get to know you. She didn't commit herself, but that was all the commitment I needed. So that was it. I was hooked."

He moved to a city near her about three months later and they began to date. She had two young children from a previous marriage and was wary of making another mistake with men, but was pleased with the attention and praise that this chubby young man was giving her. Parker asked her to marry him, but she asked him to give their relationship five years first. "She saw my immaturity, she saw that she wasn't ready, and she wasn't too sure about it."

But when another sister told him that if he threatened to move, Gail would marry him, Parker had the solution to his pursuit. He put the pressure on by planning his departure and just before he left town, she agreed on marriage. "I said, if I go...and get things set up and build a life in a few months, a year, whatever, would you agree to come if I send for you? I'll get a house ready, and furniture, you know. She said yeah."

Parker's plan didn't work out exactly the way he had hoped, but later that year he and Gail did get married, down in the United States. In August, 1981 they were living in an apartment with the two children. "So here I was in a damn machine-shop job, which I hated, working 10 hours a day. Didn't even have furniture in the apartment, except for beds. Didn't have a phone. Had a car, that's about it. So the payments for just all that alone kept me down. I could never afford to get anything. So she was very depressed. The kids were unhappy."

He stopped going to the Witnesses' meetings, talked of suicide, and wallowed about the house in self-pity. Parker also found out that he and Gail were not sexually compatible. Witness doctrine prohibits sex before wedding vows, and Parker was very inexperienced. "I'd only had a few, a couple, three experiences before in my life. And the times we did have sex together, Gail and I, it was very tension-filled, it wasn't pleasurable."

Parker figures that he was "oversexed" and that his wife had a "low sex drive," "so I went off and watched pornographic movies, probably once or twice a week. There was a triple X-rated drive-in that I would go to." He started stealing again and was picked up in a supermarket, trying to change the price label on some hamburger meat. He spent the night in jail but he and his wife never talked about it. "I thought how strange that felt when I got into bed that night and she was still up and we just didn't talk. It was like it just didn't happen...we couldn't talk, really, very close. I wanted to, wanted to talk close but I didn't know how to verbalize things without getting upset or feeling hurt. And she felt very protective, being a very private person, like she was."

At one point during this time he sexually molested his stepdaughter, feeling that he was being deprived of sex with his wife. On another occasion he and his wife had a physical fight. "She struggled and she ended up scratching me around the face somewhere. This infuriated me...I just bent down and I bit her very hard on her shoulder and we ended up scuffling. And I threw her down on the bed and got on top and that was it. We were both breathing heavy and I was looking down at her and holding her hands down and little droplets of blood were coming down and falling on her face."

Within three months, Parker's wife left him; she was helped financially by his older brother. "He couldn't help our marriage get back together but he could help her leave safely. He knew my state of mind, he knew that Gail wanted to leave. Gail had called my brother. She respected him and trusted him, even though he wasn't a Jehovah's Witness."

For the next three years Parker continued to pursue his wife in Canada; she was the focus of his life. He was helped in his obsession by Witness ideology. "They said, look, you need to go back home and get yourself straightened out and scripturally she has an obligation to come back to you. So right away, I realized the bond, the power, the influence this religion could have in keeping my wife."

In the fall of 1984, he moved back to Canada on a visa, and was reunited with his wife. He recalls that things went well for about two weeks, and then the arguments began again. At first the elders among the Witnesses took his side, urging her to be more accommodating; according to Parker, they gave her a "stern lecture" and she was devastated.

He says of their sex life, "She would say things like, you know, it's hard to get horny over a blimp, I'll do my best, I'll be like a good little Christian wife and spread my legs...things that were unheard of, you know, for a JW wife, I thought."

Eventually she left, and his support among the elders finally began to crumble. "I had squeezed all the sympathy out of all the members of the congregation I could and they pretty much had decided to forget about the situation and accept her back in the congregation in good standing. Which just infuriated me...the tables were turning. They were sort of sympathizing with her 'cause she was still a strong Witness and I was getting weak, spiritually weak, you know. I was whining and depressed."

Parker was worried that his wife would tell other members of the congregation that he had sexually abused her daughter, and he was starting to hate her. "I started fantasizing about how pleasurable it would be for her to be knocked out and for me to be able to have sex with her. I even went to the library to check out different chemical ingredients and different poisons that were available that make people die."

Ultimately, he decided on a shotgun. He kept it around for three or four months before he confronted his wife. "The door was open. She kept it unlocked, and this was around 11 a.m., and I opened the door very quietly, took the gun out of the bag and walked in and closed the door very quietly. She was sitting there talking to her mother over the phone."

Gail Parker told her mother that she had to get off the phone because she had a shotgun pointed at her. When her mother asked if she wanted the police, she said yes and then hung up. Gordon Parker was now even more panicky. "I thought, well, this is no longer going to be a private thing, it has to happen now."

He found the kids in their bedroom and told them that no

one was going to get hurt, that he was just going to talk. When the police called the house he told them that they couldn't talk him out of it, and asked them to stay away. He also told them that he didn't want to have to kill anyone. "I had already planned to kill them and I knew it was going to happen. Stay away was what I meant. But I knew I couldn't let them know that. I started closing the curtains, locking the doors so that nobody could see in...barricading them in place."

For over an hour Parker kept his wife and her kids in the kids' bedroom. The little boy and girl sat on their bed and his wife on a tiny stool while Parker rattled off his litany of self-pity, "all the things she had done to hurt me, and why didn't she answer my letters, and why doesn't she talk to me, and can't you see I loved you, and what's wrong with you, blah, blah, blah...."

He told her that what he was about to do was "warped" and he apologized in advance, saying that he hoped he "had the guts" to take his own life later. He asked her when she stopped loving him, and just after she said she wasn't sure, he fired the gun. "I shot her in the head. She immediately fell backwards, straight backwards, almost like in slow motion...and I'll never forget the image of that. I remember her falling backwards and having a lot of damage done to the side of her head and she started moving around...moving around in the sense that she was shrugging her shoulders and moving her hands a little bit and her mouth was moving...this terrified me...I've since learned that she was instantly dead, that this was just body movements, muscle contractions, it was nerves and things."

The little boy screamed and the little girl froze. Parker loaded his gun again as quickly as he could and shot the girl in the face at point blank range. "She went back against the wall and then stayed upright. And then Bob went...tried to get away by going to the end of the bed. Then I looked at him. It was like he obeyed me. He did the only thing he knew how to do, and in my mind he was a very heroic and brave little man — he went over to his dead sister, put his arms around her...and looked at me and waited to die. About a second later, I killed him. This all took about 20 seconds.''

Parker pointed the gun at himself, but could not pull the trigger. He says now that he was ''a wimp — afraid of the pain it might cause.'' He walked outside the house and was immediately arrested. He says that he told police he wanted to be extradited to the United States, to receive the death penalty that he deserved.

At trial, however, he was trying to beat a charge of first degree murder. ''Even at that point I probably wasn't able to admit that, yes, I stooped that low, that I actually premeditated. I was taking the blame but I was also justifying by saying she pushed me, she was such a hard woman ...which she wasn't at all. She, ah, she did nothing wrong. She just got stuck with a man who was obsessed and flew into a rage.''

Gordon Parker was convicted of first degree murder; he will not be eligible for parole until well into the next century. ''It's hard to comprehend. I cannot imagine spending 25 years in prison. It's just inconceivable, you know. Five years, 10 years maybe I could conceive, but try to conceive 25 years. I can't conceive it. I guess what keeps me going is the same thing that kept me going [in another jail], that is, that I felt that, well, it won't be that long. You'll end up finding some good way to work...you can kill yourself or...it just won't be that long.''

The Canadian Murderer: A Profile

Gordon Parker was not like most people who kill. He was found guilty of first degree murder, one of about 25 men who are convicted each year of that offence. With 650 killings annually in Canada, Parker's crime falls among the worst 5% of all homicides — he has been judged as more deserving of punishment than 95% of those who kill. But as with most killers, his victim — or in this case, his victims — knew him well.

Thirty years ago he probably would have been hanged for this offence, selected from the average of about 100 convicted murderers each year and executed. He might well have been one of three or four hanged annually during the late Fifties and early Sixties. The details of some of this history will be described later, but first let us consider some general information about the kinds of people who commit murder, and the circumstances under which the crime occurs.

About 80% of all culpable homicides (killings) occur as the result of a social dispute; angry men and women kill their families and their acquaintances. A further 10% can be classified as killings for money, about 5% are committed by people who might be said to be emotionally disturbed, and a further 5% are killings for sex.

These categories are not entirely watertight; often there is some overlap across specific kinds of murder and some exceptional cases may be difficult to classify. The sizes of particular categories contain a margin of error of 5-10% in any given year.

But the evidence that we have from Canadian police forces, Canadian courts and the files of murderers, characterizes the crime as more tragic than evil in at least nine out of 10 cases — the result of men and women making desperate decisions in desperate circumstances. The Canadian murderer is typically not a person who coldly disposes of anyone who stands in the way of economic or sexual conquest; the men or women who stand in our courtrooms charged with first or second degree murder generally bear little resemblance to the calculated and socially polished murderers of most television dramas. In statistical composite the murderer in Canada is most likely to be a single unemployed male between the ages of 16 and 40, a man with few economic resources who kills for reasons of "revenge," "jealousy," "anger or hatred," or "during an argument or quarrel."[2]

The best information that we have about Canada's murderers is kept by our police forces. The *Homicide Return* is a document that is prepared after each homicide and sent to the Canadian Centre for Justice Statistics for processing and analysis. In each of 600-700 cases annually police fill out this form, specifying the precise details of the offence, and giving characteristics of the accused — age, sex, marital status, occupation, relationship to victim, weapon used, and apparent motive.

The one limitation of this information is that we have no data about trial outcomes — there is no systematic record of the sentences for murder that are handed down in Canada's criminal courts. While police categorize over 90% of all homicides as murders, empirical research and warrants of committal to Canadian prisons have shown that there are acquittals in approximately 25% of these cases. Almost a third of these acquittals involve a finding of not guilty by reason of insanity; the other two-thirds is an amalgam of cases in which the police have a suspect, but not enough evidence, and cases in which the accused is genuinely innocent.

The profile of those convicted departs quite radically from original police perceptions. A little over 60% of these convictions are for the offence of manslaughter, a little over 30% for second-degree murder, and about 5% for first-degree murder.[3]

There is little reason, nonetheless, to doubt police descriptions of the general characteristics of those who are defined as guilty of murder and manslaughter. Violence is a male problem, and murder is no exception. Between 1961 and 1974, about 98% of the more than 700 people convicted of murder were male, and there seems little reason to believe that this figure has changed drastically in the intervening years.[4] Young and poor adults are most likely to be involved in culpable homicide, about 90% of murder suspects are between the ages of 16 and 40, and about two-thirds are unemployed.[5] In over 80% of all killings, there is either a family relationship, or a social or business relationship. The two most common means of killing another human being, shooting and stabbing, are responsible for about 80% of all homicides; beating and strangulation follow in relative frequency.

As I noted in my introduction, the murderer of 1988 doesn't seem to have very different motives from the murderer of 1958. Police report that "revenge, jealousy, anger, hatred, and argument or quarrel" are the motives for the vast majority of homicides; the categories of robbery, sexual assault, and "mentally ill" explain many fewer murders.

Killing cannot always be set apart from other crimes of violence and interpreted as an entirely separate phenomenon. The difference between a conviction for assault — or even a less serious offence — and a conviction for first degree murder could amount to a misplaced punch or a bad fall on concrete. And culpable homicide — killing — isn't necessarily the cruelest act that one human being can perpetrate on another. Adults who inflict years of sexual and physical abuse upon children can be more cruel. While the taking of life is certainly tragic, and final, the degree of moral blameworthiness varies as one moves from case to case. Gerald Eaton, a man who killed an eight-year-old girl with a tire iron during a sexual assault, was a very different human being from Elizabeth Workman, a woman who beat her husband to death with a piece of wood — after enduring his physical abuse for many years. Canada hanged both Mr. Eaton and Mrs. Workman, albeit in quite different historical periods: Mr. Eaton in British Columbia in 1957 and Mrs. Workman in Ontario in 1872.

We also need to place culpable homicide in context alongside other kinds of violent death. Traffic deaths and suicides are numerically more significant than killings. Over the past 10 years the annual suicide rate in Canada has fluctuated between 12 and 15 deaths for every 100,000 Canadians, — about 10 suicides per day over each of the last five years. The rate of traffic deaths has declined markedly over the past decade, dropping about 25%, in absolute terms, from about 14 per day to about 11 per day. The reasons for this latter reduction in violent death can be narrowed down to two possibilities: improved safety technology in motor vehicle construction and changes in driving behaviour among Canadians.

But while murder accounts for less than one half of one per cent of all crimes of violence in Canada, and the national suicide and motor vehicle death rates are about six times as high as the murder rate, killing remains more socially relevant. A society with too many killings is one that ultimately flirts with civil war. Our murder rate is a reflection of our ability to live in peace, and so it seems natural that we focus more intensely on killings than on either self-inflicted deaths or accidents.[6]

The rate at which we kill each other does say something about the kind of society that we live in. The city of Detroit has 30 times the murder rate of Canada. The United States taken as a whole has four times as much killing as we do, in absolute terms 20,000 murders to our 600. The poverty and desperation of urban ghettoes are a pervasive feature of crime in America.

What ultimately unites homicide, traffic deaths, deaths at work, and suicides are similarities in intention and behaviour. It is not only violent death that brings these categories together. There is also reason to believe that the motivations behind violence do not always change as one moves from culpable homicide to traffic death to suicide. The boundaries that we draw around each kind of behaviour are not as definitive as we might believe. The young man who tried to impress his friends by driving very fast and then careened his car into a concrete wall, killing two passengers, didn't mean to kill, but he was reckless as to the consequences of his behaviour. In the same way, an outraged husband didn't mean to beat his wife to death, but was reckless. The man who shoots his partner and his children and then turns the gun on himself spans two categories, as a matter of definition — he is a murderer and a suicide.

In addition, we don't know how many traffic deaths or accidents at work might be better classified as murders or manslaughter, or how accurate we are in making distinctions between murder and suicide; the interpretation of the causality that underlies violent death is not an easy task. So-called "smoking guns," suicide notes and statements from surviving passengers are not always available. What we can be sure of, though, is that people defined as murderers will continue to be seen as more morally blameworthy than people who kill themselves or people who kill others in traffic accidents. And this takes us towards some important questions. How have we defined murder in the past, and how should we define it in the future? What kinds of behaviour are the target of the law?

Defining Murder: Creating Categories of Morality

The legal definition of murder has always reflected a preoccupation with the specific question of who should die for what crime, and with the more general issue of capital punishment itself. Discussion about murder has taken place on the floor of the House of Commons for over a century, focussing again and again on two questions — should we execute, and whom should we execute? In the summer of 1987, the House of Commons rejected a return to capital punishment by a narrow margin. We have now lived over 25 years without an execution.

Prior to Confederation the native people of Canada used a variety of responses to murder; the form of punishment could include payment of compensation to the victim's family, a killing to avenge the death, or banishment.[7] The response of the English and French colonists, about to declare Canada their dominion, was not as flexible; for a wide variety of crimes offenders were hanged in public spectacles in the market-place, drawn by a horse to the scaffold on a wooden cart, and there dispatched. In 1833, Ontario reduced its catalogue of capital crimes from over 100 to 12 — murder, treason, rape, child molestation, homosexuality, bestiality, robbery, robbery of the mail, burglary, arson, and accessory to murder. And throughout the nineteenth century English and French colonists acted to reduce the use of the death penalty, to restrict its application to fewer and fewer categories of crime.[8]

By the time of Confederation in 1867, there was increasing support for executions in the confines of the jail, for covering the face of the accused on the scaffold, and for further restricting the range of crimes punishable by death. Canadians were becoming less comfortable with the spectacle of public hanging. They continued to support the use of execution, but they wanted the act itself to be out of sight.

The young nation state moved quickly to follow the lead of Britain and Western Europe in abolishing public executions, using the British experience as a justification for introducing the legislation in the House of Commons. The bill provided that executions would take place behind prison walls. The sponsor of the legislation argued that "privacy in executions was better for the right state of mind of the criminal himself in his last moments..." and "better also...by avoiding the injurious consequences which result from the immense crowds gathered together to witness such exhibitions."[9]

This was the beginning of the end for the spectacle of execution. For the next 107 years the government of Canada gradually withdrew from the business of hanging, restricting the application of the law to smaller and smaller categories of behaviour, and finally rejecting "the ultimate sanction" in 1976 and again, in the summer of 1987.

The essential structure of the legal description of murder in Canada has not changed significantly since it was set out in our first *Criminal Code* of 1892. The government of Sir John Sparrow Thompson based this initial legislation on Stephen's Draft Code, a British reform proposal.[10] Culpable homicide was said to be murder, first, "if the offender means to cause the death of the person killed" or second, "if the offender means to cause...any bodily injury which is known to the offender to be likely to cause death and is reckless whether death ensues or not."[11] These conceptions of direct intention and of a more indirect recklessness remain in our current *Code*; culpable homicide is murder in 1988, "where the person who causes the death of a human being means to cause his death, or means to cause him bodily harm that he knows is likely to cause his death and is reckless whether death ensues or not."

The *Code* of 1892 also defined the act of trying to kill one person, but mistakenly killing another, as murder; this provision can be found virtually untouched in Section 212(b) of the *Code* of 1988. Death that occurred during the commission of certain criminal offences, piracy, escape, rape, forcible abduction, robbery, burglary, and arson, was cast as murder, "whether the offender means or not death to ensue, or knows or not that death is likely to ensue."[12] Again, Section 213 of our present *Code* speaks of murder in the commission of offences in language markedly similar to that of 1892. Manslaughter is still defined as a murder "in the heat of passion caused by sudden provocation."

The potential breadth of the legal definition of murder is really quite remarkable. Under existing sections of the *Criminal Code*, a person can be a murderer by intending to kill another person, by being reckless about whether death occurs, or by doing anything "for an unlawful object...that he knows or ought to know is likely to cause death." The implications of this latter definition of murder have been significant, leading to dozens of convictions of men and women who did not kill — and, in some instances, were not present when the killing took place. Until the Supreme Court of Canada's decision in *Vaillancourt* in late 1987, this doctrine of constructive murder had been upheld for over 120 years.[13]

Yvan Vaillancourt and an accomplice planned the robbery of a pool hall in Montreal in the early Eighties, with the understanding that no guns would be involved — only knives. When his accomplice showed up with a loaded gun, Vaillancourt insisted that it be unloaded and was then handed three bullets from the chamber, which he put in his glove. During the robbery his accomplice shot and killed a client of the pool hall, and then escaped; he has yet to be captured. Vaillancourt's glove and its three bullets were found at the scene of the crime. He was charged and convicted of second degree murder. As a "party" to the offence of murder he was found responsible, under Section 21 of the *Criminal Code*, for the crime itself. In December 1987, the Supreme Court ordered a new trial in *Vaillancourt v. the Queen*, Justice Lamer writing, "It is not necessary to convict of murder persons who did not intend or foresee the death and who could not even have foreseen the death, in order to deter others from using or carrying weapons. If Parliament wishes to deter the use or carrying of weapons, it should punish the use or carrying of weapons."

This decision comes almost 40 years too late for Donald Perreault. In the early afternoon of September 23, 1948, Donald Perreault and two friends, Noel Cloutier and Douglas Perreault (no relation) planned to rob the Banque Canadienne Nationale on the corner of Notre Dame and St. Juste in the east end of Montreal. Donald Perreault was driving his Cadillac along Notre Dame, with Cloutier and Douglas Perreault sitting in the car, armed with automatic pistols. Just past the bank Donald made a U-turn, and put on the brakes. Douglas Perreault and Noel Cloutier got out of the car, wearing smoked glasses and raincoats with turned-up collars. Just outside the bank they lifted handkerchiefs over the lower part of their faces.

Donald Perreault drove on in the car, parking it close to the bank. He crouched down on the front seat, pretending to fix the clutch. Inside the bank, with guns pulled, Douglas Perreault and Cloutier went about their business. While Cloutier went around the counters, taking about $2,000 from the tills, Douglas Perreault stood guard at the door.

There was no burglar alarm, but the young men with the handkerchiefs and the turned-up collars did not go unnoticed. Some "young lads" in a restaurant across the street saw Cloutier and Douglas Perreault and called police.

Constables Paquin and Duranleau arrived at the main entrance of the bank about 10 minutes later, and a flurry of shots followed. In less than a minute both policemen were dead. Cloutier and Douglas Perreault ran for the door, but Donald Perreault and his Cadillac were not to be seen. As soon as he had heard the shots, Donald Perreault had driven off.

He made his way to Longueil, picked up a friend and drove to Varennes, about 50 kilometres from the scene of the robbery. Back near the bank, Noel Cloutier and Douglas Perreault had fled on foot; Cloutier was arrested within a few minutes but Douglas Perreault managed to make his way home. Later that afternoon Donald reached Douglas by telephone. They agreed to drive north to Ottawa, and then on to Sheenboro, the home of Douglas Perreault's grandparents. They stayed there for a couple of days, and then learned that they were wanted for the murder of the two Montreal policemen. They headed west, but their freedom did not last long. At Taber, Alberta, they were arrested for breaking a gasoline pump. The false names and the Manitoba license plate did not add up, and it was quickly established that the two reckless travellers were Douglas and Donald Perreault.

At trial, Donald Perreault testified as a witness against both Noel Cloutier and Douglas Perreault. By the time he came to trial Noel Cloutier had already been hanged, and Douglas Perreault was awaiting execution. After four days in court, Donald Perreault was found guilty of murder, a party to the offence. As a local reporter noted, "Donald, who appeared confident of an acquittal during his four-day trial, paled slightly when the death sentence was pronounced, but quickly regained his composure, showing no other outward signs of emotion."[14]

Efforts then began to save Donald Perreault from the hangman. His lawyer, Alexandre Chevalier, wrote to Hughes Lapointe, the federal Minister responsible for commutation, arguing that Donald Perreault had not carried firearms, that he had testified for the Crown in three cases related to the murders, and that "he [Perreault] was given to understand and allowed to believe that the services rendered by him to the Crown and the police in testifying...would save his life." On this latter point Mr. Chevalier indicated that although "no definite guarantee of commutation of sentence had been given," a strong impression of possible leniency had been left by a meeting in Bordeaux Jail with the Crown prosecutor and an officer of the homicide squad of the Montreal police force.

The memorandum prepared for Hughes Lapointe and the federal Cabinet noted that "the only point in his favour is that, according to the evidence, he was not carrying a gun, and did not himself do any shooting.... He is 26 years of age, and married. His criminal record does not show that he ever made use of firearms to commit his offences." But leniency was not recommended. The memorandum concluded, "It should be pointed out that this tragedy...aroused great public indignation. There was no recommendation to mercy, neither by the jury nor by the trial judge. Considering the facts and circumstances of this case, the undersigned is of the opinion the law may well be allowed to take its course."[15]

The *Globe* reported the execution on page two of its Friday paper on November 25, 1949. It was just a few lines, set in small type, carried over the wire service from Montreal, "Donald (the Rat) Perreault, last of three police killers to go to the gallows for the slaying of two city constables, was hanged tonight at Bordeaux Jail here.... Tall, bespectacled, and now 26 years old, he was placed in the death cell six days ago."[16] The breadth of the legal definition of murder, took the life of Donald Perreault, public indignation about the crime guiding the operation of the law. In 1988, in the wake of *Vaillancourt*, Perreault might not be convicted of murder, much less executed for it.

This malleability of the legal definition of murder over time raises a critical question: how do we determine if an unnatural death should attract criminal responsibility? At first glance, this seems a somewhat unnecessary question, with an obvious answer. Gunshots and stab wounds speak for themselves; so do beatings, and acts of strangulation.

But there may be more subtle forms of killing — causing death by degrees, not by firing a rifle or slashing with a knife. There exists a kind of violence in the social relations of everyday life we take for granted. It is not a mean-spirited viciousness, but rather an often unconscious acceptance of the dangers inherent in our social and economic organization. Some of us work at physical labour in conditions that have a tendency, statistically speaking, to cripple our bodies prematurely and even to kill. Within industries such as mining, logging and commercial fishing, the annual death rate is often at least 20 times the murder rate. With regard to these and many other types of work, our generally accepted structure of social relations can cause death or life; the kind of job that a person has is significantly related to life expectancy and to the likelihood of dying prematurely from work-related disease.[17]

The common-sense response to this claim of analogy is that dying from working at a dangerous occupation isn't really like dying from a violent attack. Like boxers in a ring, the combatants in the workplace usually accept, at least to some extent, the terms of the social bargain. The victim of violence has much less freedom of choice. One could also argue that there is a human difference between being stabbed to death and dying of emphysema after 30 years in the mines. Direct interpersonal violence also has a tragic and frightening character that is quite separate from any sort of death by degrees, and it is fairly dealt with as a distinct phenomenon.

But the social and economic organization of Canadians at work does lead to premature, and in most senses, violent death. What unites a man stabbed to death in the downtown east side of Vancouver with a miner dying of lung cancer in Toronto's Princess Margaret Hospital is the issue of preventable pain. The victim of murder has a short painful death and the victim of existing social and economic arrangements, a long painful death.[18]

This book can only adequately cover one type of violent death, however. I leave the social problems of suicide, motor vehicle fatalities, and deaths at work to others. My concern is with open warfare on the home front, a phenomenon that I see as fundamentally similar to international conflict. Like men at war plotting a response to those who have wronged them, our domestic legislators have always been preoccupied with the question of making the punishment fit the crime.

In 1914 Mr. Robert Bickerdike first introduced a private member's bill on the floor of the House of Commons, an amendment to the *Criminal Code* to abolish capital punishment. Bickerdike was a persistent advocate, sponsoring a number of pieces of legislation from 1914 through 1917.

On second reading of his first bill, Bickerdike argued that capital punishment was not a deterrent, that innocent people could be wrongfully executed, and that vengeance was not a good reason for hanging. He concluded his lengthy speech, "Why should a government stoop to engage a man, under contract for so many dollars per head, to drive poor criminals into eternity. What is there to be gained by it? If it is not a deterrent, then why do it? If it is not a deterrent it becomes simply revenge.... The Government's motto is 'We murder to prove that murder is wrong.' "[19]

The House of Commons debated Bickerdike's bill from mid-afternoon until late on a February evening. Just before 10:30, C.J. Doherty, then Minister of Justice in Sir Robert Borden's Conservative government, rose to address the House. He congratulated Bickerdike for presenting "a view that...found its source in the impulse of his kindly heart" and for his "argument strong in reasoning, and backed by authorities,"[20] stated that his own views in favour of hanging had not been changed by anything he had heard, and moved that the debate be adjourned.

A year later Bickerdike was back with Bill 18, another attempt to abolish capital punishment. He was now armed with data from around the world suggesting that execution had no deterrent value, and he presented his statistics to the House. The leader of his party in Opposition, Sir Wilfrid Laurier, sparred with him when he claimed that Canada had executed innocent men, and the Minister of Justice was absent when Bickerdike rose to defend his Bill after its second reading.

The relationship between Bickerdike and the Minister of Justice was a little more strained in 1915, albeit remaining cordial. "I think that on reflection it will appear clear that man's right to his life is no more absolute than his right to his liberty," C.J. Doherty told the House of Commons. "If it should have to be admitted," he went on, "that one man, innocent of a crime, should unfortunately be convicted and executed, no doubt that would be a most lamentable thing. But for my part I would be quite prepared to set over against that the immense advantage...of this most extreme form of punishment."

Bickerdike chided his old friend Doherty in response, telling the House that "before he got into politics, he was a good tender-hearted judge." He concluded with prophetic hyperbole, "Now with him it is more rope, and nothing but the rope. We may not live to see the day when the millenium is here, when swords will be beaten into ploughshares and spears into pruning hooks, but we will see the day when the better elements in this country will rise in their might, and in that day they will make oakum of your halters, they will smash your gallows, and from the Atlantic to the Pacific make kindling-wood of your scaffolds."[21]

There were other private member's bills in 1950 and 1953, both calling for abolition and both, ironically enough, introduced by the late Ross Thatcher, the father of convicted murderer and former Saskatchewan politician, Colin Thatcher.[22] But the first significant legislation regarding categories of murder occurred in 1948 and 1961.

In early June of 1948, Prime Minister Mackenzie King rose in the House of Commons. "As today has been set apart for the celebration of His Majesty's birthday in Canada," he began, "I would suggest that, before beginning the day's proceedings, honourable members rise and sing *God Save the King*."[23]

It was the birthday of George VI and also the day on which Justice Minister J.L. Ilsley introduced the new criminal offence of infanticide. Ilsley explained that this new crime would apply to mothers who kill their newborn children. "It is useless to lay a charge of murder against the woman," he said, "because invariably juries will not bring in a verdict of guilty."[24] The new offence was needed to provide a more effective punishment than the present system was capable of delivering. Prosecutors faced with cases of infanticide were laying charges of "concealment of birth," a criminal charge which was not seen to have adequate penalties attached.

There was opposition, however, to the new provision. E. Davie Fulton, the Conservative member for Kamloops, spoke against the principle of the bill, "...why make it a lesser penalty and thus run the risk of encouraging persons to commit the crime? So long as they might be convicted of murder, they would be less inclined to commit the crime, but if they knew they could get a maximum of only three years, those who might be tempted might yield to the temptation to commit the crime."[25]

But there was no unanimity in the Conservative opposition on the subject of killing and its punishments. John Diefenbaker sparred with Fulton in the House, making clear his own preference for the reduced offence of infanticide and for the abolition of capital punishment. Diefenbaker pressed the Justice Minister on the procedure to be employed in capital cases, and chided E. Davie Fulton, "...when the honourable member for Kamloops suggests that a woman in that position, having just given birth to a child, will give consideration first to what the penalty will be...."

"That is not what my argument was," Fulton shot back.

"My honourable friend corrects me, but I took it from what he said that a person in that position would contemplate the penalty. I say that a woman in the condition in which she must be, alone in the world and fearful of the consequences of going out into society with a stigma upon her, does not realize the gravity of her offence until after it is committed."[26]

This debate would be replayed 13 years later, albeit on slightly different terrain and with the power of government; Diefenbaker was the Prime Minister and Fulton his Minister of Justice. In the intervening years pressures for both the restriction and abolition of capital punishment persisted. In 1954 the Liberal government of Louis St. Laurent formed a joint committee of the Senate and the House of Commons to determine whether the criminal law should be changed in relation to capital punishment, corporal punishment or lotteries.

The Committee submitted its report to Parliament in June of 1956. The members of both the House and Senate unanimously recommended the retention of capital punishment and argued against breaking murder down into two categories, one deserving capital punishment, and the other life imprisonment as the maximum penalty.

"The Committee is of the opinion that the present distinction between murder and manslaughter is quite clear and straightforward...any attempt to break murder down into degrees may lead to the creation of technical and confusing distinctions without, at the same time, creating any precise delineation between murders of differing degrees of moral culpability.''[27]

At the same time the Committee made a number of recommendations that would better protect the rights of those facing execution: abolition of capital punishment for those under 18, full disclosure of the prosecution's case to the accused, a mandatory plea of ''not guilty'' in capital cases, and an automatic appeal to the provincial Court of Appeal for all those convicted of murder. Hanging was to be replaced by electrocution because ''a small charge of electricity...is the only method of execution where it could be established that unconsciousness was produced instantaneously and that death was painless.''[28]

From 1956 to 1961 pressure for the abolition of capital punishment continued on the floor of the House of Commons, in spite of the findings of the Joint Committee of the House and Senate. Private member's bills were introduced each year, calling for restriction of the penalty of death to the act of treason.[29] At the same time, a change in government signalled a new era in Cabinet commutation of death sentences. The Conservative government of John Diefenbaker came to power in June of 1957 and began to change the longstanding Cabinet approach to the sentences of death that came from Canadian courtrooms. From Confederation to 1958 only a minority of these court-scheduled hangings were commuted by successive federal governments. During Diefenbaker's tenure, from 1958 to 1962, over 82% of all convicted murderers had their sentences commuted. In the preceding five years, from 1953 to 1957, the Liberal government of Louis St. Laurent had commuted the death sentences of 45% of all convicted murderers.[30]

But perhaps the most significant catalyst for changing the application of the law of murder was Wilbert Coffin, hanged in the courtyard of Montreal Jail on February 10, 1956. There were other important capital cases considered by the federal government during the final years of hanging in Canada, but there was probably no case that cast a darker shadow on the practice of state execution.

Coffin was a 40-year-old guide and prospector working in the bush near Gaspé, Quebec, when he crossed paths with three men from Pennsylvania who were on a hunting holiday, hoping to kill some bear. It was early morning on June 10, 1953, when 45-year-old Eugene Lindsey, his 17-year-old son Richard, and his son's friend, Frederick Claar, met Coffin for the first time. The three American hunters had a stalled truck and diagnosed the problem as a defective fuel pump. They asked Coffin to drive into Gaspé with young Richard; Coffin agreed, shared a breakfast with them, and then headed off to town. A new pump was purchased and Coffin suggested a trip to his brother's garage in order to get some information on how the old gas pump could be repaired.

According to Coffin's affidavit evidence, young Lindsey had explained to one of his brother's employees that there was a little pin inside the old pump that wasn't working.[31] The employee, a man by the name of Jack Hackett, then took the new gas pump apart and explained its operation to the young visitor. Coffin also had time while in town to go to the bar at the Gaspé Hotel, where he drank a beer and told bartender Murray McCallum that he had been going across country prospecting when he ran into three American bear hunters. He explained to McCallum that the hunters' truck had broken down and that he was on his way back to the bush with a new fuel pump.

Coffin finished his beer and took another five with him in a paper bag. He picked up young Lindsey and they drove off into the bush. It was the last time that Richard Lindsey was seen alive; Wilbert Coffin was seen again about 48 hours later in Gaspé, drinking beer at the Harbour Hotel and telling the bartender who asked him about his American $20 bill, "I got that from some hunters I brought from the bush to get some repairs done on their car."[32]

What happened during those intervening 48 hours is still unclear. The prosecution — and ultimately the jury — believed that at some point during this time Coffin shot and killed all three hunters, leaving their remains to be mauled by the bears that they had been stalking. The motive for the killings was said to be robbery. Binoculars, a knife, a gas pump, four blue towels and a valise were all found in Coffin's possession a month later, all property identified as belonging to the three Americans.

Coffin argued, after trial, that the knife had been given to him as a gift by young Lindsey for helping with the truck and that he had taken the other articles from the Americans' truck when they did not arrive at a planned rendezvous on the 12th of June. According to Coffin, after he and young Lindsey arrived back with the gas pump on the afternoon of the 10th, he was given $40 American for his trouble. He then went on his way, promising to check back after a couple of days of prospecting to see if the hunters needed any more help. He acknowledged that the $40 payment was quite a generous reward for his services.

At the same time that he met the Lindseys and Claar on the 10th, Coffin noted a jeep with Pennsylvania license plates, carrying two men who said they were also bear hunters. "I would say they were around 35 to 40 years of age, they were just dressed like ordinary men, had kind of overalls or 'jeans' on," he told police.

Two days later Wilbert Coffin came across the abandoned Lindsey truck and waited for a couple of hours for the hunters to reappear. When they didn't show, he packed the valise, binoculars and fuel pump into his truck and drove to Gaspé, his inclination to steal apparently fortified by alcohol.

Over the next couple of days Coffin made his way down to Montreal, to the home of his common-law wife, Marion Petrie Coffin and his five-year-old son. Although the two had never legally married, Marion Petrie signed all her correspondence as Mrs. Wilbert Coffin and in Montreal, Val d'Or and Gaspé was thought to be Mrs. Coffin. From 1945 through 1953 Wilbert Coffin "had looked after her maintenance."[33] For about a month, Coffin stayed in Montreal; a local grocer testified at trial that Coffin was in the habit of coming to the store where he worked two or three times a day during this period to buy cigarettes, soft drinks, and beer; he would usually take away about eight or 10 beer each day.

On July 5, Frederick Claar's father phoned the Quebec Provincial Police in Gaspé and asked them to find out what had happened to his son and the two Lindseys. A search party was struck a few days later and on July 10 the hunters' abandoned truck was found on Tom's Brook Road. There was still a lot of equipment in the back, but no sign of the hunters. The search continued and on July 15 the first body, that of Eugene Lindsey, was discovered at the side of a brook. There were just bones, gnawed by bears, and little pieces of cloth left. It wasn't until a week later that the bodies of the two younger men were discovered. The bones and clothes were scattered about, the skulls separated from the bodies, and the large leg bone of one body still sitting in its boot. Bullet holes were found in young Lindsey's shirt and sweater, the sweater bearing the inscription "Hollidaysburg Tiggers."

Wilbert Coffin was the last man known to have seen the Americans alive, and he was ultimately arrested and brought to trial for the murders. There was a lot that didn't add up in his favour. He had the hunters' property at his wife's home in Montreal and he had been spending a lot of money, some of it American currency, while in Gaspé and en route to Montreal, just after coming out of the bush.

At trial in the summer of 1954, Coffin's first lawyer did not call any witnesses, believing that the Crown had not made its case. This tactic meant that Coffin did not take the stand; the judge and jury heard no explanation of where the money might have come from, no explanation of how Coffin came to steal the binoculars, valise, and fuel pump, and no questions were raised about a jeep with Pennsylvania license plates, seen in the area at the time of the shootings. Coffin was silent in the face of all this circumstantial evidence, and the jury found him guilty in less than an hour. He was scheduled to be hanged on November 26, 1954.

Early in November defence counsel Francois Gravel appeared before a Quebec court and won a first reprieve for Coffin to March 12, 1955, pending the outcome of the case before the Provincial Court of Appeal. The argument had yet to be heard by late February, and Gravel went back to court to win a further reprieve to June 12. By early June there had still been no decision from Quebec's highest court; a fourth date for hanging was set, September 23, 1955.

The Quebec Court of Appeal unanimously denied Coffin's appeal during the summer and his counsel had only one more appeal to the courts remaining, a request to a single member of the Supreme Court of Canada for a final hearing by that court. A further reprieve for this application was given to October 21.

In early September the Supreme Court's Justice Abbott refused Coffin's application for an appeal in the court of last resort. But in an unprecedented move the Chief Justice of the Court then advised the Minister of Justice that three members of his Court would have granted Coffin's application for an appeal. On October 14, just a week before Coffin was to hang, the Cabinet asked for a Supreme Court review of the case, a significant break from any established procedure in the *Criminal Code*. "Cabinet Asks Court Review Coffin Case," said the headline on the front page of the *Globe and Mail* of October 15.

Two other events might have influenced the decision of the federal Cabinet. In early September Wilbert Coffin escaped from the Quebec City Jail on the Plains of Abraham and flagged down a taxi travelling along St. Foy Road. Coffin explained to Gaston Labrecque, the taxi driver, that he wanted to go to the Quebec bridge, about five miles away. He offered Labrecque a cigarette, and sat smoking in the back of the cab. When asked about his destination, Coffin was continually evasive.

Finally the taxi driver pulled over and stopped. Coffin explained that he had just escaped from jail, and offered to pay for his fare with cigarettes. He didn't have any money and didn't want to leave without some kind of payment. The two men kept talking and within a short time Coffin suggested that they should head back into Quebec. He said that it was hard for a man to control his nerves when he was innocent, and that he was very discouraged.

He told the taxi driver that he would go back to jail, but first to his lawyer Raymond Maher, and then to the prison. Taxi driver Gaston Labrecque concluded his statement to police a day later, "At no time at all did Wilbert Coffin threaten me or try to get any money or help from me to escape. He continued mentioning to me that he was discouraged; that it was too much for a man to have bad news for the last two years when [he] had nothing to do with the death of the three American bear hunters."[34]

In early October 1955, a 13-page statement from Wilbert Coffin was released to the press. The release explained that he had stolen certain items from the back of the Lindsey truck, but that there had been a jeep and two hunters with the three Americans when he returned from town on the 10th of June. Subsequent affidavit evidence did establish the likelihood that there had been a jeep with American plates in the vicinity at the time of the murder.

The money that Coffin spent just after the murders, travelling from Gaspé to Montreal, could be explained by payments made to him for staking claims. Thirteen different people had paid him a total of almost $600 in May, June and July.

Early in the new year the Supreme Court handed down its judgement. The seven member panel split, deciding 5-2 in favour of letting the verdict stand. Justice Cartwright wrote the judgement for the minority, saying that he could not be sure that in a new trial, without the errors made, Coffin would again be convicted.

Wilbert Coffin's life was now in the hands of the Cabinet. A memorandum prepared for the Minister of Justice in early February noted that Justice Cartwright had something of a leaning towards the accused in murder cases: "out of 10 capital cases (including Coffin) there have been six in which there were dissenting judgements. Mr. Justice Cartwright is the only Judge who dissented in all six cases. Mr. Justice Locke dissented in three out of the six."

A memorandum two days later continued, in its discussion of new evidence about the American money spent by Coffin, "there must be some doubt as to the accuracy of the memories of these persons who, after 27 months, say that they paid to Coffin relatively small amounts of money (ranging from $10 to $50) in a certain month." New affidavit evidence concerning other Americans in jeeps in the vicinity was set out in the memorandum, but not discussed, "[Gerald and Alwyn Tapp] said that they had some conversation with an American hunter dressed in part in American Army clothing; he said he was in the Gaspé for the purpose of bear hunting and that he was just waiting for his guide or his driver...a second man came in...and the American asked whether everything was in the jeep, ready to go, whereupon the two of them left."[35]

On the morning of February 9th, 1956, Wilbert Coffin was told that the Cabinet saw no reason to interfere with his sentence of death. About six in the evening he was brought a final meal of fried chicken, but he didn't touch it. He sat talking to the Protestant chaplain, sipping coffee. Coffin talked about his family, his work, and the people he loved, his conversation dotted with the persistent question, "What time is it?"

He was upset that his appeal to marry his common-law wife, Marion Petrie, and thus "legitimize" his son had been turned down by Quebec Premier Maurice Duplessis. Duplessis had been furious with the Cabinet's decision to have the Supreme Court review the case; he saw it as an assault on the integrity of Quebec's Court of Appeal. He refused to explain his reasons for denying the marriage in any detail, saying only that "it would not be in the public interest."[36]

At about midnight Coffin handed his prayer books and his Bible to chaplain S.L. Pollard, and took communion at an altar set up outside his cell. Dressed in his street clothes, with two clergymen leading the way, he walked towards the scaffold chanting the psalms offered by the clerics. Earlier in the day he had again declared his innocence. On top of the scaffold he said his last words, "Into thy hand, O Lord, I commend my soul...." The lever was pulled and Coffin was hanged by the neck until he was dead.

But the Coffin case didn't go away quietly. It was the subject of discussion on the floor of Parliament on a number of occasions, with Ministers of the day briefed on how to respond to questions from the opposition.[37] Also the subject of indignant newspaper and magazine articles, the conviction of Wilbert Coffin seemed, at the least, a very close call. There was more than a reasonable doubt of his guilt. Arthur Maloney, who had become one of Coffin's legal team towards the end, wrote in a feature article in the *Star Weekly* a few weeks after the hanging, "No one can say categorically an innocent man has been hanged... And no one can say categorically he was guilty so long as a real doubt exists and the case is surrounded by mystery...."[38]

In late May of 1961, Conservative Justice Minister E. Davie Fulton introduced Bill C-92, an amendment to the *Criminal Code*, in the House of Commons; it was the most significant restructuring of the legal definition of murder in the history of our country. He and his government had been working on the legislation for some time; a memorandum prepared for Cabinet in February noted that Britain had divided the crime of murder into two categories with its *Homicide Act* of 1957; similar moves had been made in the United States and in a number of countries in Western Europe. Fulton proposed that "deliberate and premeditated" killings should be classified as a separate category of murder, and should be punishable by death. He also argued for two other kinds of capital crime, the killing of a police officer or prison guard, and a killing "committed in the course of a crime of violence, such as arson, rape or armed robbery."[39]

The Bill was brought up for debate and was the major business of the House of Commons for two weeks in late May and early June. Again and again speakers in the House of Commons rose to speak about capital punishment. The politicians knew that the bill was a compromise. Harold Winch, the C.C.F. member for Vancouver East and a persistent ad-

vocate of abolition, made the point, "I stand here this afternoon as I have on previous occasions, believing that the right
thing to do is to abolish capital punishment. In saying that,
sir, I do want to give credit to the Minister of Justice for having
introduced Bill No. C-92, which is without doubt one of the
first and therefore one of the most progressive approaches
made toward this subject for many years."[40]

Those who were opposed to the legislation were afraid that
it was the beginning of the end for capital punishment. As
one member argued, "I realize that the piece of legislation
now before us is not a bill for the abolition of capital punishment. However, we know it is one more step which will
inevitably lead to a reality if we go on indulging in this false
sentimentality."[41]

For his part, Justice Minister Fulton believed that the legislation could steer his government away from persistent public
criticism of the process of execution and from the need to commute a high percentage of death sentences. Fulton was in
favour of capital punishment and he hoped that his reforms
would allow hangings to take place with greater public acceptance.[42]

Bill C-92 passed into law in much the same form as had
first been proposed to the House of Commons. Section 202A
of the *Criminal Code* now defined murder as either capital
or non-capital. Capital murder was defined as any "planned
and deliberate" killing, as a death during "piracy,
escape...resisting lawful arrest, rape, indecent assault, forcible abduction, robbery, burglary or arson" or as "causing
the death" of a police officer or prison guard. All other murder
was to be "non-capital," with a sentence of life imprisonment
attached upon conviction.

The legislation did not end the clamour for abolition. The
Diefenbaker government continued to commute most
sentences of death, in spite of the new category of capital
murder. Those Conservatives in favour of capital punishment
— Fulton, and later, Donald Fleming — could not sway
Cabinet from the path of commutation.

When Pearson's Liberals came to power in 1963, they commuted all the capital murder cases that came before them. From a tactical point of view this practice placed the government in something of an awkward position. They had created a precedent of commuting the very "hardest" of cases: a man who had murdered a 12-year-old girl after hours of repeated rape (Meeker) and a man who had shot and killed two police officers during a bank robbery (Marcotte). In April 1966, a motion to abolish capital punishment went down to defeat in the House of Commons, 112 voting for abolition and 143 voting for retention. In July, with the death sentence of Roger Fulton before the government, a memorandum was prepared for the Solicitor General. D.H. Christie, in a document labelled "strictly confidential," wrote, "The question then is should the vote be taken as requiring a change of policy, namely, whether, in effect, there should be a re-introduction of capital punishment and, if so, what guidelines might be looked to in the implementation of such a policy."[43]

Christie argued that the government must either allow the execution and announce "a firm policy that...commutations are to be the exception rather than the rule," or continue to commute. The danger foreseen by Christie was inconsistency; there would be two or three executions "merely out of deference to the vote and the existing situation will soon again prevail." "It may well be," Christie concluded, "that to continue to commute and to face up to the almost inevitable charge that the will of Parliament as manifested by the free vote is being ignored will prove to be the better course in the long run."[44]

In 1967 Pearson's Liberals introduced a further amendment to the *Criminal Code*, an attempt at a further reduction in the scope of capital punishment. Again, as in 1961, the discussion on the floor of the House of Commons was mainly about capital punishment and not about the specifics of the proposed legislation. Bill C-168 provided, among other things, a single category of capital murder, killings of either police officers or prison guards. Murder in the course of a crime such as sexual assault or robbery and planned and deliberate murder were now to be classified as "non-capital" crimes. Killing a police officer, a symbol of order, was now the worst crime, apart from treason, that a person could commit.

The legislation passed into law in November 1967, but not without a struggle. One proposed amendment would have added the murderers of children under the age of 16 to the category of those deserving death; another amendment suggested that the murderers of "any female person" would also be subject to hanging. Eldon Woolliams, after the failure of the proposal relating to child-murder, told the House, "if these people [police officers and prison guards] are to be placed in a special class we should add another group to that class, the women-folk of this nation. I feel that this must be done in order to protect females against the kind of people who, whether sexual deviates or not, attack females and kill them in the course of such attacks."[45]

The legislation, like the 1961 amendment, was a compromise between abolitionists and retentionists. Andrew Brewin of the New Democratic Party rose in the House and moved abolition of capital punishment, but also voted in favour of the bill. The restriction of the possibility of hanging to police killers was perceived as a step forward, generally endorsed by the Liberals and the NDP and generally opposed by the Conservatives. As Solicitor General Lawrence Pennell told the House, "I realize that...I am open to criticism both from retentionists and total abolitionists. I have to accept such criticism for the sake of the survival of the bill.... I had hoped to reduce the categories to the very minimum consistent with getting the bill through."[46]

The House of Commons passed the legislation after third reading with a vote of 114-87. The law was to stay in force for five years, and could then only be extended by the introduction of a new bill on the floor of the House. Between December 30, 1972 and January 1, 1974, the definition of capital murder reverted to what it had been in 1961, planned and deliberate murder, murder during the course of certain crimes and murder of a police officer or prison guard. Time had run out on the five-year experiment, and in 1973 the House of Commons passed a new piece of legislation extending the 1967 law until December 31, 1977, giving it a further trial. The 1973 legislation also applied retroactively to the period between December 30, 1972 and January 1, 1974; any murders committed during this time would be responded to "as if the offence had been committed after the coming into force of this Act."[47]

All this led us to our latest compromise, *The Criminal Law Amendment Act* of 1976, which abolished capital punishment for all crimes but treason. In a confidential letter to the Deputy Solicitor General in late 1975, General J.A. Dextraze had argued strongly for retention of the death penalty for this offence.

"To put the matter very simply," he wrote, "it would be illogical and even incongruous to argue that the State, which must authorize the members of the Armed Forces, as its agents, in time of war...to kill in its defence, should nevertheless not expose to the death penalty one of its own citizens for acts which place in jeopardy the lives of many or the security of the State itself."[48]

This was the first of two compromises that the Liberal government of Pierre Trudeau would need for its bill to succeed; the other compromise was in the longer terms of imprisonment that the new law would provide for. Prior to abolition in 1976 the *Criminal Code* required that convicted murderers spend 10 years in prison before parole; our present law requires that those convicted of first degree murder spend at least 25 years behind bars and those convicted of second degree murder, from 10 to 25, at the discretion of the trial judge. The principal spokesman for the bill, then Solicitor General Warren Allmand, considered that these more substantial penalties could be tolerated, given the possibility of abolishing the death penalty for all domestic crimes.

Through May, June and July of 1976, the debate continued; the Liberals and New Democrats were generally in favour of the Bill, the Conservatives generally opposed. The retentionists, most notably, Simma Holt, Leonard Jones, Claude

Wagner, Tom Cossitt, Sinclair Stevens, and Benno Friesen, all rose to express bitterness and anger with the government's proposed legislation. As Sinclair Stevens said on the day before the legislation passed the House of Commons, "...the government, aided and abetted by its Socialist friends to my left, has, by bringing forward this legislation, ignored the public will.... I intend to make sure, in my area, that in the coming election, whenever it is called, the cards are laid squarely on the table to show who stood for what insofar as the retention of capital punishment is concerned."[49]

In the early afternoon of July 14, the House voted on the third and final reading of Solicitor General Allmand's motion, and capital punishment was abolished. It was the last item of business before the summer recess; the yeas totalled 130 and the nays 124; the hangman was out of business, if only by a hair's breadth.

And then in the summer of 1987 we went through it all again. At the outset, early in the year, it seemed sure that some form of execution would be reinstated. The Prime Minister wanted to honour his pre-election commitment to a free vote on capital punishment. Conservative backbencher Bill Domm championed the cause, and a number of kindred spirits rushed to his side — Alberta MP Paul Gagnon urged, "hang 'em high and hang 'em often."

These good old boys were no match for the opposition — the entire NDP caucus, all Liberal MPs but one, the Canadian Civil Liberties Association, prominent Toronto criminal lawyer Edward Greenspan, and the Prime Minister himself. Having created the opportunity for a change in the law, Mr. Mulroney ultimately chose to fight against the very monster he had created. When the vote was counted, the nays carried the day by a slender margin. Canada affirmed its civility in the face of the largest Conservative majority in our history.

We are still asking ourselves about the kind of murderer who deserves death and we are still trying to reach agreement. We know that some murders are more morally blameworthy than others, that sexually assaulting and strangling an eight-year-old is a more socially offensive killing than the "planned and deliberate'' bludgeoning of an abusive husband by a long-suffering wife.

And yet both murders could be called first degree, one planned and deliberate, and the other a murder in the commission of sexual assault. Within each of our current categories of first degree murder, planned and deliberate killings, contract killings, killings of peace officers, and killings in the course of hijacking, kidnapping, or sexual offences, there is considerable variation. The circumstances, motives and relative morality of police killings differ as we move from one case to the next. And the same scattered pattern of moral blame can be seen in the remaining categories; planned and deliberate murders cannot be easily described, for example, as invariably coherent.

Our recent past suggests that it is difficult for the courts to separate first degree murder from second degree murder. In the next five chapters you will read of men and women convicted of both first and second degree murder — and you will find that consistency and reliability in the distinctions made is very elusive. A number of the people convicted of second degree murder have committed crimes that seem to be better described as murder in the first degree, and a number of the people convicted of first degree murder might better be classified as deserving conviction for murder in the second degree.

When the stakes underlying this kind of decision were life or death, successive Canadian governments were no better than our courts are today. They were attempting to draw some kind of consistent moral line between those deserving hanging and those deserving commutation, as they exercised the federal prerogative of clemency. This process of deciding about death is the subject of the last section of this chapter. I will have more to say later about these almost inevitable limitations in human judgement.

But first we need to place murder in Canadian society in some kind of perspective. How much violent crime and how much murder do we have? How did we get it and what can we do about it?

Canadian Murder Rates: Have We Become A More Violent Society?

From at least 1879 to the present, Canadian police forces have been keeping track of criminal offences — the alleged crime, the province in which it occurred, and, in some years, the number of convictions and the penalties attached. We haven't always been consistent in our record-keeping. From Confederation to 1920, crime statistics were supplied by a small number of municipal police forces across the country. From 1920 to 1961, reporting procedures improved, with an increasing percentage of the forces involved in the information-gathering process. But it wasn't until 1962 that we began to get a reliable picture of the extent of homicide, or other criminal offences, in Canada. January 1, 1962, marked the beginning of the Uniform Crime Reporting System, an initiative of the Dominion Bureau of Statistics, assisted by the Canadian Association of Chiefs of Police. Every police force in the country was given standardized offence definitions and rules for compilation of offences were established.

We have to be careful, then, in evaluating crime statistics prior to 1961; the numbers provided by the Dominion Bureau of Statistics consistently underestimated the number of murders, as well as other crimes. Fortunately, however, some researchers have calculated criminal homicides in Canada from 1926 to 1975, using coroners' reports to fill in the gaps prior to 1961.[50] Equally fortunately, we can also use the incomplete figures of the old Dominion Bureau of Statistics to sketch out at least some of the patterns of murder in Canada more than 25 years ago.

What these data reveal is that the Canadian murder rate in 1930 was 2.14 killings for every 100,000 Canadians. In 1986, there were 2.19 killings for every 100,000 Canadians — current levels of homicide are not entirely without precedent. In the long term, that is, from 1867 to the present, the murder rate has fluctuated between one and three deaths per 100,000.

There have been some significant fluctuations over time, what one might call cycles of criminal homicide. Throughout the late Twenties and early Thirties, the murder rate hovered close to two deaths per 100,000 annually. Over the next 30 years, there was a gradual drop to a rate of about 1.2 killings per 100,000. The Forties and Fifties were a period of relative stability insofar as interpersonal violence was concerned. And then in the late Sixties and early Seventies, we experienced what we might call a homicide "boom", an increase to about three killings per 100,000, going from less than 200 murders annually to over 600. This second cycle of violent crime ran from 1966 to 1975, and has since reached a kind of plateau, if not a modest decline.

The following five charts give the reader something of a statistical backdrop; they are designed to represent, in visual form, the development of murder in Canada over time.

Figure 1 indicates that the motivations underlying killings in Canada do not seem to have changed much over the past 25 years. While there have been increases in all kinds of murder — killing family, killing acquaintances, killing for money, and so on — the categories themselves have remained relatively stable. The killings of family and acquaintances still account for about 80% of all homicides in Canada. Police report that "revenge, jealousy, anger, hatred" and "argument or quarrel" are the motives behind these crimes. Death at the hands of another human being is, most of the time, the consequence of a social dispute.

Figure 2 reflects police classification of offences prior to trial, and shows clearly the dramatic increase in murder in Canada from 1966 to 1975, with a levelling off since that time. The rate of manslaughter is perceived by police to be relatively constant and insignificant. But *Figure 3* shows what happens when murder cases go to court. First, 35% of cases do not result in a conviction. The defendant is found not guilty of murder, not guilty of manslaughter, or not guilty by reason of insanity. About 25% of defendants are found guilty of murder and about 40% are judged guilty of manslaughter.

What we have in Canada, then, is not so much an increase in our murder rate from 1966 through 1975 as an increase in our manslaughter rate.[51] *Figure 2*, while commonly represented as a reflection of Canada's murder rate, is only a total of the criminal charges that the police first considered appropriate to lay in cases of criminal homicide. It also reveals that we have a lot more killings in Canada in the Eighties than in the early Sixties.

Figure 4 reveals that there are marked differences in homicide rates as one moves from east to west, and that these differences have been remarkably stable over time. The Maritimes have traditionally had the lowest murder rates, and British Columbia the highest. These differences can also be seen, (and again they reflect the same east-to-west direction) in the reports of the Dominion Bureau of Statistics from 1879 to 1961. At one point, between 1880 and 1890, British Columbia's murder rate averaged in excess of five killings per 100,000 annually — with the probability of incomplete reporting of all homicides.[52] The province's current rate of just over three killings per 100,000 pales in comparison. The presentation of consistent geographical differences in Figure 4 suggests a need to understand murder in Canada as a regional phenomenon.

Finally, *Figure 5* places murder and manslaughter in the context of two other kinds of violent crime, sexual assault and robbery. Again, these are police data; these figures cannot encompass or comprehend the results of courtroom decisions. But the increase in these kinds of violent crime seems ominous: a more than 100% growth in sexual assault and robbery rates in less than 25 years. Murder and manslaughter rates, as insignificant as they are relative to the rates of other crimes of violence, have nonetheless doubled.

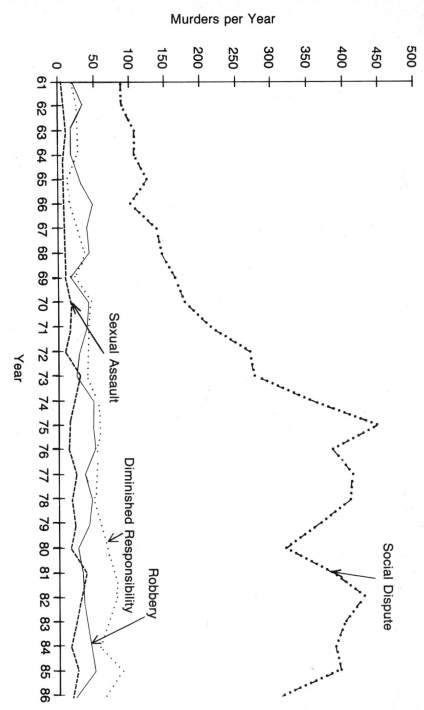

Figure 1: The Motives of Murder, 1961-1986

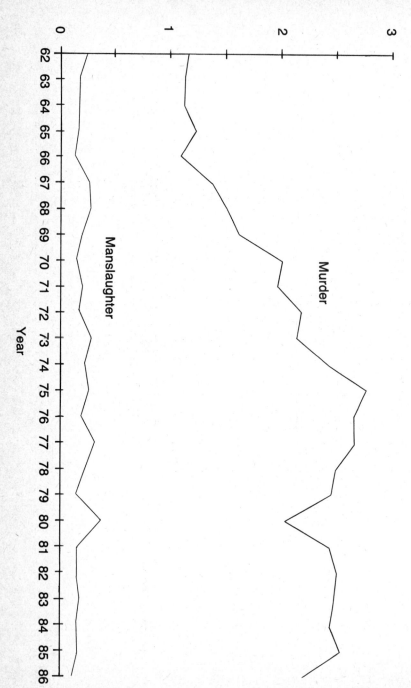

Number of Murders per 100,000 Population

Manslaughter

Murder

Year

Figure 2: Canadian Murder and Manslaughter Rates, 1962-1986

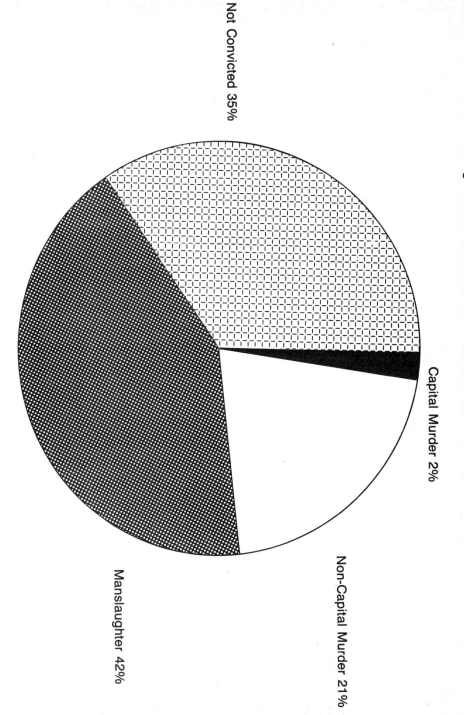

Figure 3: Trial Outcomes in Canadian Murder Cases, 1961-1974

Not Convicted 35%

Capital Murder 2%

Non-Capital Murder 21%

Manslaughter 42%

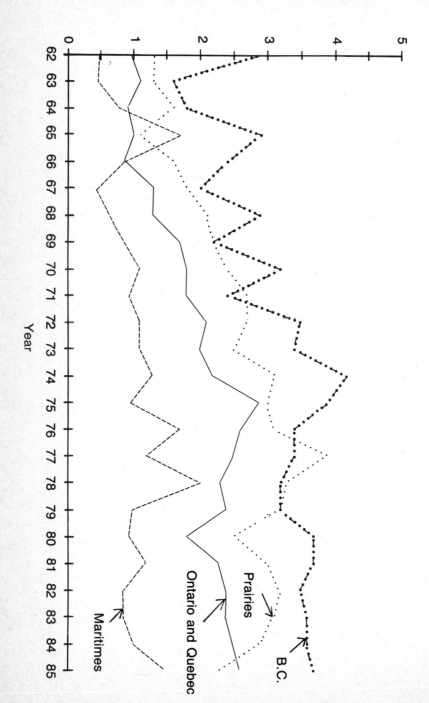

Number of Offences per 100,000 Population

Figure 4: Canadian Murder Rates by Region, 1962-1985

Number of Offences per 100,000 Population

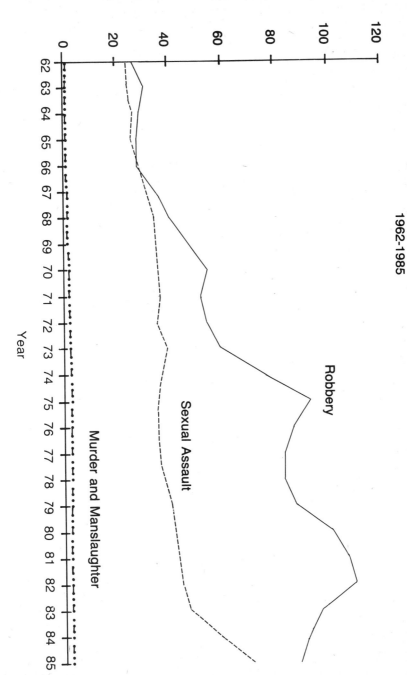

Figure 5: Canadian Sexual Assault, Robbery and Homicide Rates, 1962-1985

There are good reasons for being skeptical about whether these numbers measure real changes in behaviour. First, there have been some changes in police organization over time. The number of police officers per 100,000 Canadians grew from about 150 in 1962 to a peak of about 200 in the mid-Seventies. With more police officers per capita, more crimes of violence will be uncovered and more offenders prosecuted. And, where in 1962 the police officer might intervene in a dispute and resolve a complaint informally, the police officer of the Seventies and Eighties might be more inclined to proceed to court with an offender. The police officer may be less the "man on the beat," less familiar to the community, and more the impartial administrator of the law. The reported crime rate is inevitably influenced by the way we structure the organization of criminal justice.

As my introduction indicated, there was also a change in the composition of the Canadian population between 1962 and 1986. The post-war baby boom produced a disproportionately large number of Canadians entering the 16 to 24-year-old age bracket during the late Sixties and early Seventies. Given that these are the years in which a person is most likely to commit crimes, some increase in Canada's rate of violent crime should not be surprising.[53] Finally, the reported increase of sexual assault may not indicate any real increase. With increasing power in social life, women may simply be more willing to lay charges against the men who have attacked them.

But the baby boom, changes in police organization and practice and changes in reporting practices, taken together, cannot easily explain much of the increase in violent crime. In any event, arguments about changes in reporting practices are less plausible in the case of murder or manslaughter. Sexual assaults and robberies may or may not be brought to the attention of the police; dead bodies are almost always reported. We are, without doubt, a more violent country than we were 25 years ago.

The punishments meted out in the criminal justice system do not appear to have played a critical role; the murder rate has both increased and decreased while hanging has been permitted — and the murder rate has increased and decreased when hanging has not been permitted. We have reliable information about homicide from 1926 to 1986 and these data tell us that the number of murders is not related in any systematic way to the death penalty. Specifically, the changes in the law in 1948, 1961, 1967, 1973, 1974, 1976 and 1985 do not seem to have had any measurable effect on behaviour.

To explain the increase in such violence, we must look at changing patterns of social and economic organization. Killing in 1988 is, like killing in 1958, generally motivated by a social dispute. As a consequence, the problem for policy makers has a troubling breadth — to introduce measures that will reduce, in some rather unknown and indirect way, the 650 murders that now occur each year in Canada.

There are so many changes that might account for the increased violence that we are experiencing. Some would cite more killings as a reflection of a nihilistic world rotating in the shadow of nuclear war; others would note more killings committed by a generation moved by the messages contained in the mass communications revolution of the past 20 years — the have-nots can now see only too well the relative wealth of those who have. We have experienced the gradual erosion of the extended family, fuelled by increasing urbanization and by the economic accessibility of air travel. Canada's children have spread across the country, tied to home by the umbilical cord of the commercial jet and by the telephone, lacking roots and a sense of belonging to a community. And finally, at the level of the individual, it is argued that there is more murder because there are more angry and frustrated men around, unable to express their fears and affections.

But what is consistent amid all this sociologizing and psychologizing is the role of social and economic organization in changing rates of violence. Murder rates seem to have gone through two periods of rapid increase, first in the late Twenties, and later in the late Sixties. As these cycles of violent crime cannot be explained by reference to changing penalties, more useful explanations would seem to flow from changes in our culture.[54] And as I argue in the introduction to this book, the keys to understanding can be found in fundamental economic and sexual changes in male-female relations, a significant increase in alcohol consumption, and the expansion of the black market in illegal drugs. In fact, the penalties that we impose on those who kill would seem at times to be almost beside the point, had it not been for our 96 years of life with the hangman.

Capital Punishment: Discrimination and Death

When I was young — not yet a man
The sun rose and set upon our land
We were the chosen ones
My native son. . . .
> — Bryan Adams and Jim Vallance, "Native Son"

Frog Lake, Alberta, is a community of about 1300 people, spread out over thousands of acres, close to the Saskatchewan border. The lake itself is about 10 miles long by five miles wide, with a few small islands, the habitat of whooping cranes and eagles. There is a general store, a school and a garage, a halfway house, and a band office; a new band hall is being built. The native people who live on the Frog Lake Reserve work at woodcutting, farming, and teaching school. There aren't too many people "from the outside," just a few who have married their way into the band.

In April 1885, Frog Lake was a small community of white colonists; there was a Hudson's Bay store, a Catholic church, a general store, the police barracks, and a few houses. This was also the territory of the Woods Cree and Plains Cree Indians; the white settlement was situated on the boundary of two large reservations. This was the spring of the Riel uprising, and the native peoples and the colonizing forces of young Canada were locked in battle.

In late March a group of Métis won a battle with government forces at Duck Lake, Saskatchewan, dispatching an army of over 100 police and volunteers. News of the victory reached the Plains Cree quickly. They had been having their own difficulties with the Canadian government; the Indian agent in Frog Lake, Thomas Quinn, was limiting rations to the Cree, until they either did more work on a local merchant's mill, or cleared land that was to be sold to incoming settlers. Quinn was one of several Indian agents known for his dislike of native people; the Cree called him "Dog Agent" and "The Bully."

The white settlers had also heard of the Duck Lake skirmish and were worried about their safety; they sent a lot of ammunition off to Fort Pitt. Thomas Quinn then contacted the Indian leaders, Big Bear, Wandering Spirit, Four Sky Thunder and Miserable Man. Through the day on April 1, Indian delegations met with Quinn. He told them that they would be looked after as long as they stayed on the reservation, but when they asked for more rations, Quinn refused. He would not bend his rules. One native by the name of Ayimasis offered a compromise: give the food to Big Bear and his men as a gift; that way Quinn would not be seen as giving in to pressure. Again, Quinn refused.

On the morning of April 2, a band of about 100 Plains Cree rode into Frog Lake, whooping war chants. They went to Thomas Quinn's house, broke the lock, and quickly took him prisoner. William Cameron was ordered to dispense tobacco to the Indians from his Hudson's Bay store, and Quinn was forced to turn over an old ox for meat. Within a few hours the Cree had looted the stores of Frog Lake, helping themselves to alcohol and dressing in the suits they had taken from the stores. Most of the whites were attending church, while the Indians, by now quite drunk, "came in and out of the church, singing, shouting, howling and beating drums, storming around and strutting...." As one observer said later, "It was getting hard to be optimistic. The Indians were getting drunker and drunker, more and more provoking. The crazy games they were playing with firearms, an accident was sure to happen."[55]

The accident occurred when Thomas Quinn refused to move from the Frog Lake settlement to the camp of the Cree. When

Quinn remained steadfast, Wandering Spirit raised his rifle and shot him in the head. The war chants accelerated; Wandering Spirit urged his fellow Cree to kill all the whites. Chief Big Bear ran towards Wandering Spirit, yelling at him to stop.

But it was too late; in just a few minutes nine white men were dead, with blood all over the melting snow of early April. The two white women at Frog Lake, widows of two of the dead, were taken prisoner, along with William Cameron, the Hudson's Bay storekeeper. Cameron was a young man who spoke fluent Cree and had very good relations with the natives. The rebellion continued for a few months, and the prisoners travelled with their captors, the Métis and the Cree; one of the women later wrote a book about the experience, *Two Months in the Camp of Big Bear*. Mrs. Delaney had been very frightened at times by the Cree but was treated well by a Métis man, John Pritchard, who had "purchased" her from Big Bear's Cree for $30.

But Riel and the dreams of the fighting Métis and Cree could not survive; with the Rebellion over, the government soon set out to arrest the Frog Lake killers and bring them to trial. Wandering Spirit, Round the Sky, Bad Arrow, Miserable Man, Iron Body, and Little Bear were all tried, convicted, and sentenced to hang at Battleford, Saskatchewan, on November 27, 1885. All of the men had been seen shooting at the murder victims, and although Bad Arrow and Little Bear had not fired fatal shots (Little Bear's two shots missed entirely), they were technically as guilty of murder as the others; they were all parties to the offence.

The public execution was to take place at 8 o'clock in the morning; the six Frog Lake murderers were to be hanged alongside two other natives who had killed whites during the rebellion. "The Battleford Execution to Take Place Today, Six Frog Lake and Two Battleford Indians To Be Sent to the Happy Hunting Grounds"[56] read the headline in the *Manitoba Daily Free Press*. Toronto's *Globe* was less enthusiastic. In an editorial titled "A Year of Blood," the influential paper called the execution "a spectacle at which humanity must shudder.'' The news headline read, ''Wholesale Butchery: Eight Indians Suffer the Extreme Penalty of the Law.''[57]

The morning of November 27 in Battleford, Saskatchewan, was dark and cloudy, with a light frost on the ground. About 150 police were guarding the scaffold, a massive wooden structure built for the occasion, allowing all eight men to fall to their death at the same instant. The original plan had been to hang the Indians two at a time, but a single drop was ultimately decided on. The throng of policemen stood around the scaffold, wary of an outbreak from the crowd; there was ''no excitement among the whites'' about the execution and a number of Indians from neighbouring reservations were there to watch the hangings. They had camped out on open ground near the scaffold and they sang the death chants of their tribes through the night.

At about half past seven the procession from the jail began. The natives' arms were pinned and they were each escorted on both sides by a policeman as they walked over to the scaffold, up the stairs, and to their spots, each on one of eight trap doors. When asked if they had anything to say, Wandering Spirit addressed the crowd in his native Cree. He blamed himself for the crime, said that he deserved death and warned the audience not to make war with the whites; they are our friends, he concluded. Miserable Man then spoke, saying that the sentence was just, and warning the crowd to stay clear of such disturbances in the future. The eight men then began chanting their death songs to show that they did not fear what was about to come; eight white hoods were slipped over their heads and the death chants continued. All the while the priests could also be heard, reciting prayers.

In the midst of this desperate mix of song, a bolt was drawn and all eight men fell to their death. The *Globe* reported the event in its Saturday edition, ''The eight Indians concerned in the Frog Lake Massacre were hanged here at 8:15 this morning. There was no hitch whatever.... The Indians who stood at a distance and witnessed the affair were very quiet and the silence was only broken by the wailing of the wives of the condemned men. The savages generally set out for their reserves after the execution, and those who remain show no special signs of excitement.''[58]

In 1987 native Canadians still figure prominently in murder. Although comprising only 2% of our population, they represent about 13% of all murder victims and 18% of all murder suspects. In contemporary Canada, native people usually kill each other after a domestic or social dispute. Killing during sexual assault or robbery is significantly less common among natives than among any other racial or ethnic group. While the annual murder rate in Canada is about two deaths per 100,000, the native rate is about 15 deaths per 100,000.[59]

Native Canadians were also more likely to be hanged than members of any other ethnic or racial group, other things being equal. Economist Ken Avio's recent study of 440 capital cases between 1926 and 1957 held constant the features that one would expect to be associated with execution: premeditation, no use of alcohol and no mental disease, a lack of provocation, no confession and no judge or jury recommendation for mercy. Race and ethnic origin emerged as a predictor of execution, independent of these traditional extenuating circumstances.

There have been two major pieces of research to date on execution in Canada, David Chandler's in 1976 and Avio's in 1987.[60] For as long as capital punishment existed in Canada, successive federal Cabinets had to make final decisions about life or death; Chandler and Avio have placed these hundreds of cases under the microscope of statistical analysis. Chandler analyzed 378 capital cases between 1946 and 1967, and Avio studied 440 capital cases between 1926 and 1957.

Chandler reported in 1976 that people who murdered during a sexual assault or robbery were more likely to be put to death than murderers out for revenge, a finding confirmed by Avio. Both studies found that, other things being equal, ethnic and racial origin remained a statistically significant variable in Cabinet judgements. Native Canadians and French Canadians were more likely to be hanged than English Canadians. Chandler's analysis suggests that discrimination against French Canadians was most pronounced, and Avio's suggests that discrimination against Natives was most pronounced, but both argue that ethnic background is a significant variable. Avio also found two other variables not addressed by Chandler; gender, and the previous year's homicide rate. Other things being equal, women were less likely to be executed than men; execution was also more likely after a year with a high homicide rate than after a year with a low homicide rate.

There are, as well, anecdotes which suggest other kinds of discrimination in the Capital Case files. Abraham Steinberg was hanged in Toronto in 1931 for the murder of his business partner, Sam Goldberg. The evidence against him was circumstantial. Steinberg's defence was based on an alibi; four witnesses testified that they had seen Steinberg elsewhere at the time that Sam Goldberg was shot to death. Ontario Supreme Court Justice Nicol Jeffrey sentenced Steinberg to hang, and wrote in his summary to the Minister of Justice, "Steinberg is a Hebrew and that fact was referred to by Mr. Hellmuth, who defended him, and it was stressed to the jury. All of the witnesses called on his behalf are Hebrews...and [Mr. Hellmuth] particularly asked the jury not to be influenced by that fact.... I carefully instructed the jury that they were not in any way to be influenced by the fact that the witnesses for the accused were Hebrews...."[61]

The death sentence imposed on Steinberg aroused public indignation and 20,000 signatures were collected on a petition opposing the hanging. Four days before the execution a memorandum was written to the Solicitor General on the option of commutation. The office of the Deputy Minister of Justice did not recommend clemency. M.F. Gallagher wrote, "Now, as to public sentiment as expressed by the petition...I would attach importance to all this if public opinion were here in accord with average common sense and intelligence and the general sentiments of the people. An *organized* expression of opinion may be quite misleading and certain sects have acquired the reputation of being more industrious than others in working upon the sympathies of their fellow men...I see no good ground left for interfering with what appears to me to have been a logical and, in truth, a sound verdict.''[62]

Leo Mantha was a tugboat engineer who stabbed his lover to death in a jealous rage in 1958; he was hanged in April 1959. Mantha's trial focussed on his homosexuality and its role in the murder. Psychiatrist Douglas Alcorn testified at trial, ''He has shown the features which I encounter frequently in homosexuals.... Society expects from the homosexual a degree of chastity and total avoidance of any expression of their sexual drives.... This in itself creates tremendous tensions which from time to time result in gross disturbances.'' A memorandum prepared for the Solicitor General 10 days before Mantha died noted three features suggesting clemency: ''(a) consideration might be given to effects of alcohol on his somewhat peculiar personality, giving rise to an explosive or irresistible impulse; (b) this can be regarded as a crime of passion; (c) there was present an element of provocation by the victim....''[63] The Cabinet was not moved; on April 28, 1959, Leo Mantha was hanged in an abandoned elevator shaft at Burnaby's Oakalla Prison, the last person to be executed in the province of British Columbia.

Cabinet clemency decisions seem in retrospect to have been something of a macabre lottery, subtly influenced by considerations of race, religion and sexual orientation, among other things. Natives, French Canadians, Jews, and homosexuals were, at least occasionally, at greater risk of dying for their crimes.

And yet the application of the death penalty changed as Canada moved from 1867 to 1962. As juries became increasingly reluctant to convict of murder and legislators grappled with the issue of capital punishment on the floor of the House of Commons, the category of murderer considered to deserve death narrowed. Increasingly, those who were hanged had murdered during robbery or sexual assault. The domestic murderer was less likely to be sent to the gallows.[64]

In the last four years of capital punishment, from 1959 to 1962, there were 42 clemency decisions made by the federal government. All of the convicted murderers were male; the Diefenbaker Cabinet decided to hang 10 and commute the sentences of the remaining 32.

The composite portrait of these 42 men is a little difficult to assemble, but their murders can be categorized by motive: 11 killed in the course of robbery, four in the course of sexual assault, three killed police officers, one was a contract killer, and 23 killed as the result of a social dispute; the motives set out in government correspondence are "anger, quarrel, crime of passion, or jealousy."[65]

In the category of social dispute, four men were hanged. They were Leo Mantha, the tugboat engineer from Victoria who stabbed his lover to death; Robert Raymond Cook, a young man from Alberta said to have killed all seven members of his family; Louis Fisher, a Toronto man who stabbed a woman to death after a long day of drinking with her in down-and-out bars; and Owen "Mickey" Feener, a hard rock miner from Nova Scotia who stabbed at least three women to death.

The one contract killer, Arthur Lucas, was hanged. Lucas was a man from Detroit who slit the throats of an illegal drug distributor and a prostitute; his motive was "racket discipline." Three of the 11 men involved in murder during robbery were hanged: Hector Poirier, a middle-aged man who killed a young man with a piece of iron; Marvin McKee, an Ontario man of "below average mentality" who killed a taxi driver; and Ernest Côté, a 36-year-old who shot a bank manager during a holdup. Two of the three men who killed policemen were hanged: Ronald Turpin, a 29-year-old who killed a Toronto constable who was trying to apprehend him; and Thomas Young, a 27-year-old who shot a policeman while very drunk and apparently hallucinating. None of the four men convicted of murder during a sexual assault were hanged.

The composite portrait of the 32 men left behind leaves us with a number of nagging questions. How was John Vollman's stabbing during a sexual assault on a 16-year-old girl set apart from Leo Mantha's behaviour, or apart from any of the cases of the 10 men hanged? Why were Pierre Patenaude and Gaston Bouchard, men who murdered a restaurant owner and a scrap dealer respectively during planned robberies, treated differently from Poirier, Côté, and McKee? What made police killers Turpin and Young so different from Eric Lifton, reprieved late in 1962?

It is virtually impossible to find consistency in the final years of execution in Canada, to feel that the prerogative of mercy was fairly applied, in spite of what were probably the best of intentions. And for Dan Robertson, a man whose sentence of death was ultimately commuted, the workings of government clemency remain a very unpleasant memory.[66] Robertson is now confined in a federal penitentiary, his parole revoked for not reporting to his parole officer. He served 13 years for his role in a killing in 1949 and was ultimately released in 1962. For most of the past 25 years he has been out of jail and he indicates that if he had agreed to continue reporting to his parole officer, first in 1978 and then again in 1986, he would never have been returned to Canada's penitentiary system.

Back in 1949 Dan Robertson was a 17-year-old boy living in a small town just outside of Montreal. He had been deserted by his parents when he was four months old and had lived in nine different foster homes during his childhood.

He was working on a farm, making a dollar a day and his room and board, when a work hand from a neighbouring farm came over one day and asked him if he wanted to make some easy money. Guy Talbot, who was about eight years older than Robertson, told Robertson to meet him in town on Saturday night.

When Robertson arrived in the small town, he was told to phone a taxi. When the taxi arrived he was told to get in the front seat with the driver. Talbot climbed in the back. Talbot told the driver to go to a place "out in the sticks," and as Robertson recalls, "So we're going down this gully and just as we get to the top of the rise he says to the cabby, this is where we want to get out, after driving about seven miles. And the first thing I know I hear this — well — it was the sound of a hammer hitting a head. And it's undescribable. And naturally the taxi driver slumps."

Robertson figures that Talbot "lost control of himself...he just went berserk. And in the meantime I'm trying to duck the blows of the hammer and I'm trying to keep the car on the road, right...well, I'll tell you, the force of the blows of the hammer on the guy's head cracked the driver's window. And I mean now, we're talking about an early model car, this was 1949...so I mean, hey, glass was strong in them days."

At the bottom of a gully the car finally coasted to a stop. Talbot pulled the taxi driver out and dragged him across the road. He still had the bloody hammer in his hand and he called Robertson over: "...he says, 'You're in this just as much as I am', and I says, 'You bet I am.' And he says, 'Well, to prove it you gotta hit him.' So I tapped him once on the forehead all right. Now as far as I'm concerned, I tapped a dead person. 'Cause I mean, his head was just a gory mess and there was blood and flesh all over the place, eh."

The purpose of the attack had been to get money in order to purchase ammunition for a robbery. A short time later Robertson walked into a store in Montreal and purchased two boxes of shells. The two men then drove to a small town and robbed a bank. Robertson stood at the entrance with a gun in his hand while Talbot walked up to a cashier and demanded money, "So finally he gets his gun out and I mean, hey, you look at a .45 like this, I mean, it's not pleasant. It looks like a cannon, right."

The two men escaped with about $5,000 and took a taxi out of town, but the police were already on their trail. They were captured the next morning after hiding out in a barn overnight and went to trial on charges of murder and armed robbery, "And I mean, everybody was against us. I mean this was a horrible crime, let's face it...I am surprised that a lawyer even appeared in court on our behalf. I know we weren't defended. We were just represented."

For Dan Robertson, contact with the criminal justice system was a new experience, "I had never been inside a police station, never mind commit a crime up until that time.... You see, morally I convicted myself. The court did not convict me. The court pronounced sentence.... I knew I had done something wrong. I didn't actually kill the guy, but I didn't prevent Guy from killing him...one shot in the head, that was enough...I should have right then said to Guy, 'What the hell are you doing?' or something, you know, to shake him out of it.''

Both Talbot and Robertson were convicted of murder and sentenced to hang. Robertson told the court that he was ''just as guilty'' as Talbot. ''Not once did I ask God to forgive me for leaving this family in the situation they were in. I put...the blame on myself...I mean, I was 17 years old, I lacked experience, I lacked knowledge, I don't know, I really don't know what it felt like...the realization of what the judge's words were...to hang by the neck until you are dead.''

Talbot and Robertson were placed in what were called the Death Watch cells and then in what were called the Hanging cells, ''Well, I relived my life many, many times.... I'm thinking to myself I deserve what I'm getting.... Now don't ask me why a man's thinking is so irrational or why it's so cockeyed. I will never know. 'Cause I'm not a stupid person, okay. I'm not overly intelligent either, but I'm not stupid. I'm in between, you know...if I had just thought, hey, I didn't kill this guy.''

A couple of days before the hanging Robertson was weighed and bags were filled with sand so as to correspond to his weight. He could see the scaffold from his cell, ''...and they're painting the scaffold and they're testing it, and they're dropping the sand bags. That's a horrible sound in itself.''

In the evening before he was to hang Robertson was asked what he wanted for his final meal and whether he wanted to be drugged prior to going to the scaffold. He told prison officials that he didn't want anything special to eat — ''Whatever I've been getting, it don't matter,'' — and that he didn't want any drugs.

It was now less than two hours before he was to die. ''I finally resigned myself to the fact that, hey buddy, you kiss the world goodbye, because you're leaving it.''

At about 10:30, an hour and a half before he was to hang, the door to his cell opened and he was told that his sentence had been commuted. "It was just like I had died mentally on the spot. After all, this is it, resign yourself to the fact — good-bye world." Robertson recalls that at the time the commutation meant very little to him, "We just kept walking, and all of a sudden, bingo, I'm blank. I don't recall the ride...to [the penitentiary]. I don't even remember.... And I thank God that I didn't hang. I've had a few ups and downs in my life but, hey, I've had some good moments too."

[1] "Gordon Parker" and all other names connected with this story are pseudonyms.

[2] There are many empirical sources for this statement but the following two reports probably best demonstrate the consistency of this finding from 1962 to 1986. *Homicide in Canada: A Statistical Synopsis*, Statistics Canada, Ottawa, 1976, and *Historical Homicide Data Relevant to the Capital Punishment Issue*, Canadian Centre for Justice Statistics, Ottawa, 1987.

[3] See particularly *Historical Homicide Data Relevant to the Capital Punishment Issue*, note 2, *above*, 31, and *Homicide in Canada: A Statistical Synopsis*, note 2, *above*, 105-111. See also Hann and Kopelman, *Murder and Related Offences: Custodial and Probation Sentences: 1984-85*, Policy, Programs and Research Branch, Department of Justice, Ottawa, 1987. Note, particularly, Figures 3.1. and 5.1.

[4] See *Homicide in Canada: A Statistical Synopsis*, note 2, *above*, at 109.

[5] One qualification here: there is a real difficulty in getting an adequate empirical assessment of the social and economic status of murder suspects. Only 3,000 homicide returns of the 10,000 completed between 1962 and 1985 indicated employment status; of the 3,000 reporting, approximately two-thirds were unemployed at the time of the offence. *Historical Homicide Data and Other Data Relevant to the Capital Punishment Issue*, note 2, *above*, 26.

[6] See *Historical Homicide Data and Other Data Relevant to the Capital Punishment Issue*, note 2, *above,* 14.

[7] M. Nagler, *Perspective on the North American Indians*, McClelland and Stewart, Toronto, 1972; H. F. McGee, *The Native Peoples of Atlantic Canada*, McClelland and Stewart, Toronto, 1974, R. Strickland, *Fire and the Spirits*, University of Oklahoma Press, Norman, 1975.

[8] For a description of hangings in Canada prior to 1867 see Frank W. Anderson, *Hanging In Canada: A Concise History of Capital Punishment In Canada*, Frontier Publishing, Calgary, 1973.

[9] Government of Canada, *House of Commons Debates*, 2nd Session, 1st Parliament, April 28, 1969, 95.

[10] A. Mewett, "The Criminal Law, 1867-1967," *45 Canadian Bar Review*, 1967.

[11] *Statutes of Canada, "The Criminal Code,"* chapter 29, 55-56 Victoria, 1892, s.227.

[12] *Ibid*, s.228. For a discussion of the development of constructive murder see J. Ll. J. Edwards, "Constructive Murder in Canadian and English Law," 3 *Criminal Law Quarterly*, 481-509, 1961.

[13] Section 21 of the *Criminal Code* provides that "Every one is a party to an offence who..."abets any person in committing it," indicating that one does not need to commit a criminal offence in order to attract a criminal conviction. The person who assists the murderer has been, until the Supreme Court's decision in Vaillancourt, as guilty of murder as the person who pulls the trigger or inflicts the fatal knife wound.

[14] "Letter from André Chevalier to the Honourable Hughes Lapointe," *Capital Case Files, RG 13 Series, Donald Perreault*, November 17, 1949, National Archives, Ottawa, Canada.

[15] "*Rex v. Donald Perreault*, Memorandum for the Honourable the Solicitor General," *Capital Case Files, RG 13 Series, Donald Perreault*, 1-6, 6.

[16] *The Toronto Globe*, November 25, 1949, 2.

[17] Harry J. Glasbeek and Susan Rowland, "Are Injuring and Killing at Work Crimes?" 17 *Osgoode Hall Law Journal*, 507-594, 1979, particularly 507-510.

[18] See, for example, Charles Reasons, Lois Ross and Craig Paterson, *Assault on the Worker*, Butterworths, Toronto, 1981.

[19] *House of Commons Debates*, February 5, 1914, 489.

[20] *Ibid.*, 510.

[21] *House of Commons Debates*, February 18, 1915, 281.

[22] Colin Thatcher was convicted in 1984 of the first degree murder of his estranged wife, JoAnn Wilson; his conviction was upheld by the Supreme Court of Canada in May 1987. Ross Thatcher moved from the House of Commons in the 1950s to provincial politics, becoming Premier of Saskatchewan in 1964; during his time in the House of Commons he was a member of the CCF party, and later in Saskatchewan a Liberal with a penchant for the rhetoric of free enterprise. *The Canadian Encyclopedia, Volume 3*, 1805, Hurtig Publishers, Edmonton, 1985. For discussion of his private member's bills see *House of Commons Debates*, June 6, 1950 3277 and February 20, 1953, 2259.

[23] *House of Commons Debates*, June 7, 1948, 4837.

[24] *House of Commons Debates*, June 14, 1948 5185.

[25] *House of Commons Debates*, June 14, 1948, 5187.

26 *Ibid.*, 5187.
27 *Report of the Joint Committee of the Senate and House of Commons on Capital Punishment. Corporal Punishment and Lotteries*, Queen's Printer, Ottawa, 1956, 17.
28 *Ibid.*, 22.
29 See, for example, *House of Commons Debates*, August 1, 1958, 2977, and June 19, 1959, 4960.
30 Guy Favreau, Minister of Justice, *Capital Punishment: Material Relating to Its Purpose and Value*, Queen's Printer, Ottawa, 1965, Appendix D.
31 "Statement of Wilbert Coffin," *Capital Case Files, RG 13 Series, Wilbert Coffin*, 1956, National Archives, Ottawa, 5.
32 "Condensed Summary," *Capital Case Files, RG 13 Series*, Wilbert Coffin, 30.
33 *Ibid.*, 37.
34 "Affidavit of Gaston Labrecque," *Capital Case Files, RG 13 Series, Wilbert Coffin*, 2-3.
35 "Memorandum for the Minister of Justice and the Solicitor General," February 5, 1956. *Capital Case Files, RG 13 Series, Wilbert Coffin*, 3.
36 Stanley Handman, "Coffin: He Died Seven Times," *Weekend Magazine*, Volume 6, Number 19, 1956, 2.
37 See, for example, *House of Commons Debates*, December 13, 1963, 5850
38 Arthur Maloney, "Did Canada Hang An Innocent Man?", *The Star Weekly*, Toronto, March 3, 1956, 4.
39 "Memorandum for the Cabinet, *Re*: Criminal Code Amendment Bill," *Department of Justice Files Relating to the Criminal Law Amendment Act, 1976*, February 20, 1961, received under the Access to Information Act, September, 1986.
40 *House of Commons Debates*, May 23, 1961, 5230.
41 *Ibid.*, 5240.
42 E. Davie Fulton, *personal communication*, October, 1985.
43 "Memorandum for the Solicitor General," *Capital Case Files, RG 13 Series, Number 1497*, July 6, 1966, 3.
44 *Ibid.*, 6.
45 *House of Commons Debates*, November 23, 1967, 4608.
46 *Ibid.*, 4609.
47 "The Criminal Law Amendment (Capital Punishment) Act," *Statutes of Canada*, c. 38, ss.8-9, 1973.
48 "Letter to Roger Tasse," *Department of Justice files relating to the Criminal Law Amendment Act, 1976*, released under *Access to Information Act*, September, 1986.
49 *House of Commons Debates*, July 13, 1976, at 15313 and 15315.

[50] M.C. Urquhart and K.A.H. Buckley, *Historical Statistics of Canada*, Macmillan, Toronto, 1976, at Z21-27 and Z15-21.

[51] We know this from the Statistics Canada publication *Homicide in Canada*, note 2, *above*, released in 1976. The researchers tracked homicide cases through the court process for the period 1961-1974 to determine the ultimate outcome. Courtroom conviction data is currently not being kept; we can only infer from statistics that were kept between 1879 and 1961 and from this 1961-1974 study that manslaughter convictions have always been about twice as common as murder convictions. For some empirical confirmation of this finding in more recent years see Hann and Kopelman, *Murder and Related Offences*, note 3, above.

[52] *Criminal Statistics — 1980, Dominion Bureau of Statistics*, Table IV, 190-191.

[53] See, for example, J. Fox, *Forecasting Crime Data*, Lexington Books, Lexington, Mass., 1979, and B. Hasenpusch, "The Rise and Fall of Crime in Canada: An Attempt at Criminological Forecasting," *Crime and Justice*, Volume 6, 1978, 108-123.

[54] See, for a discussion of this concept of cycles of crime in Britain, Canada and America, Paul and Patricia Brantingham, *Patterns in Crime*, Macmillan, New York, 1984, particularly chapter 8.

[55] Bob Beal and Rod Macleod, *Prairie Fire: The 1885 Northwest Rebellion*, Hurtig Publishers, Edmonton, 1984, 198. See also, on the Frog Lake Massacre, C.P. Mulvaney, *The History of the North-West Rebellion of 1885*, Hovey and Co., Toronto, 1886, and Heritage Series, *Frog Lake Massacre*, Frontier Books, Surrey, B.C., 1984.

[56] *The Manitoba Daily Free Press*, Winnipeg, November 27, 1885, 1.

[57] *The Globe*, Toronto, November 28, 1885, 1.

[58] *Ibid.*

[59] See *Homicide in Canada: A Statistical Synopsis*, note 2, *above*, at 86, and *Homicide in Canada, 1984: A Statistical Perspective*, Ottawa, Statistics Canada, 1986, 35 and 38.

[60] David Chandler, *Capital Punishment in Canada*, Toronto, McClelland and Stewart, 1976, and K. Avio, "The Quality of Mercy: Exercise of the Royal Prerogative in Canada," *13 Canadian Public Policy*, 1987, 366-379.

[61] "Letter to Hugh Guthrie," *Capital Case Files, RG 13 Series, Abraham Steinberg*, National Archives, Ottawa, 10.

[62] "*Re* Steinberg Capital Case," *Capital Case Files, RG 13 Series, Abraham Steinberg*, 2. Emphasis on "organized" retained from original.

[63] "Memorandum for the Solicitor General," *Capital Case Files, RG 13 Series, Leo Mantha*, National Archives, Ottawa, April 17, 1959, 3.

64 With the 96 cases that I selected from 1867 to 1962, there were marked differences between the periods 1867 to 1900 and 1901 to 1962. The categories of murder during robbery or sexual assault accounted for 18% of all cases prior to the turn of the century and for 33% of all cases between 1901 and 1962.

65 "Department of Justice Memorandum," *Capital Case Files*, National Archives, Ottawa, February 28, 1966.

66 "Dan Robertson" and all other names connected with this story are pseudonyms.

Chapter
Two

KILLING FAMILY

I've loved you for a long long time
I know this love is real
don't matter how it all went wrong
that don't change the way I feel
I don't believe
that time can heal this wound I'm speaking of
there ain't no cure
there ain't no cure
there ain't no cure for love

Leonard Cohen, "There Ain't No Cure for Love"

Jenny Buchanan and her husband Rob grew up in eastern Canada. Married when she was 19 and he was 20, they were always described as each other's best friend. Within a few years he was working in a stock brokerage and she was at home with two babies, but still going to school. It was the mid-Sixties; Canada — and the Buchanans — were just about to experience the Woodstock generation.[1]

Jenny Buchanan recalls, "We weren't particularly flower children but we certainly questioned social values very sincerely.... We had enough money that we were living comfortably at a very young age. We decided we didn't want to just be working for money the rest of our lives. We preferred to enjoy our life."

The Buchanans went to Europe with their young children, travelling for two years. When they returned to Canada they found that their values had changed. They didn't want to return to suburbia, so in the early Seventies they bought a farm in the Maritimes and went to live there.

The most prominent feature of their 12 years on the farm was alcohol. "We both drank. It's sadly classical. When we changed our scene to Europe, our North American drinking habit stayed the same. We enjoyed liquor but we also added wine to our daily intake. In the Maritimes on the farm we started to make our own beer so we had unlimited amounts to drink. We'd often buy wine and liquor on the weekend. Our tolerance kept increasing. We were both aware we had a drinking problem and we didn't really want to do much about it."

Jenny Buchanan went to a psychiatrist about stresses in her marriage but didn't talk about her drinking, just about her changes in mood. She was prescribed valium, and so added a second drug into her cycle of abuse. She says of her life on the farm, "There were good and bad times in the Maritimes. Years went by and economically we were finding it difficult.... My husband had been offered a job with [the post office] in the city for a year, and we agreed that it would be a good idea. We didn't want to sell our farm."

The Buchanans moved away from the Maritimes in 1983 and found that they liked life in the city after 12 years in the country. They were both working, and enjoying the challenges that their jobs presented, but they were both still involved with alcohol. "We would meet after work and we'd go and both work out and then we'd have a few drinks. And, my God, the city had happy hour, when drinks were two for one, but we had doubles and we had three or four...and it was too difficult to carry beer around...so we were buying more and more hard liquor, instead of just beer and wine...every day of the week and heavy, heavy drinking on weekends."

The Buchanan's lifestyle started to disintegrate while they were in the city. Rob Buchanan collapsed at work one morning. "My husband had a serious heart attack. We both avoided carefully diagnosing what had happened to him...he was kept in the hospital for, I believe it was just about six hours; I don't recall him being held overnight. At that point he was somewhat overweight. He had a current and severe history of high blood pressure. His own father had died of a heart attack at 42, or about that age.''

This situation made Jenny Buchanan "very, very unhappy." She was now facing unemployment in the Maritimes and she had very little sympathy for her husband's medical problems. "His health had been seriously undermined and although he was not to smoke and not to drink, he upped his smoking, upped his drinking and upped his eating. It was sort of a reaction. I knew that when I went back to the Maritimes and I was alone on the farm I'd drink more at home."

They went back to the Maritimes in the fall of 1984 and she too began to lose control of her drinking. "I mean, when you drink as much as I drank, you figure it's under control if you're functioning at all the next day. It's a sad story."

In the new year, she tried to pull herself out of her alcoholism. She started going to fitness classes and swimming, "And I'm feeling so good that just around Easter time I rejoiced in all this fitness and took myself off skiing. Had a minor skiing accident, cracking an ankle bone, which put me out of commission, in a cast...which was of course a great excuse to go back to 292s, other prescription drugs and drinking."

She lost control of alcohol almost completely, "(Normally) I had to give myself 36 hours between heavy drinking and the point at which I could really appear without tremors, without any appearance of this heavy drinking. I couldn't do that any more. I couldn't stop for 36 hours."

Rob Buchanan joined his wife in these drinking sprees and conflict would flare between them occasionally. She describes one particular argument about money and employment: "He grabbed a pillow and shook it and started to hit me with it. He kept hitting and as he hit me, the feathers in the pillow shrank to one corner of it, until it became a bludgeon. And he continued to beat me as I ran up the stairs, into our bedroom, till I cowered on the bed and covered my head to protect my face, to protect my glasses...and he kept beating me till the pillow actually exploded. The result was that I was covered with bruises. I couldn't go anywhere, I couldn't go to any classes or anything 'cause people would have seen them. I couldn't use my arm the next day — the nerves in my elbow had been smashed to bits.''

By the spring she was beginning to feel that something had to be done. She made arrangements to enter a detoxification centre and had her husband drive her up there. She drank a bottle in the car as they drove — she had been told by one of the A.A. members that she shouldn't try to do it ''cold turkey.''

Rob Buchanan was not happy about leaving his wife at the detox centre; he thought the whole idea of treatment was crazy and he didn't like the centre, which he viewed as a ''rundown, derelict kind of place.'' What the centre had to offer was, in Jenny Buchanan's words, ''too little, too late.'' ''I didn't know what I needed. I don't think at that point I was prepared to stop drinking. I guess all I needed was for him to say come home and I did. He went back on the Sunday. I got a bus on the Monday. I stopped at the liquor store and picked up a bottle on the way...and a bottle of sleeping pills.''

Five days later Jenny Buchanan shot her husband. ''My husband and I spent a fairly normal Sunday for us. I woke up before my husband, went down and poured a drink. I know he came down an hour later and said, pour me one too, and we started in again. The day progressed...we had sex. Our older daughter was still living away from home, our younger one had spent the night in town. That pattern was not unusual...part of a work situation and partly to avoid the drinking in the home.''

She remembers only bits and pieces of the evening. Asked when she first became aware that she had shot her husband, she responds, ''Sunday evening, at the time that he died. Yes, because I was very aware that he'd been shot — that I had done it. I called the police and reported it. I don't know how whatever was going on in the house got me into a state where that would happen. I honestly just don't know. It's like taking a reel of a movie film and cutting out chunks. I tried to put it together and it's just not there.''

The Buchanans were both very drunk at the time of the killing. "My husband's body was autopsied and the alcohol count was well over 300. That was very, very high and he weighed a huge amount more than I did. He pushed over 200 pounds. And we'd been drinking the whole day. The intoxication was not a figment of my imagination.''

She was tried and convicted of second-degree murder; a defence of manslaughter was not accepted. "My lawyer was in tears. He had assured me...that it was certainly not going to be a murder conviction and that I was probably looking at seven years under a manslaughter conviction, 'cause that's what normally came down in this kind of case. He didn't bother getting a change of venue, even though I came from a small town where my husband was the president of the Chamber of Commerce and on the Board of Directors of the hospital. I'd been there 12 years. I knew they were very puritanical. When the verdict came down that I was guilty of second degree murder I was totally unsurprised. I think any other verdict from a Catholic community of that nature would have been totally unexpected.''

The alcoholism of the Buchanans was documented in criminal court and was difficult for Jenny to accept. She was sentenced to life imprisonment with a minimum term of 10 years before parole eligibility. "I think one of my strongest recollections during a court recess is standing in one of the entranceways feeling slimy and dirty. I literally felt like a little wormy animal somebody had lifted up from under a rock. That's the way I felt about myself when they were talking about the drinking and boozing that Buchanan had done. I didn't want to hear that in public.''

Jenny Buchanan figures that society "deserves a guarantee that I'll never drink again. I can say, yeah, sure, if I drink again, I'll take my own life. Who says that I won't take somebody else with me in doing it? Obviously I have proven that I am a very dangerous woman when I drink.''

She doesn't drink as she serves her time in Kingston's Prison for Women. "There is stuff around if you want to get it, but I come from a Scotch and martini background and I'm not really into shoe polish and Tang." She believes that prison is a fool's paradise for her, an alcohol-free environment that doesn't test her skills for coping with everyday life.

Mostly, though, she just misses the man her daughters described in court as her best friend. "It's two years and a bit since my husband died. My deepest wish is that I could do whatever time I have to do and we could be together again. I wish that we had a chance to make up some of the mistakes that we made because there was just so damn much good between us."

Her voice begins to tremble. "That's what I wish with all my heart. I still don't see what the hell use it is to go on living. I had a life that I enjoyed."

We are most likely to kill the ones we love. The killing of family is the largest single category of homicide, defined in the police Homicide Return as "a combination of immediate family, other kinship relationships, and common-law family categories." Statistics Canada reports over the past decade suggest that 40% of all homicides involve a domestic or family relationship between suspect and victim. In any given year approximately 200 Canadians will kill an intimate, a person with whom they were sharing a life.

These domestic killings make up about one-third of all killings by males, and over 70% of all killings by females. When women in Canada kill, they usually kill their husbands; they are rarely involved in killings for economic gain and they virtually never kill for sex. Their taking of life is, at least in some sense, a result of passion and hence more understandable.

With most murders of family members, the motive for the killing is all too clear — revenge, anger, jealousy, or argument. The vast majority of men and women confess guilt and make little effort to avoid detection. The people that I will tell you about in this chapter — Elizabeth Workman, J. B. Pirie, Kevin Bourne, Cordelia Poirier and others — did not ultimately deny their guilt. Understandably, many of them put forward justifications for their actions. Killings, although not easily forgiven, can usually be explained.

The domestic killer is treated less harshly than any other by Canadian courts; the crime is usually defined as manslaughter. Killing family is much more likely to involve "provocation" or "the heat of passion" than killing acquaintances, or killing for money or sex. While almost 60% of those who kill during the commission of another crime are sentenced to life imprisonment, only 20% of family killers receive this penalty.[2]

What we are about to hear in this chapter, then, concerns the worst of Canada's family killers, those who have been defined as murderers by our courts. These are the men and women who were said to be beyond the pale of provocation or passion. I found three basic themes underlying their crimes — alcohol, sexual betrayal and financial disputes. The chapter opened with Jenny Buchanan and the tragedy of her alcoholism. I turn now to Steve Galloway and another facet of the way in which this drug can increase the probability of violence.[3]

Galloway was raised in a small town in central Canada along with two sisters and two brothers. When he made mistakes as a child his father would hit him. "I probably deserved most of mine, I don't think I was a prize pupil by any means. I think I caused a lot of shit when I was younger, but his only answer to it was, do what you're told or else, and then get whacked on the side of the head or get the belt."

Galloway was aggressive himself as he went through his teens and twenties. He has a criminal record that was built on assaults — five or six convictions for assault causing bodily harm, obstructing a police officer, and common assault. There were also many other incidents that didn't result in court appearances. "If I was drinking then I would always end up in a fight. If I wasn't, then nine times out of 10 I'd walk away and say, okay, it's not worth the aggravation. I'd get into a lot of problems if somebody was bothering my friends. Like, if they didn't want to do something about it then I was quite willing to step in there and do it for them. The bars, that's basically where everything happened all the time."

Galloway married Brenda when he was in his mid-twenties; a couple of years later she gave birth to their little boy. He was working in a factory and active in community sports, refereeing and coaching minor hockey. The marriage couldn't have been too stable. She left and came back a number of times. He remembers one angry confrontation. "There was four of us. We were playing cards, and I forget what the argument was about, but anyways, she kept laughing. So I got really hot and I walked out of the room and ripped the phone off the hook, off the wall.

Steve Galloway is a very strong man — as he pulled, part of the wall came out, along with the cord and a lot of wiring. This only made things worse. "I always told her, like I said, lookit, when I'm mad, just leave me alone, I'll go off by myself and straighten it out. But that day she didn't, she had been drinking too. And she was trying to get me to settle down and I was getting mad. I just needed that few minutes just to settle myself down, but she kept coming on."

He pushed her out of the way, went into the bedroom and smashed his dresser. "I really got twisted that night. I shoved her up against the wall and just told her to get the hell out of my way. I said, just leave me alone." It was the first time that Galloway had shown any real violence toward his wife, or any woman, and it disturbed him.

On the day of the killing Galloway had been out drinking around town, first at a restaurant and then at the local Legion, mixing wine, whiskey and beer. He started at about noon and didn't finish until about one in the morning. In the evening he and his wife went out with some friends to a birthday celebration.

Galloway doesn't remember what happened that night. "I woke up the next morning and the baby was crying. And so I hollered out to my wife to go feed him. I figured she was up and about already. And I got no response so about five minutes later I said, shit, I guess I'm going to have to get up. So I got up and walked into the baby's room, picked him up, and walked out in the living room and then I seen my wife on the floor. And...went crazy. I didn't know what had happened.''

For about three days after his arrest he figured that he hadn't killed her. "It was while I was sitting in the bucket, I don't know, this is kind of weird, but it was almost as if she was sitting there with me, her presence. And so she said, yeah, it was you. And from that time on I accepted responsibility for it but still don't have the details.''

He knows now that he strangled her, apparently during an argument over who should have taken the babysitter home. He was charged with first degree murder; he pleaded guilty to second and was given a minimum of 10 years before parole eligibility. "I was told afterwards I could have done better but part of me didn't really care. I wanted to survive it.''

He fears that his inability to remember important details of the killing may compromise his chances for parole. "I think it rubs people the wrong way. They don't accept it. They accept the responsibility, they can take that, but that doesn't mean as much to them as being able to provide details of exactly what happened that night. So that in itself is something that I don't know how to deal with. I just tell them and that's it. If they don't accept it, they don't accept it and there's nothing more I can do about it.''

Some eight years after the killing he has made some changes in his life. First, and probably foremost, he has put alcohol behind him. "I never had to drink. It wasn't something I had to do, like drinking water. But when I did drink, I drank too much. That, to me, is the easiest thing I've solved. That part's history.''

At the same time he is aware of the temptations that the street will offer. "People that've known me before could say, Steve, come on, let's go for a beer and I'm going to say no. Well, what to do with that, I don't know. So I still got problems to face with some friends when I meet them again. If I have to go another way and look for new people to hang around with, then fine. That's something I'll have to do.''

Galloway is also working on his relationship with his son,

now an eight-year-old boy. Scott has been brought up by Galloway's sister and brother-in-law; he comes in about three or four times a year, usually for an extended trailer visit. Galloway recalls, "when he first started coming up to see me that way, it was always 'Steve.' I was just somebody called 'Steve.' I didn't really call him...but he asked me if I was his dad one time. And I told him I was. He says, I got two dads and one mom. I said, yeah, you do. I said, you're kind of fortunate, aren't you?"

Galloway suspects he will be something of an outsider to his son. "I'll spend as much time as I can with him, bringing him up wherever." He's very proud of the way his son is turning out, but he is concerned about his boy's aggression. "The only thing right now is that he likes to fight. Shades of his dad. I don't know how I'll work that out, but I'm telling him that's not the way to go. He says he does it to stick up for his friends. And I'm sitting there going, Jesus Christ, I used to say that too."

Steve Galloway will, with any luck, be able to begin his return to the street within a few years. He figures that a relationship with a woman will be the most difficult issue that he has to face. "I don't know how I would explain it to somebody. I'm not too sure of how they would react to it and I'm also afraid that I would lose somebody because of that. So I don't know what to do, really. Casual relationships, then there's no problem because you don't have to delve into your history. But something where you get more serious than that, then I would feel obligated to tell the person. I think they would have to know."

Steve Galloway and Jenny Buchanan leave us with a very similar appreciation of alcohol as a stimulant for marital strife. To borrow the imagery of Jenny Buchanan, these two people have had huge chunks cut out of the films of their killings; they can only remember bits and pieces of the entire evening in question. Alcohol is a relevant factor in 40% of all family killings; over the past decade there have been close to 100 of these crimes in any given year.

The relevance of alcohol is not always to be found, however, in the intoxication of the convicted murderer. Consider the case of Elizabeth Workman, who lived with her husband James in Sarnia. One night in the fall of 1872 she beat him to death with a piece of wood as he lay in bed. He was known in the community as an abusive drunkard; at trial, neighbours recounted prior incidents when Elizabeth Workman fled the family home after a beating.

The couple was not held in high esteem by the local aristocracy. Workman's lawyer wrote to Prime Minister John A. MacDonald, "All the parties were of a very low class. The murdered man was a drunken brutal cruel husband. A licentious loose life had weakened or destroyed all fine domestic feelings on the part of husband and wife. Coarse language and blows were common and no one seemed surprised that their wretched life ended as it did."[4]

The jury found the accused guilty, but unanimously recommended mercy; the judge, sentencing Mrs. Workman to hang, told her that, despite the jury's inclinations, he did not hold out much hope for commutation. Most of the blame for the crime focused on Workman's husband; both Sarnia City Council and Lambton County Council sent petitions to the federal government, requesting a commutation of sentence.

In early June of 1873 Lambton County Council unanimously passed a motion that councillors John Mackenzie and Robert Rae travel to Ottawa to attempt to obtain a commutation for Mrs. Workman. The written motion noted that Workman was "quiet and mild in disposition" and "sober and industrious in her habits."

"There is a widespread feeling amongst all classes of the community," the councillors wrote, "that this unfortunate woman, if guilty of crime, has been far more sorely tempted than human beings usually can be...there are such extenuating circumstances in this case as would justify His Excellency in commuting her sentence to imprisonment...."

Few citizens in Sarnia were interested in an invitation to the June 19 execution; not many of the black-bordered cards were given out. The government of Sir John A. MacDonald declined to interfere with the sentence of death, and in the early morning young Elizabeth Workman walked up the scaffold, assisted by three ministers. She carried a white handkerchief and a bunch of white flowers as she stood on the trap door. Amidst prayers said by her ministers, she fell to her death. Some 20 minutes later her body was lowered into a coffin, the flowers and handkerchief still clutched in her hand.

These are the tragedies of alcohol abuse in the home — Elizabeth Workman, Steve Galloway, and Jenny Buchanan represent only three of the thousands of such cases that Canada has experienced from Confederation to the present. But while alcohol abuse is a lubricant or accelerator of violence, sexual betrayal is a motive in itself. I am now going to tell the stories of three men who killed because they felt betrayed, and a woman who betrayed and killed her husband, in concert with her lover.

Kevin Bourne and his wife Joyce first moved in together at 16 or 17, as teenage lovers — and they soon had two children and marital difficulties. Bourne figures that the story of their life together ought to be called Kids Having Kids.[5]

His father was a longshoreman and his mother was a housewife. Bourne never imagined that he would go to jail. "My brother, he's younger than I am, he was always getting into trouble so our whole family thought, well, if anyone was going to jail it's him. I worked most of the time and never did crimes or anything like that."

During their last year the couple had a number of violent conflicts. At one point Bourne told his wife that things just weren't going to work out, that he was going to leave the city. But he came home that night — after his promise of departure — and found the apartment full of people. He waited outside.

After a while, his wife was alone with another man and it didn't seem that he was about to leave. Joyce was apparently talking to her guest about staying the night. "And this guy he said, oh, what about the kid? And right then, I just thought, who the hell...he was talking...like a sack of potatoes or something."

Bourne began to plot against them, "So I thought, okay,

you know, I'll wait. I'll wait until you guys get in that bedroom and I'm going to come through that bathroom window and God help both of you.''

About 2 a.m., the manager of the building was out doing his rounds and saw Bourne. He let him into the building and knocked on the apartment door. As he stood outside with the manager, Bourne could feel his anger rise, wanting to kick in the door, hearing his daughter crying inside.

His wife opened the door. Bourne stormed in. ''I just threw my coat down and went into the bedroom and he wasn't there. I went into the kitchen and he wasn't there. . . . I opened the bathroom door and he was standing in front of the mirror, combing his hair. I just said to him, well what was this about...oh, you know, what about the kid? And he says, I don't know what you're talking about. That's when I dropped him right then and there. And he got up and he was wearing glasses. I'd smashed the glasses and the glasses had cut into his nose.''

Kevin and Joyce remained together after this incident. The building manager called the police but they didn't push for any courtroom intervention, after they realized that Joyce had not asked for them. For the next five months the couple tried to patch their lives together but without much success. Kevin Bourne finally left the city, setting up a relationship with another woman in a city hundreds of miles away.

But eventually he was drawn back to Joyce and his two children. This second time around produced even greater conflict. As Bourne describes it, ''My buddy was passed out in the chair and we started arguing. I went and got a drink. She threw a cup at me and I just kept drinking, and then I got pissed off at her and went to throw the glass at her. And then she took a swing at me and that was it. I grabbed her and I started beating on her and beating on her, and I can remember saying, this is the last time you're going to take a swing at me, or hit me. And then I started kneeing her and kicking her and booting her...it must have been going for at least a minute or two and then finally my buddy woke up, he pulled me off and threw me against the wall.''

Bourne's wife went upstairs, after she could pull herself together, and called the police. Bourne was taken to the city jail and then to court; he was convicted of assault and fined $100. When he was released, he swore that he wouldn't drink again — he had been very drunk at the time of the assault and decided that this was the problem that he had to overcome. But he also took a cab from the jail to a local hotel and started drinking again. He didn't contact his wife, left the city a couple of days later and kept himself out of trouble with her for about six weeks.

Once again, though, he couldn't stay away. He started calling her and she kept putting him off — she didn't want to see him. At one point a man Joyce was working with told Bourne to stay away. But Bourne decided that he had to see her. For a third time the couple reunited, under his relentless pressure.

As he puts it, "Now I know that she didn't want me, you know. She said all that in court...and then I get a letter from her in the remand centre. She starts telling me things I didn't even know that would have made a big difference to me if she had said something to me, but I think she was scared. You see, I wouldn't talk. Or I'd talk, but I was hard to get along with back then."

Many years later he still finds it very difficult to talk about the killings, becoming very emotional when he describes what happened. On the night of the crime Bourne wanted his wife to be home by nine. He was following her around, checking up on her and at a little after nine she was still at a meeting in a local hotel. He went back to the apartment, furious, and waited. He was becoming more and more angry and started making phone calls to her boss, and to the welfare office, telling them to come and pick up the children. He was leaving, he said, and the kids needed to be looked after.

He hung up on the welfare office, walked over to a nearby shopping mall, walked back to the apartment and paced around feverishly. Not long after coming back to the apartment he placed a pillow over the faces of his sleeping daughters, one about a year old and the other about three.

The notes that were left at the scene were signed "don't love Daddy," and the note to his wife said, among other things, "I hope you're happy now" and "you don't have to worry about me or the kids."

Bourne left the apartment before his wife came home. He didn't go far, standing outside and watching fire trucks go by, a couple of ambulances, and police cars. In just a few minutes, with police cars combing the streets, back and forth, back and forth, Bourne was using alleyways to move around and still stay close to the apartment building.

He found a quiet back yard, and was standing there, leaning against a fence, both arms on top of it. He was thinking about how he was going to get around all the police cruisers parked out on the median, red lights flashing in the night.

"And finally I just said, fuck it and I walked out. I remember walking straight toward this police car...cars slamming on their brakes. And I just kept walking straight, and then the driver's door opened just two or three inches and [he] kind of half-assed leaned out and said, are you...? And I said, yeah, and then they both jumped out of their car, grabbed me and turned me up against the car, patted me down. They handcuffed me and turned me into the back of the car and started driving...started asking me all these questions."

Kevin Bourne was convicted of second degree murder and sentenced to life imprisonment. The way he sees things now, he might not be able to walk right by his wife if he saw her on the street, but he also wouldn't want to find her again. He believes that he deserved to be sent to prison — "Right from the beginning I thought I should be doing the time" — and that he is a better person now than he was five years ago, "I say I'm glad I came [here] because I know I just didn't care about things out there. All I cared about was drinking. I worked and drank and that's all I did from day to day."

"I remember that all I wanted to do was kill, kill, kill Joyce. All I wanted to do was kill her. Every night that's how I fell asleep — I was thinking up different ways of torturing her, and I'm not bullshitting. Every night, that's how I went to sleep."

Ben Costello didn't have the same drive to hurt that Kevin Bourne did at the time that he killed. Costello's stabbing of his "old lady" was less of a statement of vengeance, but again, it was motivated by a betrayal. Ben Costello and Alice had been living together for about a year. He had been hospitalized for depression: "They don't fool around. You're into the hospital and they nail you with the bug juice. And I mean, really nail you with it. You're a walking zombie."[6]

Costello is maintained today on the antidepressant drug lithium, a chemical that seems to keep his "hyperness" in check. He has had a constant battle with depression all his life and is one of those killers who does not fall neatly into a single category of explanation. There are some who might say that he was emotionally disturbed at the time of his crime. His outbreak seems to have been brought on by drinking, by an apparently deteriorating relationship with Alice, and by an evident genetic susceptibility to depression — there is a history of the illness in his family.

Costello found Alice in bed with another man once at her mother's home. They were sleeping when he walked into the room. "I didn't scream or nothing, I just ran upstairs, I couldn't believe it. And I just.... I scooted upstairs."

The situation was driving him crazy, but he left — "just took off." Now, a few months later, he was facing a similar situation. An old friend told him that Alice "was really going at it last night" at a party. The old friend didn't know that Ben and Alice were living together.

Costello was upset and drunk when he confronted her later that day. "Well, did you have a good time at the party?"

"How did you know I was at the party?"

"Oh, I know. Did you have a good lay?"

Alice started laughing and Costello "just flipped right out." Having finished off three-quarters of a bottle of liqueur, he grabbed a butcher knife and stabbed her. "And I turned around...I threw the knife...we had a couple staying over...well, he came out, and I grabbed the knife — another knife — and I tried to kill myself. I just grabbed the damn thing and I was just going to pull it in, and he grabbed my arms. So I wrestled away from him and I ran out on the balcony and I dove off.''

Costello landed on some rocks below and received three stitches later at the hospital; his wife died there later in the day. It was an unexpected end to their relationship; there hadn't been physical violence between them before. As Costello recalls, the only person in this family who had been hit was Don, Alice's baby from a previous relationship. ''Yeah, she smacked Don a few times. But I mean smacking her would be ridiculous. It was just the point. I couldn't believe what I had done when I had stabbed her.''

Costello had one previous conviction for impaired driving; he was convicted of second degree murder and sentenced to life imprisonment. He will not be eligible for parole for about 10 years. ''A lot of people don't realize how I feel,'' he says now. ''I mean, I loved her. I'm the guy that's got to live with it. And it ain't much of a life, you know, to live like that....''

Not all of those who kill family over a sexual betrayal are as sorry as Ben Costello or Kevin Bourne. Victor Morrison believes that killing his wife was quite justifiable. When he was told by police that she was dead, his comment was, ''Good, at least I've done something right in my life.'' While the vast majority of those who kill family are caught up in the heat of a moment, there are men — and very occasionally, women—who kill without remorse, imposing ''just'' punishments on those who have betrayed them.[7]

The difficulties between Victor and Stella Morrison began in 1973, when Stella left her husband for another man. According to Morrison, ''Stella didn't do things the way an honest thinking person would. She was a person who liked to find somebody else first and if it worked out, then she could dump me.''

The couple began divorce proceedings, but later got back together. As Morrison recalls, he drank heavily during the separation, but otherwise handled it in good shape. His business was doing well, and their 10-year-old son was staying with him. His wife's affair did not come out of nowhere; it had been developing over a two-to-three year period. But when

Stella left him again in 1982, he was in his fifties. As he put it, "I was getting old, and I felt that I was being rejected and dumped."

Morrison had been out of town for a few days, on a bus trip to Reno with his brother-in-law. His son met him at the bus station and the three men drove to the apartment where they found a note on the refrigerator. As Morrison recalls, the china cabinet had been stripped of its wares and the note explained that his wife was leaving him for a man she had been to Reno with — a man she found very attractive, younger and more athletic than Morrison.

For a few months Morrison coped on a comfortable income; his son moved into the apartment with a girlfriend. But Morrison was still angry and still looking for his wife. He found her in an apartment not far from his own, and asked her to come back to him.

"Of course you miss your wife," he says now. "If you love a woman and you've lived with her for 20 years and gone through hard times and gone through good times and raised a fine son and had everything that married people in Canadian society expect you to do...naturally you miss your wife."

One day in May, 1982 Morrison confronted his wife and her lover out in a shopping mall, where they were selling pictures. As Morrison describes the scene, "Now, this is the thing that really hurt me. All the years that I had this business, and it was a good business, my wife didn't give a shit about that business. All she'd give a shit was when there was a hundred-dollar bill in the till, you know, take it and buy some new clothes or buy something for her family. I mean, when I think back, it's no goddamned wonder she's dead. It's no wonder. And there she was, out selling goddamned $5.00 reprints — art reprints for this guy on the street corner...."

Morrison telephoned the couple and threatened them, telling them they were both "dead ducks." He drove down to the U.S. to try to buy a gun, with no luck. He took a long knife, though, and slashed the tires on the man's car; he also smashed in their car's windshield. A detective from the local police force went over to Morrison's apartment and talked to him. The upshot of the meeting was that no charges were laid, but the detective urged Morrison's son to keep his father at home for a few days.

For the next three years Victor Morrison drifted across Canada and the United States, a competent salesman and a person who could fend for himself, but also an increasingly embittered man. He remembers an evening with some friends in the southern United States as particularly significant. He and his wife had known George and Gail for years, through a shared interest in playing bridge at the duplicate bridge clubs.

"We'd had supper and I felt comfortable, but I didn't feel that comfortable. I was enjoying myself. So Gail made a drink...well, I said, oh, I don't think I'll have a drink, I can live without it. And so she brought me a drink anyway, a light drink, and she came up and she put her arm around me...'Vic,' she says, 'I just feel terrible about you and Stella.'"

As Morrison puts it, "something snapped." He went back to his apartment that night and cried. "I felt terrible. It bothered me then, everything. That was almost the start of the murder...the wheels, the wheels up here started to turn."

A few months later, in the summer of 1985, he returned to Canada. He had purchased a number of guns, a .357 magnum and a couple of .38 specials. He was prepared to kill his wife and her lover. "I had a plan. The plan was well orchestrated; it was well done. If I would have got away from the scene of the murder, they'd never have found me."

At this point Morrison was becoming increasingly depressed. He went to see a doctor about his depression; he was given a drug, and told to come back in a few days if he didn't feel better. Morrison also applied for welfare, got himself a cheque, and cashed it. "That sort of gave me a little bit of a lift," he recalls.

But he was also casing the store at which his wife worked. He took his gun and went down to the mall. He saw his wife and her lover. "She looked 15 years older than when she left me, and he looked...like a good target."

For several days he made the trip to the mall, "getting deeper" into the idea of the killing. One Thursday morning he walked into his wife's place of work.

"What's this about the divorce?", he said.

"Oh, when did you get back in town?"

"I've been in town for a day or two. I guess we should get this divorce thing finished."

"Well, I've got the thing all ready. You just have to go up to this guy and sign the papers."

As Stella Morrison went to get the address, her husband of 24 years pulled out his gun, saying, "I'll give you a fucking divorce you won't forget," and shot her. She was facing him when she fell. He walked a few feet closer, leaned over the counter and pumped the remaining bullets into her. He threw down the gun and walked out of the shop.

He didn't get far. His "well orchestrated plan" for escape fell apart within minutes. There were police everywhere; an employee from another store had seen Morrison leaving. He was arrested and tried, convicted of second degree murder, and sentenced to life imprisonment.

He has no complaints about the way he has been treated or about the sentence imposed. "I can honestly say that even in the police station, I was treated with dignity and respect. They brought me coffee, and they knew that I was in bad shape. I think that the arresting officers and the detectives were very sympathetic to me.

"Maybe I possessed my wife," he explains. "Maybe I never did love my wife. Maybe my wife was one of my possessions, maybe, maybe, I don't know what love is. Maybe, like the doctor claims I'm a narcissist, that I don't love anybody but myself.

"But I was certainly a good husband to my wife. But you see, the people at the pre-trial and the police and the lawyers and this circle of friends that runs this stuff, they love a guy like me. 'Cause here I am, they got somebody they can charge with first degree murder, and in his own mind he's done nothing wrong.

"Of course, I have some personal things that...like I don't like civil servants and I don't like Jews. This is from my own reading and my own education...not that I would go out shooting them. I'm just saying that I think they're the cause of the problems we have in the world today — the bureaucracies and the Jewish money people, but I'm not going to get into that this time.''

For the present, Victor Morrison is quite content to spend his time in prison. ''I'm very comfortable in jail.'' He concludes, ''You must understand I worked hard for 35 years. I never had very much holiday in my life, and prison to me is a holiday. It's a rest; I have time to think about the past.''

Like Victor Morrison and his wife Stella, Cordelia and Isidore Poirier had an unhappy marriage. They were living near St. Scholastique, Quebec, in 1898. At the turn of the century, St. Scholastique was a part of rural Quebec; today it's the home of Mirabel Airport, an international destination, and, to many, a white elephant.

Isidore Poirier was a builder, a man who liked to drink a little; he was neither loved nor liked by his wife Cordelia. She had told a friend just a few days before the killing, ''If ever you get married, marry a man you love; one is too unhappy with a man one does not love.''

Cordelia Poirier did have a lover — Sam Parslow, a local labourer whom she had been seeing for at least a couple of years. The trial heard evidence that at one party Sam Parslow was sitting on Mrs. Poirier's knee, with his arm around her. There was more proof, in the testimony of a neighbour, who witnessed ''conclusive presumptive evidence of adultery.''

''One day in the spring of 1897, Poirier being absent at St. Jerome, the witness Hall saw from his house...Parslow and the female prisoner together. After [Mr.] Poirier left, the female prisoner came to the door of her house and spoke to Parslow, who after a few minutes, went back into the house with her. They stopped in the house for a while and came out and sat on the verandah and talked together. They remained there for over an hour and as Parslow stood up to go away, he stooped down and kissed the female prisoner.''[8]

On Monday, November 22, Isidore Poirier was found lying across his bed; he had been stabbed six times, and his throat was slit from ear to ear. The opinion of doctors who performed the post-mortem was that Poirier had been stabbed while sleeping; he had struggled about the room a little, but had quickly been subdued. The cut from ear to ear had been inflicted methodically, probably after Poirier had stopped moving.

Poirier's body was discovered by his wife Cordelia and by his neighbour, blacksmith Noél Bouvrette. Cordelia Poirier had stayed at her father's Sunday night, and then gone on to church, where she played the organ, as she usually did at Catholic wedding services in St. Scholastique. After she returned from the wedding, she asked Bouvrette to help her into the house. As Bouvrette noted at trial, Mrs. Poirier's response to her husband's corpse was unusual. She put her hands over her eyes and seemed to be crying, but she did not cry very much.

The most compelling evidence against Cordelia Poirier was her own confession, and that of Sam Parslow. Police detective McCaskill indicated to her that Sam Parslow had confessed, and she consequently made a statement in which she indicated that she was an accomplice; she hadn't been present at the killing, but she knew that it had taken place. Sam Parslow confessed that he had stabbed Isidore Poirier, but added that Cordelia Poirier had been with him. In fact, he said, it was Cordelia Poirier who was the instigator — she had been nagging him to kill her husband since New Year's.

The memorandum prepared for the Minister of Justice agreed with this interpretation, concluding that, "the result of all those confessions leaves the cut on the throat from ear to ear unaccounted for. By which of the two culprits that wound was inflicted remains a mystery, or at least a matter of conjecture.... The impression left upon my mind by reading the evidence is that the woman was the master-mind in the crime. The evidence given on Parslow's behalf shows him to have been of a soft and pliant disposition and easily influenced."[9]

Sam Parslow and Cordelia Poirier were both convicted of murder and sentenced to hang in March 1899, less than four months after their crime. There were petitions on behalf of both convicted killers, and in mid-February of that year, Cordelia Poirier wrote from her prison cell in St. Scholastique, hoping to avoid her quickly approaching date with death.

"It is from my cell and on my knees," she began, "that I am writing these few lines to implore your mercy and pardon.

"I know I do not deserve much compassion, or even perhaps the slightest sympathy, but could you not at least discover in some remote part of your good heart a particle of pity towards the most unhappy of all women....

"I am, of your Excellency, the most devoted and unworthy servant," Poirier concluded.

The government of Wilfrid Laurier was not moved by this appeal or by others. About a week before the hanging the Minister of Justice indicated to the Cabinet that he was unable to see any reason for recommending interference with the sentence imposed by the trial judge.

On the morning of March 10, a crowd of about 2,000 gathered outside the prison at St. Scholastique and about 600 people had been given passes to come inside and watch the double hanging. It was a rambunctious crowd, both within and outside the jail.

The crowd inside the jail had been allowed to walk by and "gaze on" the prisoners in their cells during the previous evening; Cordelia Poirier's father had to push his way through the crowd for a last visit with his daughter. Both Parslow and Poirier slept a few hours, and were then awakened a little after 4:00 a.m. They spent an hour at mass between five and six, and then had a light breakfast of toast and coffee. The Toronto *Globe's* reporter said that both Poirier and Parslow "seemed to relish it."[10]After breakfast both prisoners were given a glass of brandy, "a stimulant for the terrible ordeal through which they were so soon to go." A few minutes before eight a rustling in the corridor announced the beginning of the procession to the scaffold and the crowd fell silent. Sheriff Lapointe led the way in uniform, followed by Cordelia Poirier; she was supported by Father Meloche. Sam Parslow walked behind his accomplice, held up by Father Lalonde.

As she walked up the scaffold, Poirier hitched up her long black dress with each step, not wanting to trip. At the top of the landing, she walked over to the trap **door; she** and Sam Parslow were unable to see each other, sta**nding back** to back on the wooden platform. As the priests **whispered spiritual** consolation to the two killers, Radcliffe, **the hangman,** "with lightning-like rapidity, **strapped** the limbs, adjusted **the nooses,** and drew down the **black caps...**[he] drew the bolt **and the** trap fell. As far **as he was concerned,** the work was sk**ilfully** done."

But the very **second that Poirier** and Parslow fell, **the mob** of hundreds surged **toward the scaffold,** ripping the black **linen** from the posts at the **bottom of the platform.** The couple was now dangling in public **view, still very much** alive.

The Globe explained the "uncontrollable" behaviour of the crowd as "morbid curiosity" — these people had come to the jail to watch two killers die and they didn't want to miss any of the key moments. The paper concluded its description of the hanging, "Drs. McPhail and Lamarche officiated, and announced that the woman's pulse stopped beating in just six minutes, while that of the man throbbed for twelve minutes. An examination showed that the necks were broken, and that they did not suffer in the least."

There are other men and women like Cordelia Poirier — and Victor Morrison, Kevin Bourne and Ben Costello — involved in relationships in which violence seems to them the only way out, a punishment for some kind of betrayal. As I indicated earlier in this chapter, there are three dominant themes with people who kill family: alcohol, sexual betrayal, and financial disputes. I have given you some examples of betrayers and betrayed; now to four men who felt that they never got the financial rewards they deserved. There is a sense in which one could say that J.B. Pirie, Eugene Bigaouette, Peter Beyak and John Bateman killed for money, but ulti-mately the family dynamic is the strongest element here. What these cases and dozens of others each year reveal is the impor-tance of economic relations to marriages and other similar living arrangements.

John Buchanan Pirie, a former soldier living in Ottawa 60 years ago, was obsessed by the difficulty of his economic situation. On a fall day in 1924 he walked into the Canal Street Police Station and said that he had killed his wife and two children at the family's home on Grove Avenue. The city police found the bodies; his wife had been struck on the side of the head and smothered, and his children, aged six and five, had also been suffocated. The killings had taken place during the night and in the morning Pirie turned himself in.

He told police that he had been unfairly treated, that he was never adequately paid for his services as a soldier to the Empire. He'd joined the British Army in 1900 at the age of 19 and gone off to South Africa to fight in the Boer War. Discharged in 1912, he soon re-enlisted, joining the Military Mounted Police in Ipswich. But in 1916 he began to have some difficulties; he was "invalided with rheumatism." In 1917 he crashed while flying with the Royal Air Force, and was unconscious in hospital for eight days. In 1919 he was discharged with a $250 "wound credit" for his flying injury and given a pension at 70% of his existing pay.

Pirie's pension was cut to 50%, and then later in 1923, while he was in Canada, to 40%. He wrote in the note that he left at the murder scene of the cruel world that his family would not have to experience. By killing his wife and his two children, he was removing them from an existence that must, of necessity, be unhappy.

J.B. Pirie was a tidy, fervent little man. The question of his sanity was raised at trial, but expert witnesses could not diagnose anything more traumatic than psychoneurosis. The trial judge noted in his summary to the federal government, "The prisoner seemed remarkably intelligent and did not go into the box, but his two written statements show that he had a grievance against the British government and against the world in general for not affording him a better living."[11]

After Pirie had been found guilty the trial judge turned to him, saying, "Well, Pirie, there is a very painful duty that is imposed upon me by the law and that is to pass sentence upon you. I do not propose to say anything; I do not think that you may sustain yourself by any hope of clemency."

"I do not, my Lord."

"I do not know that you wish it."

"I do not."

"You may rely upon it that the sentence will not be carried out until the executive is fully satisfied of your sanity. I have no doubt of it myself."

"Neither have I, my Lord."

"And the jury has passed upon it. The sentence of the Court is that you be taken to the place whence you came and there be confined in close custody until the 24th day of March, 1925, and that upon that day you be taken to the place of execution and there be hanged by the neck until you are dead, and may God have mercy on your soul."

"Thank you, my Lord."

After the trial, efforts were begun by war veterans and war widows to save Pirie's life. Despite contradictory evidence at trial, The Great War Veterans' Association argued that "the mental condition of the accused at the exact time of the crime" had amounted to insanity. They went on, "We submit that Pirie is a homicidal maniac and not a criminal murderer. As a homicidal maniac, he cannot be held in law responsible for his crime."

The Ministry of Justice engaged another doctor to see Pirie and to inform the government of his mental state. Harvey Clare, M.D., concluded that Pirie was so depressed that his judgement had been "warped to such a degree that he would not know what he should do or what he should not do. He would not be able to decide what was right and what was wrong."[12]

The memorandum prepared for the Minister of Justice quoted Dr. Harvey Clare and suggested that Pirie was a person of "impaired mentality." Its author, M.F. Gallagher, concluded, "In these circumstances the undersigned is inclined to believe that the death sentence may well be commuted to a term of life imprisonment."

The federal Cabinet agreed with the recommendation, and spared J.B. Pirie from the hangman.[13] He was sent off to

Kingston Penitentiary and then to the Ontario Hospital for the Criminally Insane at Penetanguishene. In 1936, after 10 years at Penetanguishene, he was sent back to Kingston Penitentiary, now said to be cured, and readied for deportation to his native country of Scotland.

Pirie, for his part, was frustrated by his continued detention in the Canadian penal system, from Kingston to Penetang and back to the penitentiary at Kingston. He wanted to go home to Scotland.

He wrote from his cell, "Apparently ignoring 20 years efficient, exemplary and not undistinguished service to the Empire, for my first misstep, and that, when not under mental control, I receive this savage punishment. Being condemned to live, I appeal to you to cause my removal to a more congenial environment."

Pirie's view of the crime was that it occurred "during temporary insanity." He noted that he had been born and educated as a gentleman, and then "subjected to the humiliating degradation of the penitentiary and criminal lunatic asylum...for a crime, fully demonstrated, which I, with even common justice, could not be held responsible for."[14]

The last entry in the J. B. Pirie Capital Case File is dated in October 1937, almost 13 years after the crime. It is a letter from the warden of Kingston Penitentiary. Canada was closing its file on this "homicidal maniac," and sending him home.

Under Secretary of State,
Ottawa, Ontario
>   *Re: #K-996 John Buchanan Pirie*

I have the honour to report that . . . I have released the above named convict effective the 20th, instant, into the custody of an officer appointed by the Minister of Mines and Resources for the purpose of deportation. Convict Pirie is fifty-seven years of age.

This violence of husbands towards their wives and children is the most common type of family killing in Canada. For every female murder suspect alleged to have killed family, there are four male suspects. For women, killing family is just about all there is to killing; over 70% of all female murder suspects fall into this category. But for Canadian men, this is just the beginning. Less than 35% of all male suspects kill family — men are more inclined to kill people they *don't* know.[15]

These crimes will be discussed in the chapters that follow; I return now to men and women who kill family as the result of a financial dispute. There are some common features in this category — intense anger, a longstanding abusive relationship, and a sudden explosion. Like J.B. Pirie, Peter Beyak exploded, feeling economically deprived and unwanted.

Beyak and Jessie Nehbereski had been living in a common law marriage in Windsor for about three years, back in the early Thirties. Beyak had originally been a boarder at Nehbereski's home but the relationship had developed to one of man and wife; Nehbereski's first husband had been confined in an asylum at London, Ontario.

Through late July and August of 1933, the couple was working together in a small grocery and meat shop, and fighting. For two days the argument went on. Beyak accused his wife's son of stealing from the till; his wife responded angrily that she wanted him out of the store, that she had found a better man. Beyak recounted some of the scenes later for the Ontario Provincial Police,"I was going to hit her with my fist, and she stood right where she was and said go ahead and hit, she called me a damn whore and said that I must be giving money to the girls that come and see me at night. I said you are a whore yourself or you wouldn't be going with other men and causing so much trouble all the time. I told her that all other wives who had someone else besides their husbands don't live good with their husbands.''[16]

On the afternoon of August 1, Peter Beyak lost control, or as he described it to police, "we continued quarrelling worse and worse until I went crazy, then that's all I could remember until I saw her lying on the floor, bleeding; then I got scared, after realizing what I had done.'' Beyak had hit his wife repeatedly with a meat cleaver, dropped it in the store, and then panicked, running away from the scene of the crime.

Another businessman had discovered Nehbereski in a pool of blood on the floor and called police; they began to comb the neighbourhood.

About an hour after the attack Beyak was hiding in a vacant house nearby. As police approached the building, he jumped from a second-storey window, approximately 18 feet to the ground. As he described the scene to police, "I remember I was so nervous I didn't know what was going on and I started to cry. I was feeling bad. I didn't know just what to do or where to go. Then the next thing I remember someone was coming into the house and then I jumped out of a window at the back...."

Peter Beyak was found in a "dazed" state, immediately handcuffed, and taken to hospital with injuries to his neck and shoulder. A few hours after he was admitted to Metropolitan Hospital in Walkerville, his wife died there of her injuries; he was released three days later. The police formally charged Beyak with murder as he lay in hospital on the evening of his wife's death.

At trial in September, Peter Beyak was found guilty of murder and sentenced to hang in early December of 1933. Both the prosecutor and defence counsel wrote letters urging commutation to Hugh Guthrie, the Justice Minister in R.B. Bennett's Conservative government. Defence lawyer J.H. Clark noted that Beyak was a 34-year-old man with no criminal record; he had grown up in Manitoba, and moved east about four years prior to the crime; he had always been regarded in the community as "quiet, unassuming and reliable." Clark concluded of the killing that "there was no premeditation and there was certainly no malice. The unfortunate tragedy, in our opinion, was caused from an absolute and complete loss of self-control while under the heat of passion."

Crown prosecutor Alfred Morine believed that the jury had been swayed by "the gruesome instrument" of the murder, a butcher's meat cleaver; Beyak had hit his wife many times with what was essentially a small axe. As prosecutor Morine understood this feature of the crime, "...it indicated that Beyak had caused the death in the heat of passion...and I had little doubt, if any, that the provocation he attributed to the woman had really been given.'' Morine concluded his letter to the Minister with the remark, ''I venture to say that I feel that a commutation to life imprisonment would be right.''

The government declined to interfere with the sentence of death. On December 6th, 1933, Sheriff C. N. Anderson wrote the following letter to E.H. Coleman, Under-Secretary of State, Ottawa:

Dear Sir:

Re: Peter Beyak

Peter Beyak, under sentence of death, was duly executed this morning and the body has been interred in the Gaol yard.

I am sending you herewith a certificate from the Gaol Surgeon, one from the Coroner and the third one from the Gaoler and myself.

The execution passed off without a hitch.

For John Bateman and his wife, resources were the key. He wanted a share of her house; she didn't want to give it to him. Perhaps more remarkably, though, he was 77 years old (and his wife was also elderly) when he committed this crime, a ''planned and deliberate'' act of vengeance.

The Batemans lived in Whitby, Ontario, in 1911; she was his second wife and he was her third husband. They had been married for about eight years and shared her house with two tenants, Martha Kalles and Emily Colborne. The Batemans lived in an extension of the original home; they had a bedroom, and their own bathroom and cooking facilities.

The couple's life together was fairly unhappy; they quarrelled about money and about the cats that Mrs. Bateman kept. John Bateman felt that he deserved $500 from his wife; he also thought that the money spent on cats should be given to him. On at least five separate occasions he had asked doctors to examine his wife; he was quite sure that she was insane. None of the doctors asked was inclined to examine Mrs.

Bateman, but Bateman persisted. About three weeks before the murder he mentioned that his wife's proper home was the asylum and that he "would do the old woman in and set fire to the place."

On a December morning in 1911 the two tenants in the Bateman house heard a number of disturbing noises. There were four groans and the thud of what sounded like a body hitting a floor. Mrs. Bateman was heard saying, "my poor bones...my poor bones." When the tenants went to the window to see what had happened, John Bateman was standing there, blocking their view, "very pale and eyes staring and big." The tenants were frightened and went back to their part of the house.

But some time later in the morning Bateman left the house: the tenants found Mrs. Bateman on the floor inside, bludgeoned to death, lying in pools of blood. The room was also on fire; there was a lot of smoke, and some paper burning at the dead woman's feet.

One witness saw John Bateman on the street and told him that his house was burning down. "It couldn't be," Bateman replied. The witness ran toward the house, urging Bateman to open the door. He refused, and the witness told him that he was going to call the police.

"Go ahead and do it, if it will do you any good," Bateman replied.

The people outside the house began to demand that Bateman go in and take his wife out. "I shan't go in," he said. The house was now smoking badly, billows coming out of the windows and under the eaves. As one person prepared to go in, Bateman warned him, "You had better be careful what you are about."

And then as a crew finally moved to extinguish the fire, John Bateman simply walked away. He was found later, sitting in a chair, in the public part of the police office, apparently waiting to be charged with his wife's murder. A bloodstained axe was found in the barn; coal oil had been smeared through the house. On arrest, Bateman's concerns were essentially twofold, that the house had burned down and that his wife was dead.

He claimed to police that he had not committed the crime, and mentioned other matters, "something about being lynched."[17]

At trial the jury took only half an hour to find Bateman guilty of murder, though they did recommend mercy. The trial judge spoke to John Bateman after conviction, "...what have you to say why the sentence of the court should not be passed upon you for the crime of which you have been found guilty?"

"I had no intention, my Lord, of killing that woman."

"John Bateman, a jury of your fellow countrymen has found you guilty of the crime of murder. You have had a fair trial; you have been very well defended by your counsel.... The jury has recommended you to mercy. Mercy is the function of the Crown; but I can hold out to you no hope whatever that mercy will be exercised. What you should do, as it seems to me, is to prepare for the ending that must come to you...."

But the letter sent from this trial judge to the federal government did recommend clemency, and John Bateman was not hanged. Mr. Justice Latchford wrote, "The crime...was murder, without any doubt; but the extreme age of the prisoner appeared to me quite to warrant the recommendation which the jury made." The memorandum prepared for the Minister of Justice also quoted approvingly from the letter sent by the trial judge, "In view of the opinion of the learned judge who presided at the trial, although it must be admitted that the crime was a horrible one, committed with premeditation and deliberation, the case is one in which the Minister of Justice would be justified in recommending the commutation of the death penalty to life imprisonment." John Bateman was to die, not on the gallows, but in the penitentiary.

For Eugene Bigaouette, there was no such mercy. Bigaouette represents a small number of people who kill family, those who kill their mothers. His case is also one which, like those of John Bateman, J.B. Pirie, and Peter Beyak, reveals some of the cracks in the typology that I am using to define murder. My five categories overlap on occasion and in the case of Eugene Bigaouette we may be looking at three of them — an emotionally disturbed man who killed family for money. The killing of family may be the most noticeable feature of this crime, but one cannot ignore either Bigaouette's state of mind or his expressed interest in his potential inheritance.

This 41-year-old man, known in his Quebec City community as "Bigaouette the Fool," apparently strangled his 76-year-old mother, and left her lying across a chair in her bedroom. The evidence against Bigaouette was entirely circumstantial. He would not participate in either of his two trials; he wouldn't even respond when asked if he wanted to plead guilty or not guilty.

In November 1925, Eugene Bigaouette was living in his mother's house in Quebec City. He had been back in Canada for about three years, after spending most of his adult life in the United States. The house had four separate apartments; Mrs. Bigaouette's other sons lived in two of these units; a third was rented by a Mrs. Laliberté, and Eugene Bigaouette lived with his mother in the fourth unit.

Eugene was regarded as something of an eccentric. At trial a number of witnesses spoke of his peculiar conduct, which included placing notices in his backyard (in both English and French) warning all neighbourhood cats to keep off the grounds after nine o'clock in the evening. Other witnesses noted that Bigaouette never spoke unless spoken to, that he played with children on the street as if they were his own age, and that he "took delight" in scattering nails and broken glass on the street to puncture the tires of passing cars. When he succeeded, he was said to show "childish glee."[18]

At the same time, Bigaouette had financial responsibility for his mother's business affairs; in clinical terms, he was a person of average intelligence. At trial, prosecutors made sure that this latter evidence was placed before the jury. It was said to demonstrate that Eugene Bigaouette was "in full possession of all his mental faculties."

On the morning of the killing Bigaouette left the house a little before noon. He walked past his sister-in-law and his neighbour and went to see the family doctor, a man by the name of Bédard. He told Bédard that he had left the house at eight in the morning and that when he came back at 11, his mother was dead. He had not told his brothers or neighbours of the death because he was afraid that he would be blamed.

Bigaouette and Dr. Bédard went to the house shortly after noon. At first Bigaouette claimed that he did not know where the body was, but he soon led Bédard into the bedroom. An autopsy revealed that death had occurred by strangulation prior to eight in the morning. The evidence, although circumstantial, leaned strongly towards Eugene Bigaouette. He was the only person who could have had access to his mother at such an early hour, and he was heard mumbling to a police detective, "If I pleaded guilty I would get 10 years, 15 years. Would I get my money afterwards?"

The money that Bigaouette referred to was his inheritance from his mother. She had made a will leaving him all that she had, about $5,000 in cash, as well as the house itself and furniture. Other evidence brought out at trial was similar in its implication; the other lodgers in the house indicated that they were afraid of Bigaouette and even his mother had apparently suggested that she was not entirely comfortable when left alone with him.

In April 1926 Eugene Bigaouette was pronounced fit to stand trial, and was ultimately convicted of murder and sentenced to hang. He was weeping openly as he awaited his sentence in the prisoner's box. When asked if he had anything to say, he replied in a very feeble whisper, "Nothing."

The trial judge then spoke, "Twelve intelligent, fearless and courageous men, forming a jury to try you, have entered a verdict of murder; they have found you guilty of killing your old mother by choking her. They did not even think it was proper to recommend you to the mercy of the Court; they probably considered that a man guilty of matricide did not deserve any mercy whatsoever. The verdict was a just one and I have already had the occasion of congratulating the jury upon their decision."

The verdict of Chief Justice François Lemieux was, however, overturned by the Supreme Court of Canada and a new trial was ordered; the court held that Lemieux had not put the case for the defence fairly in his charge to the jury.

But the second trial in May 1927 also closed with a verdict of guilty, albeit in this instance with a strong recommendation for mercy from the jury. The defence argued that although Bigaouette might not be considered insane, he was "suffering from a mental weakness" that made it difficult for him to conceive of the crime; he was, in many respects, like a child of 10 or 12.

But the memorandum prepared for the Minister of Justice did not support this view. M.F. Gallagher wrote, "...the circumstances of this case make the prisoner's deed more particularly repulsive, it was so cowardly of him to strangle his aged and decrepit old mother.... After a careful analysis of the case the undersigned has reached the conclusion that if the prisoner is mentally deficient to any degree, his mental impairment is not such as would warrant interference by the Executive with the carrying out of the sentence of the Court."

On the morning of August 19, 1927, Eugene Bigaouette began to cry when he was told that all was ready for his execution. He walked, nonetheless "with a firm step" up the scaffold. A reporter from the *Montreal Gazette* described the scene, "Hangman Ellis and his assistant first mounted the gallows. Then came the chaplain and Bigaouette.... When [Bigaouette was] standing immediately under the noose...the chaplain spoke. 'Remember what I told you,' Canon Beaulieu said to him, 'Ask God to forgive you all your sins....'

"Bigaouette shrugged his shoulders, said not a word and when his confessor presented the crucifix to him, he kissed it as though he hardly realized what he was doing...with great speed, Ellis clapped the black cloth while the assistant strapped the feet. Hangman Ellis drew the lever, the trap beneath the feet of Bigaouette opened, and the man who murdered his mother paid the extreme penalty of the law...."[19]

It is a rare person who will murder his mother for money, perhaps only a man like Eugene Bigaouette, not really an adult and not really a child. But even more rare is the conviction of a man who is probably innocent. I found two men who were said to have killed family — in the absence of persuasive evidence. It seems very likely that at least one of these men was innocent and certain that both were hanged without proof beyond a reasonable doubt.

John Davidoff might have been innocent. He was said to have murdered his son in order to collect $2500 from an insurance policy; twenty-year-old Joe Davidoff was shot with a .303 rifle while sleeping.

British Columbia's Kootenays were home to the Davidoffs. The towns and small cities that make up the district are less than a half-hour drive apart — Trail, Rossland, Nelson, Grand Forks and Castlegar; this district of mountains and lakes has a cool winter and a hot dry summer. Nelson is the gem of the district, placed on the side of a hill overlooking the expanse of Kootenay Lake; the craft of older stone buildings downtown has been maintained and embellished by recent development.

The Kootenays are also home to the Doukhobors. In 1908 Peter Verigin led about 6,000 of these Russian dissenters to this part of southern B.C. The Christian pacifist sect has changed considerably since that time, splintering into Orthodox, Sons of Freedom, and Independent groups. Only about half the Doukhobor descendents actively follow the original culture, using the Russian language, endorsing pacifism as an ideology and abstaining from meat and alcohol.

John Davidoff, the accused, was born a Doukhobor, but he wasn't much liked among his own people. He was described by the RCMP as a "typical Doukhobor" but he was in fact unpopular in his community for supporting Canada's war effort — renouncing his pacifist heritage. His son John had been in the Navy, and Davidoff himself had served in the army during the Second World War. As he put it, ". . . when I reached the age when I could look around and see how ridiculous this religion was, I broke away to live like the people of Canada and to uphold the laws of society to the best of my ability."

In early April 1951 the banner headline in the *Vancouver Sun* read, "Youth in Bed with Corpse — Mysterious Slaying in Douk Community Probed."

"A 16-year-old youth slept beside a corpse here Monday

night," the story began, "without knowing his bedmate was dead from a murderer's bullet." The newspaper noted that a suspect had been arrested and that police were working to establish a motive for the slaying. Apparently, Willie Koochin had come home about 11 p.m. and got into bed beside an already dead Joe Davidoff. He did not realize that his friend was not alive until he woke up the next morning.

John Davidoff wasn't in the house; he had spent the night a few miles away, at the home of his sister. It now became very important for him to account for his whereabouts the previous evening. Davidoff had left the house about 7 p.m., after having dinner with his son and Willie Koochin. The two young men were going to a concert, and he was going into Castlegar, a six-kilometre walk from their home in the Doukhobor village. He stopped at his cousins', the Argatoffs, for a couple of hours; they lived just a few minutes' walk from his home. According to the Crown prosecutor at the trial, he then went back home and killed his son. He fired standing over him, just an inch or two from his body, through a quilt. He quickly left and walked with the .303 rifle towards Castlegar, dumping it off the Kootenay River Bridge at about 10 o'clock.

Davidoff's version of the previous evening was very similar; he had gone to the Argatoffs', he had walked over the Kootenay River Bridge into Castlegar and spent time at both Fred's Billiard Parlor and the hotel bar, before going on to his sister's. But he told police that he had never been back home. He had been making a straight line for Castlegar — the Argatoffs, the pool hall and then the hotel bar.

Davidoff was seen just before 10:30 p.m. at Fred's Billiard Parlor in Castlegar. He went from there to a hotel bar, and then to his sister's home. No one at the pool hall or the hotel noticed anything unusual about him on that particular evening.

The evidence against Davidoff was circumstantial. He was the sole beneficiary of his son's life insurance policy. He had been seen walking across the Kootenay River Bridge. He knew where his neighbour's .303 rifle was located — and a .303 rifle turned up under the bridge, apparently thrown off on the night of the murder. The police reported that "the accused is of a questionable character and feared by many of his neighbours. Davidoff is a widower and the appearance of his home suggests that the family have been living in conditions bordering on poverty."[20]

But the case put forward by the prosecutor, the trial judge and the police, and believed by the jury, did not add up. The police reported that "he had been seen by six individuals crossing the Kootenay River Bridge at 10 p.m."; the trial judge reported that Davidoff had been seen crossing the bridge at 10 p.m.

But John Davidoff could not have been on the bridge at 10:00, and at the pool hall in Castlegar before 10:27, the time of closing. This 48-year-old man with an injured foot could not have travelled the four-kilometre cross-country route in less than 27 minutes. Both the trial judge and the police agree that Davidoff was in the pool hall before it closed, but both fix the time he crossed the bridge as 10 p.m.

The most significant problem with the case against Davidoff is timing. There seems to be agreement that he didn't leave the Argatoffs' until about 9:30, and that he arrived at the pool hall before 10:27. In 57 minutes he is said to have walked home, expecting his son to be at a concert. He then notices that his son is asleep in bed, gets a .303, loads it, and kills him. He walks to the bridge, throws the rifle off, and continues on to Castlegar for an apparently ordinary evening at the pool hall and the bar. He walks almost seven kilometres and kills his son — in under 57 minutes. The average adult walks at a pace of four kilometres an hour.

The evidence against Davidoff was also contradictory. One group of three Doukhobor boys saw a man with a rifle on the bridge in rough working clothes; a second group of four Doukhobor boys saw John Davidoff walking across the bridge in a suit. The motive of killing for money was disputed by the defence. There was evidence that Davidoff had asked for a loan from a cousin in order to buy property and evidence that the cousin had agreed to lend him the money. The $2500 insurance policy does not seem to have been important.

But John Davidoff was convicted of murder in July 1951 and sentenced to be hanged in December of the same year. The trial judge concluded in his summary of the case for the federal government, after pronouncing a verdict of guilty and a sentence of death, "If the accused murdered his own son, he must be exceedingly depraved or insane. I would strongly recommend that he be examined by one of the best psychiatrists." Defence counsel A.G. Cameron wrote to the Minister of Justice, "Nearly all the witnesses were Doukhobors, many of them young, people still suffering from a Cossack complex inherited from the original members of their sect. Further, these Doukhobors are inclined to colour their statements in a manner they think pleasing to their interrogators, in the first instance, and can be made, under stiff examination, to admit certain things which the examiner wishes them to admit, due to the fact their English is uncertain and to their wish to escape lengthy questioning."

Local Member of Parliament Herbert Herridge wrote to the Minister of Justice in support of commutation of Davidoff's death sentence, "I know the strong feeling that exists against the Doukhobors with some people in the District and that it is quite possible for the judgement of some persons of unquestionable integrity to be subconsciously influenced by their dislike for these people."

The federal government did not fail to see the political importance of hanging a Doukhobor. The Commissioner of the RCMP was asked "whether the carrying out of this sentence would disturb the Doukhobor situation in British Columbia." The response from his Assistant Commissioner in B.C. was, "Have heard nothing that would indicate hostile reaction if Court sentence carried out in Davidoff case, which is considered extraneous to general situation."

Examination by psychiatrists established that Davidoff was not legally insane. Dr. George Davidson concluded, "Nothing was brought out in this examination that would suggest that this man is suffering from mental disease.... He tells his story in a straightforward, unemotional manner and one suspects that his ideas regarding the Doukhobor population are factual and are not based on inference, as is usual in mental disease."

For his part, Davidoff wrote to the Minister of Justice a month before he died, "...you can see how biased the doukhobor people are where I am concerned. Now we are back to my case at present — that the biased evidence of the doukhobor witnesses put me in this position...my belief is that the bullet was meant for me, not my son. Look into the trouble the doukhobor people have been having, also the religious beliefs. Then you will see I am innocent, and a victim of circumstances. If the present sentence is carried out on December 11, the person or persons guilty of this crime will be without worry, but if you commute my sentence I will be able to continue on with the search for the guilty party...."

The front-page headline in the Vancouver *Province* of December 11, 1951, read, "Doukhobor Dies on Gallows — Ate Hearty Last Meal." "Davidoff was hanged at 6 a.m. today," the paper reported, "The 48-year-old Doukhobor maintained his innocence to the last and was convinced that as a member of the sect he was discriminated against in a court of law."

Almost 10 years later and just a few hundred miles away in the province of Alberta, another man was hanged without cause. I have phoned witnesses and police who were involved with this case and looked at hundreds of pages of information. And I feel at least as strongly about Robert Raymond Cook as I do about John Davidoff, Wilbert Coffin and Abraham Steinberg. I just cannot believe that he was guilty.

Bobby Cook wasn't an honest, law-abiding citizen. He stole cars, and had a string of break and entry, and theft convictions stretching from 1952 to 1957; he had been sentenced to jail terms on 10 separate occasions, in Calgary, Red Deer, Winnipeg and Edmonton. It was always the same with him — break and enter, theft and theft of auto, a year or two in jail, and then back to the bars and the highways of Alberta.

On a Sunday morning in June 1959, the bodies of his father, his stepmother, and his five young stepbrothers and stepsisters were found in the greasepit of their garage in the small town of Stettler. The mother and father had been killed by blasts from a shotgun; both had died in a matter of seconds. Ray Cook had been shot in the heart and his wife Daisy in the head. The five young children, ranging in age from three to nine, had their skulls smashed. The rotting bodies lay on top of each other in the greasepit, covered only by cardboard and planks; the smell of decaying flesh had directed the three investigating Mounties to the grave.

Bobby Cook had been released from Prince Albert Penitentiary five days before the discovery of the bodies. His prison suit was found under a mattress in the Cook house, splattered with blood. The *Globe and Mail* reported the killings on page one of its Monday edition under the headline, "Find Alberta Family of 7 Slain in Garage Near Home." The article noted the arrest of a suspect on the same day.

"Robert Raymond Cook, 22, was charged with the murder of his father, a 53-year-old mechanic. Police said he is the son of Mr. Cook by a previous marriage."

Bobby Cook's mother died when he was 10, and about a year and a half later, his father remarried. Ray and Daisy's five children were born while Bobby Cook was a teenager. Though Cook had been in and out of jail for years, he stayed in close contact with his family.

The first thing that Bobby Cook did when he got out of Prince Albert Penitentiary on the morning of Tuesday, June 23, was to go drinking in Saskatoon with his friend, Jimmy Myhaluk, also released on the same day. Cook, for his part, had spent over two years in the penitentiary. The two men partied into the early hours of the next morning and then caught a late night bus to Edmonton. Years later Myhaluk remembered the moment, "two happy young drunks with nothing more on their minds or in their futures than a triumphant orgy of B & E."[21] After arriving in the city, Myhaluk went home to his parents on the south side of the city, and Cook checked in at the Commercial Hotel.

Bobby Cook didn't sleep much, if at all. After washing up, he had some breakfast and went out to look for a car. He didn't try very hard to find it legitimately. At about seven in the morning on Wednesday, June 24, he was in the back row of a used car lot on the Calgary Trail, hot-wiring an older model with silver paper. According to his testimony, he drove the car to Bowden, some 200 kilometres south of the city to dig up a buried stash of over $4,000 in bills, the proceeds of robberies committed over two years ago.

Later in the day he was back in Edmonton, talking to car salesman Carl Thalbing at Hood Motors about trading in a 1958 station wagon that he had back in Stettler. Cook was interested in a splashy Chevrolet convertible with fins, a typical art deco of the late Fifties. He explained to Thalbing that he was in business with his father, working as a mechanic. According to Cook's testimony at trial, his father had promised him one of the family vehicles, a '58 station wagon, when he got out of jail. For the moment Cook was only setting the deal; as Thalbing noted at trial, Bobby Cook mentioned that he would come in again on Friday.

Cook then went back to his room at the Commercial Hotel and caught his first good sleep since leaving jail. A few hours later he headed out with his friend Jimmy Myhaluk for a night of partying with some "alumni from the Penitentiary." The drinking continued to closing time at the Selkirk Hotel and then moved to the Pan American Hotel, where Cook caught another few hours' sleep on a couch.

Early Thursday morning, June 25, Cook and another friend borrowed a truck and drove down to his home town of Stettler. This friend, Walter Berezowski, told the trial that the existence of Cook's stash of bills was well known in the penitentiary; Cook hadn't been particularly tight-lipped about his cache. Berezowski also claimed that he had seen Cook's roll of money on the drive to Stettler.

The two men arrived in town about noon, and went out for coffee before Berezowski headed back to Edmonton. Cook was nervous about going home; it had been a couple of years, and he spent the afternoon wandering around Stettler, "reminiscing." At about nine in the evening his father saw him standing on the sidewalk. Ray Cook parked his '58 station wagon and walked across the street to greet his son. As a prosecution witness noted at trial, the meeting was friendly.

The two men walked back to the car, Ray gave Bobby the keys, and Bobby drove around the corner to the Royal Hotel for a beer.

About half an hour later they drove to the Cook home. According to Cook's testimony, he stayed about an hour. He gave his father $4100 of his $4300 stash and kept $200 for his current needs. He didn't tell his father that the money came from break and entries of businesses, but he was pretty sure that his father knew. "We both figured I had paid my debt to society in doing that two years."[22]

While at home Cook changed out of his blue prison suit and took his father's ownership papers for the car. According to his testimony, his father tried the prison suit on, and was wearing it when Bobby left the house for Edmonton. Ray Cook was also said to have given his son his wallet and car keys. Later on, his father asked for the key case back and took out the key to the truck, returning the case to Bobby. Cook consistently maintained in testimony later that at around 10:30 p.m. he drove off to Edmonton to party with his friends.

A little after midnight two shots were heard by a neighbour, a woman who came forward only after the first trial, and then testified at the second trial.

According to Cook's testimony he arrived in Edmonton at about 12:30 a.m. on Friday, June 26. An hour later, he said, he was involved in the break and entry of a dry cleaning business on the south side of the city. As owner Hy Estrin explained at trial, Cosmo Cleaners was broken into that night, his desk was ransacked and money taken from the till. Sonny Wilson, a prisoner at Prince Albert, testified that he met Cook just outside the Pig 'n Whistle Cafe, after which he got into Cook's car, and they drove over to the dry cleaners, breaking in at about 2 a.m. Another associate from Prince Albert, Jack Mitchell, testified that he met Bobby Cook in Frankie's Cafe some time between midnight and 1 a.m. He told the court that he and Cook had coffee together.

It was crucial for the prosecution to establish that Cook had remained in Stettler until at least midnight. If they failed, Cook would be acquitted. His travels Friday and Saturday were observed, not only by convicted criminals, but also by Edmonton car salesmen, Camrose police, and the local residents of Stettler.

Whoever killed the Cook family committed the crime some time Thursday night or Friday morning, after the family had gone to bed. Ray Cook did not show up for work on Friday, which was seen by his co-workers at Modern Machine Shop as quite unusual. No member of the Cook family was seen alive after Thursday evening.

Just before 8 a.m. on Friday Bobby Cook went to South Park Motors in Edmonton, asking about a white Pontiac convertible on display in the showroom. He then went back to Hood Motors and made a deal, trading in the '58 station wagon for a '59 Chevrolet convertible. The '58 station wagon was in his father's name, and his father's papers, inside the wallet, made the transaction possible.

The car deal took most of the day; Cook agreed to pay $1,700 for the convertible, $100 a month for the next 17 months. He was to take possession at about five in the afternoon and busied himself transferring the contents of one car to the other. The salesmen described the Cook deal as "a fairly easy sale," adding that the sale of a convertible to a young fellow usually is fairly easy.

Just before five Cook drove off in his new car. There were still some papers to be signed; left behind was a puzzled car salesman, scratching his head over his client's sudden departure. From Hood Motors Bobby Cook drove to the Commercial Hotel, and then went on to Camrose Friday evening. He and some local teenagers went to a dance, drinking beer that Cook had supplied. They partied until well past midnight, and were finally asked to leave the hall in the early hours of Saturday morning.

Cook then drove to Whitecourt, a town about 275 kilometres from Camrose, looking for another alumnus from Prince Albert, a man named Gene Cebryk. Three of the teenagers went along for the ride; it was about 4 a.m. when they took to the highway. They arrived in Whitecourt in the morning, stayed until about noon and then drove back, never having found Cebryk. They returned to Camrose about five o'clock Saturday afternoon.

Cook drove back to Stettler, arriving in town a little after seven on Saturday evening. Witnesses said he seemed to be flaunting his flashy new car. Local resident John Newsham stepped onto a crosswalk, noticed a car coming, and stepped back. But the driver of the car, Bobby Cook, stopped and motioned him across.

At about 7:30 in the evening Cook returned to his home, drank a beer and noticed some suitcases packed by the door. He put them in his car, along with a green metal box. He was only home about half an hour and didn't notice anything unusual, anything that would suggest foul play.

About an hour later he was stopped by the Stettler RCMP and asked to come to the police station. He drove over voluntarily and was questioned about the purchase of the convertible. By this time Hood Motors had called to complain about the car deal, having noted that Bobby Cook did not line up with the Ray Cook who was documented as the owner of the car. Cook explained that he had given his father $4100 to help him buy a garage and that he had been to Edmonton to trade in the '58 station wagon for the new convertible. He couldn't have made the deal without Ray Cook's identification.

About 11 that night Sergeant Thomas Roach of the Stettler RCMP dropped by the Cook house to try to locate the family, to straighten out this transaction over the car. He shone a flashlight into the living room and the bedrooms, turned on the kitchen light, and walked through the garage. He did not see anything unusual and nothing in the house aroused his suspicion.

Shortly after 11 a.m. on Sunday morning of June 28, the RCMP went back to the Cook house for a more careful inspection. They found large bloodstains on the parents' double bed and near the bunk beds where two children slept in the same room as the parents. There were also bloodstains on the mattresses of the three children sleeping in a separate bedroom. The family had evidently been killed in bed. They had then been wrapped in blankets, carried through the house and dumped in the greasepit of the garage. When found, they were in "night attire."

The RCMP's Sergeant Roach told the court that he first read the charge of murder to the accused on Sunday afternoon. The transcript tells the tale:

Now, the charge of murder was first read to the accused, I believe on Saturday?

On Sunday afternoon.

Sunday afternoon, and is it correct that he was very shocked?

Very emotionally. I informed him of the murder charge involved in the death of his father Ray Cook — Raymond Cook, and he said "Oh no, not my father, not my father," and he became very upset and emotional.

Is it correct, Sergeant, that he was so upset, that you went back again —

Yes.

— and read the charge to him about an hour later?

Yes, a good hour later.

Because you were not sure that he had fully comprehended?

I wanted to make sure that he fully comprehended the nature of the charge.

From this Sunday afternoon onwards, the finger of justice was pointed at Bobby Cook, and in some respects, Cook was his own worst enemy. Because the killings had been grisly, it was not surprising that the murder suspect, once charged in court, should be sent to the mental institution at Ponoka to see if he was fit to stand trial. While at Ponoka, however,

Cook escaped. He was recaptured after an 88-hour manhunt involving the Canadian army, resulting in front page news across Alberta.

Bobby Cook surrendered meekly to police in a pig barn about 50 kilometres from Ponoka, exhausted and surrounded by his pursuers. Over the next year he was to go through two trials, and to be found guilty by two judges and two juries. A prisoner who got to know Cook at the Fort Saskatchewan jail after his re-capture near Ponoka remembers that Cook was not what he expected; he had, of course, been anticipating someone quite unusual. Bobby Cook seemed very personable, always maintained that he was not responsible for the murder, and never showed any signs of aggression in the three months that they knew each other.

What really happened? The prosecution argued that Bobby Cook killed his family Thursday night, placed the seven bodies in the greasepit, washed up, and then drove to Edmonton in the morning to trade in Ray Cook's '58 station wagon. According to this view he planned the killings from the time he left the penitentiary; on Friday he was simply taking the car to Hood Motors to complete the trade-in that he had been proposing on Wednesday. The juries believed this scenario; they did not believe that Bobby Cook was in Edmonton just after midnight at Cosmo Cleaners, breaking and entering with Sonny Wilson, or drinking coffee even earlier at Frankie's Cafe with Frank Mitchell.

And yet Sonny Wilson's evidence seems very believable. It is an unusual person who will lie, thereby incriminating himself in a break and entry, in order to protect a man who has killed his family, and dumped them in a greasepit. Sonny Wilson may be such a man, but it's difficult to see what he could have gained from such perjury; Bobby Cook was in no position to promise him anything.

Cook was known in Prince Albert Penitentiary as a "solid" guy, that is, he was well liked. The news of his arrest was quite a surprise; the only way the prisoners could understand the killing was to recall the beating, concussion, and 27 stitches that Cook had suffered recently at the hands of another inmate. This wasn't the Bobby Cook they knew; he may have done it, but it was disordered neurology that had to be the cause.

But could Bobby Cook have done this? He had no motive, no record of violence and no weapon. The shotgun that was the murder weapon didn't belong to the Cook family and Cook wasn't carrying anything when he arrived home. The 10 fingerprints that were lifted from the scene by police did not match Bobby Cook; six of them matched the victims and four were unaccounted for. The police could not find any tracings of blood anywhere on Cook, not even in scrapings around his fingernails.

No one was ever charged with the break-in at Cosmo Cleaners. In court Bobby Cook described both the loot, "about $15, a white car coat, and a man's ring with a snakehead on each side of a red stone," and the method of entry. There was no way that he could have known of this detail and these proceeds if he had not been there. He had not been in contact with anyone who could have told him of the Cosmo job; he was under guard in a segregated section of the Fort Saskatchewan Jail. Hy Estrin, the owner of Cosmo, was convinced by Bobby's description of his entry into the building. When Cook described his way down into the dry cleaning establishment — from the skylight to the drying tumblers, and jumping down from there to the floor — Estrin was sure that he had been involved. "He just couldn't have been that precise," he said recently.[23]

The key to the truck that Bobby Cook claimed his father had kept was found in the pocket of his blue prison suit under the bloody mattress. His father was wearing the suit when Cook left the house, and so it seems entirely consistent with Cook's story that the key should be found in the pocket. A shirt found with the suit could not be identified as Cook's or as belonging to the family; it was a good-quality white shirt that had become quite filthy.

The memoranda prepared for Cabinet stressed that the case for the defence, as presented by both trial judges, was "somewhat perfunctory" and "somewhat brief and general."

These documents, written in September and November, were sympathetic to Cook; commutation was urged, if only implicitly.

But the Cabinet of John Diefenbaker apparently ignored the final memorandum of November 7. They focussed on Cook's initial lies to the police about where he had been and what he had been doing. On November 8 they decided that the law should be allowed to take its course — Cook was to hang just after midnight on November 15. On November 14, Prime Minister John Diefenbaker raised the matter in Cabinet again, saying that he had had a call from a man attending Bobby Cook at the Edmonton jail; the caller believed that Cook was innocent. But Diefenbaker's interjection was not sufficient to carry the day. The majority of Cabinet noted that there was no new evidence, and hence no reason to interfere with the sentence of death.[24]

On November 16, a letter was sent from the judicial offices of the court house in Edmonton, Alberta:

Dear Sir,

Re: Robert Raymond Cook

I am today in receipt of your letter of November 14th wherein you state that the Governor General in Council is unable to order any interference with the sentence of the Court.

The execution accordingly took place at 12:01 November 15, 1960 at Fort Saskatchewan Gaol.

Yours truly,

W.A. Short, Sheriff

Who did kill Ray and Daisy and their children? The time at which Bobby Cook was released from Prince Albert was potentially quite significant. About 100 prisoners were set free on "Queen's amnesties" on the 23rd and 24th of June, prisoners who knew of Cook's cache of bills. The blue suit with shotgun shells in the pockets could have been placed under the mattress to implicate Cook. Someone just out of prison would be likely to know the significance of this clothing, tying a knot around a man's neck with the power of suggestion.

Then again, this isn't what most murder is like — about 80% of all killers know their victims. The killer may have been not one of Bobby's fellow convicts, but a man or men known to the Cooks.

Who killed the Cook family? Possibly someone just out of Prince Albert, possibly someone from closer to home, but don't put any money on Bobby Cook. He was a thief and a break-and-enter specialist, but it's unlikely that he was a murderer. As he said to police just after his arrest, "Just didn't do it at all. That's all I've got in the world. What do you think I want to hurt them for?"

[1] "Jenny Buchanan" and all other names connected with this story are pseudonyms.

[2] See *Homicide in Canada: A Statistical Synopsis*, chapter I, above, 102-103, 136-137.

[3] "Steve Galloway" and all other names connected with this story are pseudonyms.

[4] "Letter to John A. MacDonald," *Elizabeth Workman, Capital Case Files*, RG 13 Series, National Archives, Ottawa, Canada.

[5] "Kevin Bourne" and all other names connected with this story are pseudonyms.

[6] "Ben Costello" and all other names connected with this story are pseudonyms.

[7] "Victor Morrison" and all other names connected with this story are pseudonyms.

[8] "Memorandum for the Minister of Justice," *Cordelia Poirier, Capital Case Files, RG 13 Series*, National Archives of Canada, Ottawa, 4.

[9] Ibid, 20.

[10] "Disgraceful — The Hanging of Cordelia Poirier and Parslow," *The Globe*, Saturday, March 11, 1899, 22.

[11] "Letter to the Secretary of State, January 22, 1925," *J.B. Pirie, Capital Case Files*, RG 13 Series, National Archives of Canada, Ottawa.

[12] "Memorandum to Minister of Justice from Harvey Clare, M.D." March 16, 1925, *J. B. Pirie, Capital Case Files*, note 11, *above.*

[13] "Lawyers Alone Plead for Pirie to the Crown," *Ottawa Evening Journal*, February 26, 1925, 14.

[14] "Letter to The Hon. Minister of Justice from J. B. Pirie,; June 1, 1937, *J.B. Pirie, Capital Case Files*, note 11, *above.*

[15] See *Homicide in Canada*, note 2, *above*, Table 5.9, 103.

[16] "Ontario Provincial Police Report," *Peter Beyak, Capital Case Files*, RG 13 Series, National Archives, Ottawa, Canada, 2.

[17] "Memorandum to the Minister of Justice," *John Bateman, Capital Case Files*, RG 13 Series, National Archives, Ottawa, 7.

[18] "Jury Returned Verdict of Guilty...," *Quebec Chronicle and Telegraph*, May 27, 1926, in *Eugene Bigaouette, Capital Case Files*, RG 13 Series, National Archives, Ottawa, 1.

[19] "Eugene Bigaouette Hanged at Quebec for Foul Murder," *The Montreal Gazette*, August 20, 1927, 1.

[20] "Letter from Commissioner, R.C.M.P., Re: John Michael Davidoff," *John Davidoff, Capital Case Files*, RG 13 Series, National Archives, Ottawa, August 7, 1951, 3.

[21] Jimmy Myhaluk, quoted in Brian Swarbrick, "Did We Hang the Wrong Man?", *The Edmonton Sunday Sun*, February 26, 1984, 32.

[22] "Trial Transcript," *R. v. Cook (2nd trial)*, 577. Robert Cook, *Capital Case Files*, National Archives, Canada.

[23] Hy Estrin, personal communication, July 13, 1987.

[24] Privy Council Office, Minutes of Cabinet meetings, Robert Raymond Cook, November 8, November 14, 1960. The minutes indicate that the memorandum of November 7 had been placed before the Cabinet. Document obtained under *Access to Information Act*, June 1987.

Chapter
Three

KILLING
ACQUAINTANCES

Savary Island is called the Hawaii of Canada, a quarter-moon sliver of white sand beaches lying about 80 kilometres north of Vancouver in the Strait of Georgia. On a sunny day in late July it might be nirvana; the trim white, wooden cottages of wealthy city dwellers sparkle on the north side, a small forest behind them and white sand and warm ocean water in front of them.

But this is not a nirvana that can be easily reached. If you can't afford to charter a float plane from the city, you will have to take your car on the provincial ferry service from West Vancouver, drive up to Earls Cove, take another car ferry to Saltery Bay, drive to the end of the road at Lund, park your car, and take a privately operated motorboat over to Savary. By the time all these place names flash by, the better part of a day has been spent.

The best way to get to the island is to take a seaworthy boat directly up the Strait of Georgia from Vancouver, travelling either under sail, or aboard a cabin cruiser. On a sunny day in late summer the 50-foot gin palaces of wealthy American and Canadian yachtsmen sit anchored off Savary, their occupants resting up for another round of tonsillectomies, trials or corporate mergers in the cities to the south. There are also places in the sun for lesser mortals; a few smaller sailboats cruise the coastline and a scattering of fishermen in open aluminum boats cast for something to grill on the evening barbecue.

Savary Island wasn't always a desirable tourist destination. In 1893, when Hugh Lynn arrived, it was a trading post for the furs of mink, otter and bear. John Green was the proprietor of a little wooden building where he bought pelts from the coastal Indians as well as other hunters and trappers, and sold them to distributors.

Green was a 70-year-old man who liked to drink and, as several witnesses testified later at the trial, he was known to be quarrelsome when drunk. He had once thrown a hatchet at his former partner and had tried to shoot at least a couple of people. He usually moved about on wooden walking sticks, but was said to be able to walk without his sticks when he was very drunk.

In late October 1893 Hugh Lynn was welcomed by his old friend John Green to Savary Island. The day after Lynn arrived the two men travelled across the water to Lund to "have some drink," the beginning of a two-day binge featuring bottles of rye whiskey. Hugh Lynn had come with a native woman, Jennie Que-Ah-Boketo, and her seven-year-old son. Green wanted Hugh Lynn to work for him and said that he would like Lynn and his family to move into his house.

"Hughy," as he was known to Jennie, was said by those who petitioned against his execution to be "an individual of weak and defective mind,...always considered, ever since we have known him, as little better than half-witted."[1] One fur trader testified at the trial that he had purchased bear and otter skins from Hugh Lynn in January, and "had never made so much profit before."

On the night of the killing, Hugh Lynn, John Green and another man by the name of Taylor were drinking together. When they were all very drunk, Green and Taylor started arguing about who should make a fire in the stove, and who should get up and do some cooking. As Hugh Lynn looked on, a "growling" Green went to his rack of rifles, took one, and shot Taylor. He then fired two shots at Hugh Lynn, before his rifle's lever caught. Lynn rushed at Green, took his gun and ran outside the house. As he explained at trial, "I was out about five minutes. He was standing up. I thought it would be all right and he would not get another gun. [But] he had another rifle in his hand facing towards me. I might have got away, I never thought about it.... The goods did not come into my head at that time. I fired and killed him.... I was confident he was dead; his feet stuck out past the door; I stayed outside about half an hour before I went into the room.''

But Hugh Lynn did take some goods as an afterthought, $80 in bills, $10 in silver, a couple of rifles, and some bear and otter skins. He slipped away from Savary in the moist fog of late October and headed south in his skiff, leaving two dead men in a small log house.

He was arrested on Shaw Island, just south of the Canadian border. Superintendent Fred Hussey of the Provincial Police staked out a small house where Hugh Lynn, Jennie and her boy were staying. Lynn first claimed to be a man named Gallagher and then one called Newton, but ultimately gave himself up, saying, ''I expected someone would come after me. It is too bad.''

At trial Hugh Lynn's evidence was not contradicted. As a reporter for the Victoria *Times-Colonist* wrote, ''For three hours the Hon. Mr. Richards cross-examined the prisoner, who stuck to his story with marvellous exactness under the circumstances. The evidence seemed to fit the main points very well.''[2]

But the court did not seriously consider the possibility of self-defence. Hugh Lynn had stolen goods and money and left a couple of dead men, covered in blood, to be mopped up by neighbours and police.[3]

John Green had been found sitting behind the cabin door, leaning against the wall. There was blood running from his chest down to his legs; the red streaks and splatters were ''cold and stiff.'' Green was naked from his stomach to his knees, his underwear hanging around his ankles and a sock on one foot and nothing on the other. Tom Taylor was found lying face down across the room. The blood had run from his chest up around his head; the red pool around his face was caked and cold. Taylor was wearing a heavy shirt and pants and ''coarse high leather boots.'' There were bullet holes in the walls of the cabin and three empty rifle shells on the floor. The window of the trading post was smashed and there were footprints on the sill.

The blood-covered mess that Lynn had left behind on Savary was what mattered in court. In a voice trembling with emotion, Mr. Justice Drake concluded, "Hugh Lynn, after a long and careful trial you have been found guilty of the wilful murder of John Green. I urge upon you to spend what time may be left you interceding with the throne on high for that mercy which you did not show to those two unfortunate men."

The jury found Hugh Lynn guilty, but they recommended mercy, suggesting — apparently in light of his mental limitations — that he was not a man who should be hanged.

But the judgement of Lynn's peers could not prevail over the will of the men in Ottawa. A memorandum prepared for the Minister of Justice did not dispute Lynn's version of events. As the three-page summary noted, "The only other evidence as to the circumstances of the shooting is that of the klootchman [an Indian woman or wife] Jennie Que-ah-Boketo, and her account is corroborative of the prisoner's own statement. There is also some evidence that the deceased was quarrelsome when in liquor."

The Prime Minister of the day, Sir John Sparrow Thompson, was also the Minister of Justice. He was not moved by the memorandum that had been prepared for him. Four days after receiving a summary of the case, he wrote from his summer office at Port Carling, on Ontario's Lake Muskoka, "I think that the report should be that the law should take its course, unless the report from Judge Drake which is on its way puts a different face on the matter."

On the morning he was to hang Hugh Lynn woke at 4:30 and dressed. He had been praying with a couple of Presbyterian clergymen the night before until about midnight. "I deserve all I am going to get, and a great deal more," he had told the prison warden just a few hours earlier.

At about five he had a light breakfast and went back to praying. Just a few minutes before eight the hangman arrived at his cell to prepare him for the gallows. His arms were tied together in front of his body, and he began the walk across the jail courtyard and up the stairs leading to the gallows. As soon as he stood under the noose his legs were tied together. As one observer wrote later, "Lynn faced the crowd pale but firm, an occasional twitching of the muscles of the face betraying the agony he was enduring."

Hugh Lynn then thanked the prison officers for their kindness, and the hangman drew a black cap over his head and the noose around his neck. The knot was uncomfortably tight, and Lynn raised his hands and pushed it further back. The hangman moved to the lever; Lynn and the warden exchanged a "hearty handshake," and the clergyman began to speak, "Our Father, Who art in heaven, Hallowed be Thy name...."

As a newspaper reporter wrote in the next day's *Victoria Daily Colonist*, "...in the middle [of the Lord's Prayer] the bolt was drawn and Lynn was swung into eternity. The neck was broken by the fall and death was instantaneous. Not a muscle...moved. After hanging 35 minutes the body was lowered into the coffin under the gallows and later was removed for burial."[4]

Hugh Lynn was not really different from most people who kill their acquaintances in Canada in 1988. He was living a "high-risk" life that increased his chances of encountering violence; he drank excessively with men who had a reputation for violence, and lived without much economic or social foundation.

Killing acquaintances accounts for about 40% of all murder in Canada. Over the past 10 years there have been about 2,000 people suspected of killing acquaintances, over 200 each year. When we add the killing of family to the killing of acquaintances we can account for 80% of all killings in our country. Statistics Canada's definition of killing acquaintances is relatively straightforward: "This is an aggregate category of four detailed suspect-victim relationship categories: lovers' quarrels or love triangles, close acquaintances, casual acquaintances, and business relationships."[5] The people that I will be writing about in this chapter, Tom Pickard, Ronald Turpin, Louis Fisher, Ian Blenheim, Danny Harrigan and Scott Millar, can be said to represent all four categories.

The patterns of killing acquaintances are quite similar to those involved in the killing of family. Louis Fisher and Scott Millar, for example, killed sex partners in bitter rages, not unlike many of the people described in the previous chapter, Killing Family. But those who kill acquaintances tend to be different in one important respect; they are often involved in an enterprise that has been labelled as criminal. They may be distributing illegal drugs like heroin, amphetamines or cocaine, they may be carrying guns, they may be promoting prostitution — and they may already be under police surveillance.

Alcohol also plays a critical role in this type of killing. It acts as a lubricant or accelerator of violence, not only in family killings but in all other forms of culpable homicide. Running through the stories of many of the men in this chapter is a recurring thread of alcohol abuse quite similar to that found in the killings of family members.

The critical difference between the killing of acquaintances and the killing of family is that the acquaintance killers are frequently involved in using and distributing *illegal* drugs, and distributing, most particularly, the so-called hard drugs — heroin, speed (metamphetamines) and cocaine. They routinely carry guns. In the distribution of large amounts of any illegal drug, the stakes are always high. Thousands of dollars are on the line, and there are lengthy prison terms for those who get caught. When we add a person "hopped up" on stimulants or desperate for a fix to this scenario, there is a lot of tension in the air.

One difficulty in evaluating the occasional violence of illegal drug distribution is that of determining cause and effect. Do the drugs themselves promote violence, or is the structure of existing law the root of our problem? The line that we draw between legal and illegal substances is premised neither on danger to individual health nor on the collective well-being of our society. Heroin can be no more dangerous than tobacco, and marijuana is considerably less dangerous than alcohol.[6]

Granted, the reality of heroin use is frightening and depressing — it is chilling to think of a young man taking the most powerful painkiller on the planet just to get through the day, the needle puncturing his vein an act of pleasure.[7]

Moreover, injectable heroin is a drug that is highly addictive, and for most users in the illicit market, very difficult to regulate. Overdose is also a possibility, from either mistaking the strength of a dose or from a desire for suicide. And yet a regulated heroin habit is probably no worse than a tobacco habit; the drug doesn't break down human tissue in the way tobacco does and daily use is not correlated with heart disease or cancer.

Legal drugs cannot be differentiated from illegal drugs, in most important respects. Consciousness alteration is a matter of taste, formed in part by the social and legal machinery that we have inherited from past generations.

Our legal classifications are not consistent with medical, pharmacological, economic or social reality. Marijuana is not a narcotic, despite its inclusion in *The Narcotic Control Act*, and cocaine is anything but a "powerful sedative." For 80 years we have criminalized certain psychoactive substances and yet it is only in the past 20 years that most Canadians have actually learned what these drugs do to us, physically and socially. Government policy has yet to be realigned. In the interim, drug use and distribution continue to be implicated in a significant number of acquaintance killings.

For Tom Pickard, the drug of choice was heroin. Pickard was raised by his aunt; the company was a little rough, and often more than a little drunk. As he puts it, "Well, there was physical abuse. There was mental abuse, and there was some sexual abuse when I was younger. I just never really felt like I ever belonged anywhere. I guess that's basically, well, something I've come to realize now. I just never belong."[8]

When he was in his early teens Pickard began to drink heavily. For about three years he drank in the evening, from just after work to closing time at the bar, and then he drank in the morning to kill his hangover. He had a son, Donny, but he and his girlfriend couldn't make their relationship work.

Donny moved to his grandmother's, and Tom Pickard drifted into the culture of illegal drugs.

Tom began to realize that alcohol was killing him. A close friend was telling him that he had to quit. As he puts it, "I started coming out of it. I just threw the booze away. I stopped. And I felt kind of rotten, but I threw it away because I could see what was happening."

Marijuana and LSD, mescaline and MDA — it was the late Sixties and young Canadians were trying out new chemically altered states of consciousness, threatening the established order of alcohol and tobacco. Tom Pickard grew his hair long and became part of "the hippie subculture." He soon realized that if he was buying a lot of illegal drugs it would make sense to sell some of them. "I was running out of money, always looking for it, and everybody's buying the stuff, so why don't I start selling it? That way I can have the dope and I can make money too."

For about a year or so he continued this way, working during the day, selling drugs and smoking, sniffing and eating. He tried heroin once, and got into it for about five days straight, but his partner in other drugs talked him out of continuing, telling Pickard that he was killing himself. Pickard himself was "freaked out" by the experience; he went home and was sick for a few hours while coming off the drug. He felt he was older and wiser for his brush with heroin: "You know, I thought about people I knew, my uncle Bill and my aunt Betty [dead from heroin overdoses] and I just thought, my God, everybody that I've ever heard of who'd had anything to do with heroin is...nowhere."

As he sees it now, Tom Pickard wasn't doing too badly at this point; he had some money for parties, and he'd bought a motorcycle to get around on. Then a motorcycle accident in his early twenties left him in rough shape; his foot was twisted like a wet spaghetti noodle at the end of his leg; he had pins inserted in the leg at several points and was placed in a cast for a lengthy recovery.

It was during this recovery that his relationship with heroin seemed to get out of hand. It was a hot summer and he couldn't go anywhere; he had been taking 292s to dull the pain in his leg. A friend, coming over to the house with "a loaded outfit" caught him at the wrong time. Pickard pumped some heroin into his arm.

"The next thing I know I rip the cast off down here, I jump in my car; I'm driving all over town and everything. I can't feel the pain no more. I feel, oh, is this ever great!"

But the powerful painkiller wore off, and his leg began to ache; he now had the money for more heroin, and he bought it. As the next eight months drifted by, Pickard became more and more deeply committed to heroin use. He started selling the drug, and began to have run-ins with the police, after being fingered by another addict. "I'd given him hundreds or thousands of dollars for bricks of marijuana and there was never any problems, but now he was a hype, I was a hype [a user of injectable heroin]. So seven bulls jumped me. Beat the living shit right out of me. They knew exactly how many caps was in the stall before it was open. And when they analyzed it, it turned out to be sneezing powder. So, like, I didn't know whether to kiss the guy or punch him out."

Pickard felt that he could never get involved in either theft or robbery to maintain his heroin dependence, "I'm not into robbing people and stuff like that, that's just not my bag, right. And I'm not into harming guys for the bread, 'cause then you got to hurt them and I really never was into hurting people."

His motive for selling heroin wasn't really to make a lot of money. With most heroin trafficking, he says, "you're either selling him the dope 'cause you need the money in order to score for yourself, or you're fixing him because the guy's sick and you know him and you know what it's like to be sick."

Tom Pickard's girlfriend was also using heroin. When she prostituted herself a couple of times to get money for a fix, he was very upset. He didn't want her renting her body for their drug habit. As he sees it now, "the problem was I was using heroin heavily, so there wasn't much sex between us. I was into chasing the dope and getting us fixed and all of that. So I guess she was getting her sexual gratification there, but she cared so much for me...'cause she'd do anything for me and I'd do anything for her.''

For a short time Pickard managed to get away from heroin. He enrolled in a provincial methadone clinic and got a job; he and his lover would occasionally use heroin, but the methadone kept them away from the brink of obsession. "Maybe one out of four or five times we would score, and the rest of the time we'd go to the show 'cause we didn't have to." They'd walk by what was called theatre row, interested in purchasing some heroin, but not physically craving the experience.

Before long, however, Pickard got back into a higher gear, selling heroin and using large quantities himself. The stakes have always been high for heroin distributors; they carry lots of money and they're acknowledged to be the number one targets of police drug squads across the country. Tom Pickard was no different from the rest. He carried a gun, and was well known to the police. He claims that he was beaten by police several times and that on one occasion two drug squad members broke his teeth with a set of handcuffs.

The killing occurred during the time Pickard was moving heroin; he was "heroin sick," — desperate for a fix — and searching for his stash. He and his partner in heroin distribution had a policy of leaving 50 caps of the drug for each other in a city park, so that if one of the two men was "heroin sick," the other would always have something waiting for him.

Pickard wanted to get out to the park to check for a stash, but his car wasn't working. There was a van available, but one of the other passengers was a guy who would be more than happy with Pickard's heroin, and who was about 60 lbs. heavier than he. Pickard got into the van anyway — he was desperate for a fix.

He wasn't sure that he was going to be able to use his stash, but he figured that his gun would protect him. He describes the killing in the park: "I'm digging in this plant [looking for my stash] and I turn and...whack! I get it right in the pumpkin with a tire iron. He split my head wide open and now I'm all warm down here, sticky with blood, and I'm losing it."

"I think, this guy's going to kill me," he continues, "he pushes me, and I hit the ground. Something's sticking in my back. It's the piece. I pull the piece out and it jams. Now, I'm freaked. Here he comes with the tire iron, but finally it unjams and I remember firing the first shot and then I just...I went into a fog. Next thing I know, I'm running through the bushes. Then back into a fog, and I'm driving a vehicle downtown, eating some bombs [powerful sedatives]."

Tom Pickard was convicted of non-capital murder and sentenced to life imprisonment. He maintains that he didn't go out to the park with killing on his mind. As he puts it, "My intentions were to get straightened out — to get high on heroin — and to protect myself if I had to. And it was because of my lifestyle I found myself in a position where I couldn't just throw this guy out of the truck and I was so worried about getting straightened out [about using some heroin]...you know, I just wasn't thinking, right. It was totally stupid of me to do. And there's no excuse for it."

Pickard has now spent more than 10 years in jail. He feels that the first five to seven years of his sentence made sense, but that lengthy jail terms for murder are ultimately counter-productive. "Well, when they send guys to jail, I'd say that if there's any good in them at all, you leave them in jail too long and you're going to destroy whatever there is that's left in them that's good. If you're not going to salvage a human being, then why bother? But if you want to send a guy to jail for 25 years, then you might as well just turn grizzly bears loose in the city."

Pickard says that jail has been a very difficult experience for him, living with a constantly changing cast of 300 to 400 men. He has just completed his twelfth year inside and can't imagine how he could serve another 12. "You've got people looking at you when you're going to the bathroom. Some of the people do have consideration that work here, don't get me wrong. I'm not saying that all the staff are assholes, but some of them go out of their way to make you realize that you're in jail and that you have no dignity at all. That's what burns me. Okay, so you don't have no rights or you don't have the rights that you do when you're outside, okay, remind me of that. But don't keep pushing me to the point where you keep reminding me that you've taken away my dignity too, because nobody's entitled to do that.''

In the world of illegal drugs, it is not just the addicts who commit murder. For Ian Blenheim and Danny Harrigan, the drugs were a means to an end; dealing drugs was one of the various business enterprises of their bike-gang, a business that necessitated a life independent of the law.[9] Their story is important because it is representative of so many ''gangland'' killings — disputes within a community beyond the law. Like Tom Pickard, Blenheim and Harrigan killed over drugs, but they were different from him in that they were part of a relatively well-organized criminal network. Pickard may have been living life in fast forward, but Blenheim and Harrigan were speeding as fast as their Harley Davidsons could take them.

They were members of a motorcycle club who worked during the day, and took to their bikes in the evenings and on weekends. Both had criminal records for assault, and a string of convictions for other offences. Harrigan indicates that there was pleasure along with the violence. ''Adventure, you know, going around all over the country and that, with 30 guys on Harleys...that was the best part. That's the part I'll never forget about.''

Harrigan found, however, that joining a motorcycle club had made him something of a marked man with police. ''I never had no heat until I joined the [group]. All of a sudden I was getting raided all the time by the cops and punched out and charged with assaulting a cop. I was handcuffed and shackled and 10 of them start beating me and kicking me. And then they charge me with assaulting a cop while I was in the hospital. These are some of the things that happen to you when you're in a motorcycle club. And you can't do nothing about it. Who would really believe a motorcycle gang?''

The bike gang dealt in illegal drugs, but there were boundaries for acceptable drug use within the group. Ian Blenheim explains, "we would snort drugs sometimes. Cocaine wasn't even a drug then, it wasn't popular at all. I think I'd seen it once or twice. PCP was about the most common, and mescaline. Guys weren't against those drugs because they were considered non-addictive. As long as you didn't use a needle or anything like that to ingest it, there was no peer pressure." Harrigan adds, "I wasn't involved in drugs. I was in a bike club. I liked marijuana, hashish, cannabis, right. But when I was younger I experimented with LSD and I never stuck any needles in my arm. I never did speed or heroin or coke, anything like that. it was mainly PCP and LSD."

The killings were the result of a dispute in the biker community, over the illegal distribution of amphetamines. Blenheim and Harrigan were sitting in a hotel on a Sunday night, having a few beers and sniffing a little PCP, a substance first developed as a surgical anaesthetic, later approved for use in veterinary medicine, and capable of producing severe mental disorder. There was some tension in the room. As Blenheim recalls, "there were people there we didn't get along with." A third member of the club, Davis, was sitting with Blenheim and Harrigan, telling them about a problem that he was having with a speed dealer in the city.

According to Blenheim and Harrigan, Davis was suggesting that the three of them go over to the speed dealer's house and try to sort things out. Blenheim knew the dealer quite well, and apparently Davis figured that if anyone could work things out, it would be Blenheim. As Blenheim recalls, "He was a dangerous guy. But usually in the past I had no problem talking to him. I wasn't afraid of him. He was my friend and that's the way it was, right. So I didn't anticipate — it was stupidity on my part."

Blenheim and Harrigan's accounts of what happened that evening coincide. The two men went into the house first, with Davis following. There were three people there, the dealer, the woman he was living with, and his son. Blenheim tried to intervene and "smooth things out," but the speed dealer reached for his gun, taking it from the back of his pants. Harrigan describes the man, "Now this guy, he was a bad dude.

He was wanted for murder, and he was on parole for attempted murder, so you know when he pulled a gun out, I thought we were gonna get it, but Ian got him first.''

Ian Blenheim was a faster draw. He describes the scene, ''When I shot the first guy, he fumbled and dropped the gun. I turned around and shot the second guy, but I shot him twice immediately. In the meantime the first guy that pulled the gun got his gun up and fired...and it went right over my shoulder and into the wall. So I shot him again. Then he fired again. And another bullet went right near me. So I shot him two more times. So actually he was shot four times. And then he was dead.''

Harrigan explains, ''Two people were dead because [the speed dealer] got up and we shot him. Then we've got to kill everybody and get the hell out of here — get rid of this.'' Harrigan went around the room, stabbing the female witness and the other two men, both dead or dying of gunshot wounds. He describes his violence, ''I had no intentions of going there and killing anybody. None of us did. But it just happened like that, it erupted like that.'' Police reports also indicated that the three deceased had been clubbed with a shotgun.

Harrigan and Blenheim were pretty shaken up after the killings. They cleaned themselves up and smoked a few joints, trying to calm down. For months after, Harrigan had nightmares about that night. He felt he couldn't tell his wife about the killings, but he used to talk about it in his sleep. ''I woke up yelling I'd killed somebody. I remember one night she calmed me down and I said, what did I say? Well, she said, you killed somebody. I said I was just having a bad dream, got up and had a coffee and sat around.

About three years passed before Harrigan, Blenheim and Davis were arrested. They had told only a couple of people about the killings, but eventually these confessions found their way to the police. One woman in particular had been quite frightened. All three were charged with first degree murder; Harrigan and Blenheim were convicted, and Davis was acquitted.

Davis surprised Blenheim and Harrigan at trial by appearing as a crown witness. Harrigan explains, "One morning [when] he was supposed to take the stand, they brought us to the court. And there were three of us on the chain. They took Ian and I off the chain and put us in the cell and they took him someplace else. And we knew something was wrong."

On the witness stand Davis claimed that he had nothing to do with the murder, that it had all been the work of Harrigan and Blenheim. Harrigan and Blenheim now insist that Davis was involved, smashing the skulls of the three victims with a shotgun. At trial Harrigan and Blenheim lied, saying they had nothing to do with the killings, but they did not implicate Davis. As Harrigan says, "I kept my mouth shut and you know, like I was involved in it too, so I wasn't going to shoot my face off...I wanted to tell the truth at the trial but all three of us, we wanted to beat it."

It's difficult to know exactly what happened back on that Sunday night in January more than 12 years ago; what we do know is that the testimony of Davis helped to secure two first degree murder convictions for the prosecutor. The jury's finding of guilt condemned Blenheim and Harrigan to imprisonment for a minimum of 25 years. Harrigan never thought that he would kill anyone. "Like I said, I just got caught up in the circumstances and I feel that anybody, given the right circumstances, will hurt or kill. But that's probably something that will never happen again. I wouldn't put myself in that situation."

The situation that both Blenheim and Harrigan would avoid is the motorcycle club. As Blenheim says, "The only problem I seem to have is I was in a motorcycle club, you know, for nine years before I got this sentence and I've been in jail almost 10 years now. And all they want to talk to me about is that I was in a motorcycle club. Well, you know, that's like talking to me about Mars. I don't know what the motorcycle clubs are doing. I don't care what they're doing. I've got no disrespect for them; they didn't do anything to me, I didn't do nothing to them. But on the other hand they know I'm gone, they know I'm doing life."

Ian Blenheim and Danny Harrigan were probably very different people at 25 than they are at 35. Blenheim notes, "When I was younger, I was quick-tempered, easily riled up. And I know the change in myself personally because I'm older. I don't get riled up easily, things don't bother me, I take things in stride and I'm more easy going." Harrigan and Blenheim have both served 10 years in jail; they may well serve another 10 or more before they are released.

In Danny Harrigan's opinion, the lifers — the killers — are among the best prisoners in Canadian institutions, a sentiment shared by many who work inside. He argues, "There should be a lifer's joint or a wing or something. Because they know how to do time. They've been in for a few years and the other guys, they're all drugged out from the street and they come in here and they want to fight and end up killing somebody and the whole joint gets locked up because of foolishness. Most of us are sensible guys. I've met some weirdos that were doing life but the majority of lifers are quiet, passive. As a matter of fact, I said that to a screw [guard] one time, I said, they should build a joint for lifers and his first reply was, Jesus Christ, if they ever did that, I would sure want to work there."

Blenheim and Harrigan are now taking a number of university courses and beginning to think about life back on the street. Asked how he is going to handle his eventual release, Blenheim says, "It's going to be a culture shock, because it's been a lot of years, you know. But that's why I think it might be better for me to stay my full year and a half in the [halfway] house. They're not even kicking me out, because I want to ease out. I could get to socialize and do it that way, for a year anyway. Then I think about a year before I go out on my own. That way I can ease my way back into society. Because it's going to be a culture shock, for sure."

Harrigan has similar feelings, saying of an upcoming appeal against sentence, "So now we've got a little bit of hope again. Whereas before, we were doing all right and we're still doing all right but we didn't have much hope in getting out or anything." He chuckles, "We're still occupying ourselves, keeping our minds in shape as well as our bodies — and just trying to stay young."

Harrigan is very involved, along with many of the other lifers, in the Special Olympics for the mentally handicapped that the prison holds each summer. "They have special Olympiads around the country, the States and that, but they're not too bad. Like this is for people who can't get into those Olympiads — this is for the special people. And they're all right. They show a lot of affection and like all the fears I had about them, like them doing unexpected things, whatever...."

He continues, "They're always showing their love and affection and are generally really happy to be here and they don't want to leave. They come in...you know where that metal detector is there? Okay, they go out that side door...that goes way out in the yard, but halfway from here to the yard you can see them coming and they're on a dead run. Unbelievable. They're just moving. Leaving all the chaperones and everybody else behind."

For Scott Millar, drug use, legal and illegal, was an important part of business. He grew up in Ontario and first encountered the law when he was 16. By the time he was in his early twenties he had a number of convictions for assault and was actively involved in cocaine use, abuse and distribution.[10]

He started out by sniffing small quantities but graduated to larger and larger amounts. "It was easy. I'd take seven grams...just a little bag. To me it's a little bag. Pour it on the table, use a credit card [to chop it up], just spread one big line the size of the table, half on one side and half on the other side. That would take me about 15 minutes."

Millar developed a habit requiring 10 to 15 grams a day that could only be sustained by distributing the drug. He describes the toll of his abuse. "It got to the point, I'd wake up in the morning, blood's dripping out of my nose. I'd have my sink full of cold water, stick my face in the sink, suck water up my nose to get the crust, blood and stuff out. Once that was cleared up, I'd start again."

There were other drugs as well. "Really it was anything I

could get my hands on...beer, Southern Comfort, whiskey. I'm not so hot on vodka and gin and stuff like that. Yeah, it was continuous. I'd turn around and every day it was just get high, do business, get high, do business, right. I wasn't working. I had joints too.''

It was during this period that Millar committed two assaults and was sent to jail for a year. He attributes his behaviour to the paranoia and anxiety caused by his cocaine and alcohol abuse, "When [the police] arrested me I didn't know where I was...I was lost. I'd spent the whole day snorting, drinking Southern Comfort and everything. You know what I mean? I was lost."

And it was during this year in jail for the two assaults that Millar inadvertently started a chain of events that would lead to a killing. He was sharing a cell with another man in the regional detention centre. "He was a homosexual," Millar recalls, "I don't consider myself a homosexual. One night I came in and he was on his bed under the blankets. So I got in my bed, got undressed to go to bed. He got out of bed and pulled the sheets down."

Millar continues, " He gets up and says, 'Like to screw me? Like to screw me?' I got up and said, 'What are you talking about?' And he got up, bent over and said, 'Screw me.' I'd been locked up for eight months at the time. The guy said, 'Well, why not?' So I went through with it."

In the language of the prison, Millar's young friend was his "kid." "You know...taking care of him, he's your kid. You're the old man and he's the kid." The two men continued their relationship until "the kid" was released and then kept in touch by letter. When Millar was back out in the community the two of them got together on a few occasions.

But back on the street, their relationship was not the same as it had been in jail. "There was no more sexual activity between us anymore. I'm back in the street. I had a girlfriend and I was more interested in her than I was in him. I attempted to help him in some ways, moneywise, dopewise...you know what I mean. He needed money for dope and stuff like that."

Millar recalls that at the time of the killing he was "messed up.'' He was spending a lot of money, couldn't pay his bills and was dabbling in cocaine and PCP. ''The PCP buzz is — when you do it — you're not there. You lose two hours. If you do a lot of it, you lose the day. You're in a different world.''

On the night of the killing his kid was over for a visit. ''He's just all screwed up, and he's getting his welfare cheque and he owes people all kinds of money so he's trying to run away. He's all pissed up and everything to the point where he can hardly walk. I had had a couple of drinks of some whiskey and smoked a couple of joints.''

The kid liked the codeine in 222s and Tylenol and had brought a number of these pills with him. According to Millar he was also in a confrontational mood. ''He come in, started mouthing off. 'I'm going to tell your old lady you were fucking around, you fucked me in the ass when you were in prison.' I said, 'Don't even start talking about that. I'll punch your head in.' Like he was only 150 pounds and I'm 200 pounds. I said, 'I'll punch your head in, you piece of shit, just keep your mouth shut, right.' ''

Millar walked over and picked up his .22 calibre rifle — he always kept a loaded gun in the apartment for protection. He recalls the sequence of events: ''I said, 'Oh, I'll use this as a backup, punch your head in. You just keep your mouth shut. Sit down and have a drink, talk about it.' So I went into the kitchen, got him a glass, put some ice in it, poured some whiskey in it. Got some coke.''

When he came back from the kitchen the kid was beside the phone, gun in hand. ''Said he was going to call my parents on the phone and tell them, you know, you screwed me in the ass, you're queer. I put a lot of emphasis on my parents. So right off the bat, that just lit a fuse. I put the drinks down and I says, 'Don't you do it. By the time you start dialling I'll break every finger you've got in your hand.' He didn't pay any attention.''

Millar was drunk and angry, ''I started walking over to him. Well, he dropped the phone and started wrestling, the gun went off. After the fight was over, he fell down. This is how

I remember it. He fell down. I sat there and looked at him. There wasn't very much blood, 'cause there was a little hole here right through the nostril. There wasn't a second hole. I went to move him, then I seen the blood. Boom. Then it clicked in. He's dead. The bullet hole...oh, shit.''

He sat in his apartment for about half an hour, not knowing what to do. He called a friend and went over to his house to talk to him about his predicament. The advice that he received was to do one of two things, either call the police or clean up and then get rid of the body.

Millar decided on the latter course of action. He cleaned his apartment and put the body in his trunk, intending to drive it out of the country. But as he drove along the freeway, "Something popped into my head. What happens if a cop pulls me over now? Dead body in the trunk, holy fuck, I said, I've got to get rid of it. I just pulled it out of the trunk and dumped it off the side of the road. Kept on driving.''

It took police three months to tie the body beside the highway to Scott Millar, and when they did they charged him with second degree murder. He was encouraged to call his parents and tell them about the charge before the news of his arrest was flashed across television screens and radio stations. "My dad just turned 65 and my mom's 58. So they're fairly old. My mom's a diabetic and she has her nervous problems. She had cancer. Dad's the same way. He's had a couple of heart attacks and strokes. And so you just can't throw things at them.''

He was convicted of second degree murder and told the story of his prison relationship with his "kid" in the courtroom: "This Crown was really [nitpicking]. He says, well, you buggered this guy. I hadn't been to school yet so when he said, 'bugger,' I said, what do you mean, 'bugger'? He goes, 'you buggered him.' I said, 'No, I didn't bugger him, I fucked him in the ass.' And everybody in the courtroom started laughing, the jury and everything.''

Millar continues, "I said what are you talking about, 'bugger'? I don't know what bugger means. And he goes, 'Have you ever done it with anybody else?' I says, 'Have you ever been fucked in the ass?' And everybody in court was just cracking up, the judge, jury, everybody. He's turning red, all twisted out of shape.''

Scott Millar will not be eligible for release until the mid-1990s. He does not think much of Canada's correctional system. ''They're not offering you anything. If you want anything, like rehabilitation, you have to do it yourself and they suppress as much rehabilitation as possible. It's either inappropriate funding, inappropriate material, inappropriate security levels. Something's always not right and you can never get anything out of it.''

He is worried about what the future might hold for him. ''If I'm left for 10 years going through a system like this, I can imagine what I'm going to be like when I get out on the street. I find a great deal of the time I try to shut myself away from prison at all times. After work, at 4 o'clock, the first thing I do is I take my clothes off, put on my shorts and my sweat top, just an effort to get away. I'm not in prison any more. I'm into leisure time now, I've got my shorts and my sweatshirt on and...it's bad.''

Tom Pickard with his heroin, Blenheim and Harrigan with alcohol, PCP and speed, and Scott Millar with alcohol and cocaine — the drug abuse in these cases increased the risks of violence. Yet it was not the effects of these substances that were to blame. It was the lifestyle of the users and the way they used the drugs and distributed them that created so much damage.

The consequence of our existing strategy of criminalization is that some Canadians occasionally kill each other — by fighting for the right to distribute certain drugs, by punishing a breach of business ethics in the illegal trade, or by trying to stop others from using or distributing.

What we're doing now isn't working. We have gangland killings, police killings and drug store robberies. A drug like heroin, the most ''dangerous'' of illegal substances, could be regulated, legally restricted to a doctor's prescription pad. It may be that the best way to confront the organized crime of illegal drug distribution is to take over the market — in the case of heroin addicts, by giving desperate people the painkillers that they feel they need.

That kind of policy would probably have prevented Tom Pickard from killing a man. Canadians would be better served by a careful accommodation of heroin users and the users of other illegal drugs. What we have instead is a business that regulates itself with violence. If a distributor is double-crossed, he or she can't run to the police, the courts, or the Better Business Bureau. The men, and a few women, who distribute illegal drugs usually handle their disputes themselves — occasionally with gunshots, stab wounds and bodies on the bottom of the river. We have about 50 unsolved homicides in Canada each year and at least half of these can be traced to "gangland" conflict.[11]

But as we have seen, it is actually a legal drug that stands out among the rest with regard to murder. Fermented fruit and grains, that is, beer, wine and liquor, are involved in about 30-35% of all killings. Alcohol is particularly a factor in killings of acquaintances; it is seen as a key variable by police in 49% of all such cases.[12] This drug helps an angry young man, a man like Louis Fisher, to lubricate his rage.

In June 1960 the east end of Toronto had yet to be settled by the city's prosperous middle class. The Danforth and surrounding neighbourhoods were home to Greek immigrants, the poor, and the working class; the 1980s patchwork quilt of urban professionals, ethnic minorities and sandblasted brick townhomes could not easily be imagined.

Louis Fisher was raised in the east end. His parents separated when he was in Grade Four; his mother was apparently an alcoholic and his father was never close to him. "He would never have given me the shirt off his back," Fisher told psychiatrist J.P.S. Cathcart after his conviction.[13]

A neighbour described Fisher's life at home as a young boy: "The mother was an alcoholic of the worst type. There was never a day went by that she wasn't drunk. There were men in the house every day, sometimes all day. She had a couch set up in the living room and she was seen smooching all the time in front of her children. She had no control of herself at any time. The place was nothing but a sex house.''

Louis Fisher, also known as "Brad," was the eldest of three boys. He finished Grade Nine at Cosburn Junior High School and went to work. He had been an average student, liked by his teachers, but with few close friends. By all accounts Fisher was a good worker, whether earning money as a glass cutter, a warehouseman, or in a car wash.

There were a few delinquencies. When he was 16 he was fined $50 for threatening a person with a knife after he had been drinking. The next year he was fined $25 for an act of wilful damage — he had smashed a glass window when he was drunk. Fisher told psychiatrist R.E. Turner that he had a bad temper, but that he generally took out his rage upon himself, ripping his own clothing. "I am scared to hit my wife, so I take it out on myself, I'm the only one who gets hurt."

Louis Fisher married his wife Joan in 1956, when he was 20. She was about his age, with three young children from a previous marriage. The couple began to have more children — "the more the merrier," he said. At the time of Fisher's arrest, their third was on the way, a girl who was born on the day that her father went on trial for murder. Mrs. Joan Fisher later told the trial, "My husband and I had a happy life. As a husband there are none better. The children worship him. I love him. What more could a woman ask?"

On the evening of June 9, 1960, Louis Fisher finished work at the car wash at about six and drove to the Wembley Hotel for a few beers before going home for dinner. Fisher was a regular at the Wembley. As he put it, "It's a hotel near home where I drink quite frequently — I do like my beer."

He returned to the Wembley with his wife early in the evening. She was apparently there to help cash a cheque that would allow Fisher to drink with their two boarders. With this accomplished, she returned home and Fisher and his two boarders went over to the Men's Beverage Room to continue drinking.

For most of the evening Fisher engaged in his usual practice of "table hopping," going from table to table to have a beer and talk with friends. He stayed until closing time, and then planned to meet his two boarders at a nearby restaurant. He figured later that he had probably drunk about 20 to 25 glasses of beer by this point in the evening — not an uncommon amount for him.

As he was leaving, a woman by the name of Peggy Bennett was looking for a ride home. She was a 36-year-old alcoholic, recently separated from her husband, and well known to a number of male patrons of the Wembley Hotel. As Fisher's lawyer argued after his conviction, "She was a woman of the loosest moral character. She was commonly known to engage in the most perverse sexual acts with any man. I would draw to your attention the fact that the police have evidence that on the two evenings prior to her death she had slept with and engaged in unnatural acts with two men who, until these acts were performed, were strangers to her."

Mrs. Bennett had already been refused a ride home by another patron of the hotel, but Louis Fisher agreed to give her a drive. He walked back to his house, picked up his car, and drove back to the hotel to meet her.

The banner headline in the next day's *Toronto Star* read, "Hacks Woman to Death — Police Hunt 'Sadistic' Killer." The report noted that the half-nude body of Margaret Bennett had been found in a parking lot. Bennett's eyes had been blackened; she had been stabbed many times, and a knife had been driven through her heart. Her clothing had been torn, and one breast was almost completely severed from her body.

The next day a reward of $1,500 was offered by the Metro Toronto Police Commission. "No Clues Yet Found in Sadistic Slaying of Toronto Woman," the *Globe and Mail* reported. The paper noted that Mrs. Bennett's movements had been traced to the Wembley Hotel. "I don't think this was the work of a sex maniac," Police Chief James Mackey said, "There is no evidence of criminal assault but he must have become infuriated over something." The autopsy revealed that Bennett was extremely drunk; her blood alcohol reading was four times the level permitted for driving under the influence of the drug.

About 10 days later police arrested Louis Fisher and charged him with murder. A search of his home revealed a large hunting knife stained with human blood and clothing containing stains of the same blood group as Mrs. Bennett's. In a statement to police Fisher admitted the stabbing, saying that his victim had "started fondling my privates" while riding in the car. Bennett apparently continued playing with Fisher's genitals and "she had gotten me into such a state that I didn't know what I was doing."

The motive for the murder was never really made clear, but, in Fisher's words, "I knew I was in trouble with this broad, and the greatest fear was that she knew my wife. I just flipped...the knife was in the back seat, so I reached over and got it and gave it to her. I didn't think I stabbed her that many times. I really went off my rocker, I guess, or I must have been drunk or a combination of both."

Fisher was tried and convicted of murder. The prosecutor did not suggest that this was a sexual assault killing, but proceeded on the basis that Peggy Bennett had been killed in a fit of rage. The jury found Fisher guilty and the struggle to save him from the gallows began. He was scheduled to hang in February 1961 but appeals in the Ontario Court of Appeal and then the Supreme Court of Canada pushed the date to late June of the same year.

The memorandum prepared for the Solicitor General concluded by quoting from the report of the trial judge, "There...does not appear to be evidence of any antecedent, calculated premeditation, other than that which might be suggested by the statement of the prisoner." Joe Pomerant, Fisher's young lawyer, provided the Department of Justice with a seven-page plea for commutation. At one point Pomerant wrote, "I have been in communication with the foreman of the jury which convicted Mr. Fisher and he informs me that the jury was not aware that they could recommend mercy. He has told me that if he had known that a recommendation of mercy could have been made that he and other members of the jury would have made it."

Psychiatrist R.E. Turner concluded his report, "I am of

the opinion that Fisher is definitely suffering from a psychopathic personality and, as such, is a person sick in personality and should not be held fully accountable for the offence for which he has been convicted." Turner added, "I do believe he had a sudden momentarily aggressive outburst as a result of Mrs. Bennett's advances to him."

On June 22, 1961, the Diefenbaker Cabinet met to consider the fate of Louis Fisher and learned how police first came to suspect him of murder. They were told that several months before the murder a man by the name of Brad, an habitué of the Wembley Hotel, had made sexual advances to a woman in his car. The woman had pretended to faint and been pushed out the door. No charges were laid in that incident, but after Margaret Bennett's murder, police found out that "Brad" was Louis Fisher's nickname and that he was a regular at The Wembley. They figured that they had their killer. They went to his home, arrested him, and he confessed.

The discussion in Cabinet that day focussed on whether this was a sexual assault killing and whether Fisher's use of alcohol was a significant factor. On the less critical issue of drunkenness the Cabinet minutes note, "The accused had not been drunk at the time of the crime. A drunken person could not reasonably be expected to have driven his car for a distance of several miles, nor to have recalled enough to have made such a detailed statement in confession of the crime. No witnesses had testified that he was drunk."

But Louis Fisher had also had more than a dozen beers by the time he started to drive.. If he wasn't "drunk," he was certainly very much under the influence.

The Cabinet minutes note the sexual overtones in this killing. "There was no corroboration of the accused's statement that the deceased had made persistent sexual advances to him. It was equally possible, particularly in view of the similar incident several months previously, that he had made the advances. If the murder had been committed in the course of rape, it would be capital murder."[14]

The Cabinet also discussed the issue of premeditation, the

majority concluding, "His previous conviction for carrying a knife, the presence of the knife in the car, and the attempted rape of the other woman all tended to create a presumption that the murder had been deliberate."

We don't really know what happened between Louis Fisher and Margaret Bennett on that night in June, and maybe Louis Fisher didn't know either. We know that he probably "flipped out." Patrons of the car wash where he worked consistently described him as "kind," "helpful," and "courteous." We know that this killing had a lot to do with sex, but it's not clear that it was a sexual assault killing. The memorandum prepared for the Solicitor General dealt with this issue, "There were suggestions in the evidence that in character she was not too morally stable, and a jury might infer that she might be likely to consent to intercourse or could even invite it. The medical evidence indicated that the spermatozoa found in her vagina could have been deposited as early as 18 hours before death. That would have been at a time some 15 hours before she could have had contact with the prisoner."

Maybe Louis Fisher and Margaret Bennett had sex that night, and then Louis Fisher exploded. It is perhaps more likely that Louis Fisher just exploded. Or then again, maybe he raped Margaret Bennett and stabbed her to death. What was proven at trial was that two people who knew each other got into a car with confused intentions. The male brutally killed the female, in an uncharacteristic rage.

Sex was on the agenda, to be sure, but for whom and why? Both Louis Fisher and Margaret Bennett had difficulties with sexuality. Fisher told psychiatrists that when it came to sex, he "could take it or leave it." Psychiatrist R.E. Turner concluded, "It was clear that he had a markedly reduced sexual drive, both in adolescence and during his married life. He preferred drinking to sex." Margaret Bennett was an alcoholic without a lot of self-esteem, satisfying men in a drunken stupor.

On June 27, 1961, in Toronto's Don Jail, just after midnight, Louis Fisher started saying the Twenty-third Psalm, taught to him by Salvation Army Major Ivan Jackson:

The Lord is my shepherd, I shall not want;
He maketh me to lie down in green pastures.
He leadeth me beside the still waters...

The trap opened and Louis Fisher fell to his death. Chief Coroner Smirle Lawson told the press, "He was a brave man, although a bad one. I saw a sad thing tonight."[15]

The contribution of alcohol to this killing cannot easily be disputed — and yet Louis Fisher was said not to be drunk, and so to be fully responsible for his actions. While a person under the influence of alcohol may be treated with some leniency when committing a crime, Louis Fisher was not seen as deserving.[16]

Empirical research doesn't provide us with any easy answers to the problem of criminal responsibility for crime that is committed under the influence of drugs. While the use of illegal drugs can increase a sentence, the use of legal drugs can lessen punishment. But pharmacology tells us that there are no good or bad drugs, at least not in the way that our criminal law postulates.

A person under the influence of heroin is usually less dangerous than a person under the influence of alcohol — recall that Tom Pickard killed when he was having trouble getting some heroin and Louis Fisher killed when he was under the influence of alcohol. Drugs which act on the mind possess very plastic chemistries. Heroin "addicts," cocaine "fiends" and alcoholics need not be violent. The cultural context or social setting in which these drugs are taken shape the way in which the alteration of consciousness will be interpreted.

For Bill Davey, it was a legal business deal that got him into trouble — and a little alcohol. Bill Davey's problem with Ed Murray could have been resolved in Canada's civil courts. I've known Bill for about nine years, as he has bounced from one institution to another, to the street and back. I must have seen him about a dozen times over the years. I don't know him well, but I have some sense of what he's like, and I like him. Most people do; most people also say that he is his own worst enemy.[17]

Davey was an auto body man, working out on the British Columbia coast. He was married to his third wife, and while he had a criminal record at the time of the killing, he had not been involved with the law for some time. He was first sent to jail in 1957 for forgery, when he was 17. There were a number of other convictions in 1962, for break, enter and theft, escape from jail and armed robbery. He received a five-year sentence and was released in January 1967.

From that point until the killing in late 1972, he remained out of trouble, except for a marijuana cigarette. In the late summer of 1967 he was charged with possession. "I got three months for one marijuana cigarette they found. I threw it out of the motel because the cops were coming in the door. They found it on the street. I pled guilty because there was two of us, and two guys can't go to jail for one joint. Three months I did for one marijuana cigarette. And now they don't even take it away from you, probably. Just crunch it up in their hands. I've been in here so long, I don't know. Or take it home and smoke it themselves. I don't know."

Drugs have always been a problem for Bill Davey; he knows that he doesn't handle alcohol well, and he likes to take mind-altering substances quite regularly. This is the pattern of behaviour that stands between him and the street, getting high on heroin, abusing valium or getting drunk on beer. It all comes down to the same thing, avoiding what he describes as the pain of everyday life. "We all have pain. Sometimes it gets a little unbearable. I know how to cure the pain. Take a fix of heroin, a few valiums, something like that."

But drugs didn't have much to do with the killing of Ed Murray. There was a little alcohol, which Bill Davey figures didn't help. It lessened his fears about dealing with Ed Murray's anger.

Back in September 1972, Prime Minister Pierre Trudeau and Margaret Sinclair had just been married; Richard Nixon was President of the United States, and Bill Davey was going to meet his wife for a movie and a ferry trip up the B.C. coast. Because he was broke, he phoned his friend Ed Murray to collect a loan of $30. Both Bill and Ed were body men, working on the West Coast. When Bill had more work than he could handle, he would pass it on to Ed. The two men didn't know each other that well, but they had a generally friendly relationship, based on their business.

Ed Murray didn't want to talk to Bill Davey about the money that he owed him. He had been charged with breaking into a school; some stolen goods were found in his possession, and he suspected that Davey had been talking to the police. Davey insisted that he had not been talking to the police about the stolen goods, but Murray was still furious. He demanded that the two of them meet to straighten out the dispute. If Davey wasn't going to come over to his house, he would come over to Davey's body shop.

Bill Davey didn't want Ed Murray to come over to his place of work; he figured that he and his friend John Duncan could go over to Ed's and settle things down. They bought a six-pack of beer and drove over to the house, with its small body shop in the back yard. There was a rifle in the back seat of the car; Davey was planning to go target shooting with his Labrador retriever later that day.

As soon as Davey walked into the house, Murray started swinging. He was stronger and in better shape, and he grabbed a knife that Davey had on his belt. Davey used it in body work for stripping paint and fibreglass. Murray was now trying to stab Davey with the knife and ultimately succeeded, opening up a large cut in his leg.

As John Duncan noted at the trial, as a prosecution witness, Bill Davey started screaming at him to take the knife away. As Davey describes it, "Anyway, my buddy heard the noise, came running into the house, grabbed a hold of him and as I'm running out the door, [Murray] was yelling, 'Give me back the knife.''

Davey picked his .22 calibre rifle up from the back seat of the car and ran back up the stairs of the house, firing a shot through the door before he came in. It was the fatal bullet, and the only bullet. Ed Murray had been standing behind the door, and took the shot in the stomach. He fell to the floor. Bill Davey walked in and stood over him, yelling that he was not a rat, not a stool pigeon for the police. He was still furious, and not at all aware of the extent of Murray's injuries. At first he didn't want to help Murray into the car to take him to hospital. He ripped the phone out of the wall and was said to have told Murray's wife that her husband deserved to die.

In a matter of minutes, however, Davey relented. He and John Duncan helped Murray into his car, to be driven to the hospital. Davey bandaged the deep gash in his leg, and then he and Duncan drove back to North Vancouver from Richmond. Eventually they went to a popular beer parlour in Vancouver, with Davey spending most of the time before his arrest either drinking there or back at a motel room on Vancouver's Kingsway.

Ed Murray died after five hours in hospital from the bullet wound. Police were very wary of approaching Davey. They were probably frightened by his record of break and entry, armed robbery, prison escape and now, a killing. Bill Davey's wife made the transaction a lot easier for everyone. She was worried that he would be killed by the police during arrest, so she herself called them to the motel.

At this point Davey could almost have been scooped up in a basket. His leg was badly infected; he was in considerable pain. He had injected some heroin, and was asleep when the police burst into the room. He recalls that a dozen police officers converged on the motel in a van and two cars; there were at least three men with shotguns.

Davey offered no resistance. He was really only semiconscious, and was in danger of losing his leg to infection when he was transferred to Vancouver General Hospital. He stayed there 10 days before going to jail to await trial. While in Oakalla Prison he cried about what had happened. "I felt really bad. I didn't really dislike the guy. I was mad at him at the time, but if I'd had a cooling-out period he'd probably still be doing body work for me now or I'd be kind of helping with jobs. We'd probably be friends."

At the trial the prosecutor argued that this was non-capital murder while the defence argued for manslaughter, saying that Bill Davey had killed Ed Murray when provoked, in the heat of passion. The jury believed, however, that this was a murder. The heroin, and the previous convictions for armed rob-

bery and prison escape were probably just too much for the
12 men and women to accept. Even if the facts did not necessarily add up to murder, Bill Davey's past did.

Like many other lifers, Davey sees convicted murderers as
generally the least aggressive prisoners in Canada's institutions.
"All prisons try to have so many murderers because it keeps
the population cooled down. Because when there's a bunch
of bullshit going, it's usually the guys doing the life sentences
that go and tell the guys, 'Pull your socks up'. We've got something to lose. So we kind of keep the lid on the place, where
the average guy doesn't. And I think that the correctional administration will tell you that too."

Bill Davey is on the way out of prison life, if he can get
control over his use of legal and illegal drugs. He says of his
present status, "I'm in jail right now because I abuse substances on occasion. I long ago paid for my crime. I was told
that in my case management team meeting the other day. They
said, 'Bill, you paid for your crime five years ago. Now you're
paying for the fact that you did something foolish...that you
get high. Why do you do that?' I said, 'Hey, every now and
then the pain gets so fucking heavy I just have to get away
for a couple of hours. Like the guy down there who works
in the garage, he has a few beers after work. I'm not saying
it's right, but it's the truth.' "

"But when you unwind, do you unwind by having a few
beers or do you unwind by getting too high to function?"

"Well, a combination of the two," Davey tells me, "de-
pends on the occasion. Often now I'm using the heavier
drugs...heroin. You take the homemade brew that's around,
if you drink that, it ends up in violence — fights and everything. So you do heroin...you kind of sit back, you sit on your
bed and read a book or clean the house up. Every time I do
a little bit of heroin I clean the house up. I just think that
if I was put out on the street I wouldn't be a danger to anyone except myself. I may be a danger to me. I know for sure
I won't reoffend."

Bill Davey's matter-of-fact mention of drug use in Canada's prisons should not be surprising; there is a sense in which
both guards and prisoners benefit when the captives can more

easily cope with imprisonment. Prison is a constant invasion of privacy — surveillance by guards and, what is probably more significant, surveillance by other prisoners. The drugs to be avoided in this kind of environment are the mood elevators, alcohol, cocaine, amphetamines, uppers. Marijuana, valium and the opiates usually help to keep the peace, slowing down and sedating the population.

For Bill Davey, drugs are going to continue to be a problem, inside and outside prison. This doesn't make him different from a lot of people. "I'm human. And it's not that I haven't tried. I've taken alcohol treatment programs three times. I stayed straight 99.9% of the time. All the time I went out on the last six-month program, I haven't taken one thing on the outside. And it was offered, and you know, you can get anything you want out there. I have no interest in drugs...occasionally inside here, but pain, like I said earlier, the pain gets too heavy."

There is one final kind of acquaintance killing to be discussed in this chapter, the murder of a police officer or prison guard. Every year a handful of Canadian police officers are shot to death; these killings are not about money or sex, and they are usually not carried out by people who are emotionally disturbed or mentally handicapped. They are only political killings if one gives the word "political" an enormous breadth. Police officers are usually killed by desperate men in desperate circumstances; they are acquainted, killer and victim, tied together by the opposing social roles that they have chosen. To use the language of Statistics Canada, theirs is a "business relationship."

The number of police killings has fluctuated over the past 25 years, without reference to changes in law or punishment. The law has always regarded such killings as the worst of crimes, the ultimate challenge to the power of the state, the revolution of one against the collective power of 25 million. The last man that Canada hanged had killed a policeman in Toronto; Ronald Turpin was 29 when he was dropped to his death at the Don Jail in December 1962.

Ronald Turpin's difficulties began at an early age. Like Louis Fisher, he was raised in the east end of Toronto. And like Louis Fisher, he had a mother who was an alcoholic, and a father who drifted away from the family when Turpin was very young. His childhood was quite miserable; his mother and father often fought, and had sexual relations with other men and women respectively. He told psychiatrist Arthur Blair of one particular instance in which his mother placed all the family's cats and kittens in a sack and prepared to throw them into the Don River. His mother had told him that he could keep one of the animals and she asked him to pick the one to be spared from death. He was very upset, feeling that he could not just pick one cat; he wanted all of them to live. In spite of his tears and his inability to choose, his mother threw all the cats in the river.

Not long after this incident he was abandoned by his mother and taken to the Children's Aid Society. She left him sitting on a balcony and told him she would come back at a certain time in the afternoon. She had no intention of ever returning and hours later representatives from Children's Aid stepped in, taking young Turpin off to a dormitory, crying and sobbing. Turpin's mother died in 1952, on her birthday, while he was serving a sentence at the Guelph Reformatory. She had been carrying a case of beer across the road when she was drunk, and was hit by a car.

Ronald Turpin went through his teenage years, and most of his adult life, as a ward of the state. He went to foster homes, to training schools, and then to jail. His crimes all amounted to theft — forgery, break and entry, and the like. In 1960 he was released from Kingston Penitentiary, and continued to make a living by stealing. He was well known to the police and through 1961 and 1962, and subject to surveillance.

In October 1962 Turpin was involved in an incident at an apartment on Toronto's Wellesley Street. A number of shots were fired; although there were no injuries, a warrant was issued for his arrest. A detective spoke with Turpin by telephone, urging him to come to headquarters with the pistol and turn himself in. Turpin declined the invitation, saying that he would "take his chances."

Turpin then became a fugitive. From October until the

killing four months later in February 1962, he lived in a series of motels and apartments, travelling up to Haliburton and over to Buffalo, New York. On the night of February 11, he broke into the Red Rooster restaurant in the east end of Toronto, taking over $600 from the till. He left the restaurant sometime after midnight, driving a dilapidated delivery truck along the Danforth, his loot in a paper bag under the seat.

Constable Fred Nash was patrolling the Danforth just after two in the morning when he noticed that the old delivery truck had a missing front headlight. He signalled the car to pull over and stop. Turpin obliged, and Nash shone his flashlight inside the car, apparently asking for a driver's licence and ordering Turpin into the street.

What happened next is not exactly clear, but it seems fair to say that there was a gun battle. A couple driving by the scene of the crime saw Nash and Turpin standing in the street; Nash waved them along and after turning the corner the couple heard what sounded like gunshots. A streetcar driver saw Constable Nash lurch forward and fall to the pavement; he left his streetcar and walked towards the officer. At this point Turpin intervened, telling the man, "Get back in the car or I'll shoot you." Understandably enough, the streetcar driver complied.

The only evidence that we have about what happened between Turpin and Nash was given by Turpin to police while he was en route to hospital. He had been hit by bullets in the arms and the side of the cheek. "Sarge, tell me why a guy would grab a gun that is pointed at him? When he was near me he made a grab for my gun. I let him have it then a couple of times. He reached for his gun. I threw my gun down, then he fired at me from the ground. I still can't understand why he reached for my barrel. You would think when you had a gun pointing at you, you would stay where you are."[18]

Turpin had been arrested at the scene of the crime; another police cruiser arrived and he was taken into custody at gunpoint, saying, "I give up. I haven't got the gun. The gun is in the car. Look after the officer." The front page of the next morning's *Toronto Star* appeared with the headline, "Dying Words, 'I Got Him,' Suspect Shot, Charged". Nash's last words to a fellow officer were reported as "I got him. He shot first." It seems that Turpin had pulled a gun on Nash, urging him to back off, and that Nash had then moved to take the gun from him. Turpin panicked, pulled the trigger, and killed the officer.

At trial Turpin probably lied, basing his case on self-defence and arguing that he was shot three times before he returned fire. The jury was also told at trial that Police Constable Nash had been demoted from probationary detective to constable in 1961, as the consequence of a hearing into alleged police violence in the city of Toronto.

This blemish on the officer's record notwithstanding, the jury did not believe Ronald Turpin's version of events, and convicted him of capital murder. The trial judge, G.A. Gale, was also less than sympathetic. In a memorandum prepared for the Minister of Justice he wrote, "I am in complete agreement with the observation of Crown counsel that Turpin is a hardened criminal. I believe that he is a man who had come to think that he could live by his wits and a gun and that had he not encountered Police Constable Nash he would have killed some other person sooner or later. Perhaps I may be permitted to say, too, that in my opinion the morale of law enforcement agencies in this area will undoubtedly suffer if any leniency is extended to this desperado."

A few months later psychiatrist Arthur Blair conducted an examination of Turpin at the Don Jail. He argued that Turpin was of above-average intelligence and wrote, "Society has found him difficult only in that he has indulged himself in antisocial behaviour such as stealing, forgery and so forth. He certainly did not inherit a wealth of traits that if fulfilled would lead him to becoming a useful citizen. Over and above this, his early formative years were chaotic, with lack of guidance, lack of love and affection, and strife, with unstable, argumentative and physically violent parents." Having said all this, however, Blair could not bring himself to offer any prospect of treatment or rehabilitation. He concluded his report to the Minister of Justice, "With the present extent of our knowledge, modern day psychiatry can offer little to people such as he. He is not mentally ill and thus cannot be placed in a mental hospital. He is not uncomfortable, and thus would not seek treatment such as the average frightened or depressed individual.''

On December 5, 1962, the Diefenbaker Cabinet met to consider the case of Ronald Turpin; it was the last time that a Canadian government would allow a man to be hanged. The Cabinet had before it a memorandum prepared by Minister of Justice Donald Fleming. Like his predecessor Davie Fulton, Fleming was a strong believer in capital punishment. He argued for death, concluding his memorandum, ''Having regard to all the circumstances of the case there would appear to be no significant factors in favour of commuting the sentence.''

During Cabinet discussion it was pointed out that Turpin had failed to establish drunkenness, insanity and provocation as defences.[19] It was also stated that Turpin was not mentally defective. But what the minutes reveal as most significant were the comments of the trial judge. Justice G.A. Gale had written of Turpin, ''I find it quite impossible to recommend executive clemency. The accused is a thoroughly bad and vicious man.''

Ronald Turpin was, like so many killers, the product of years of neglect and abuse. He probably didn't plan to kill Constable Fred Nash, and his criminal record was one built on property crime, not violence. In the final analysis, none of this mattered. The minutes of the Cabinet meeting of December 5 close with the following standard form statement, set out for what was, as it turned out, the final time, ''The Cabinet agreed that, in the case of Ronald Turpin, who had been convicted of capital murder and sentenced to be executed on December 11th, 1962, the law be allowed to take its course.''

---

[1] ''Petition to his Excellency, Rt. Hon. Sir John Campbell Hamilton Gordon, Earl of Aberdeen, Governor-General of Canada,'' *Capital Case Files, RG 13 series, Hugh Lynn,* August 17, 1894, National Archives, Ottawa, Canada.

2 "To be hanged," *The Daily Colonist*, Victoria, British Columbia, July 21, 1894, 1.

3 The power of these images has persisted for generations. In an article written without the benefit of the trial transcript, and with substantial input from the local lore of Savary Island, C. Heather Allen concludes that Hugh Lynn was a "ne'er do well" who planned the deaths of Green and Taylor "armed with liquid courage." C. Heather Allen, "Murder on Savary Island," *Westworld*, Vancouver, Western Canada Magazines, April 1982, 43-45.

4 "Lynn Hanged," *Victoria Daily Colonist*, August 25, 1894, 2.

5 *Homicide in Canada, 1984: A Statistical Perspective*, Statistics Canada, Ottawa, 1984, at Appendix II; Glossary.

6 For ample empirical demonstration of these points see Edwin M. Brecher and the Editors of *Consumers Reports, Licit and Illicit Drugs*, Boston, Little, Brown and Company, 1972, and Weil and Rosen, *Chocolate to Morphine: Understanding Mind-Active Drugs*, Houghton-Mifflin, Boston, 1985.

8 "Tom Pickard" and all other names connected with this story are pseudonyms.

9 "Ian Blenheim" and "Danny Harrigan" and all other names connected with this story are pseudonyms.

10 "Scott Millar" is a pseudonym.

11 See Chapter 4, "The Types and Circumstances of Murder," *Homicide in Canada: A Statistical Synopsis*, Statistics Canada, Ottawa, 1976. See particularly Tables 4.1, 4.25 and 4.26.

12 See note 9, *above*. Table 4.6, 35. The percentages have been extrapolated from the table.

13 Louis Fisher, *Capital Case Files*, RG 13 Series, National Archives, Ottawa, Canada

14 Minutes of Cabinet meetings, disclosed under *The Access to Information Act*, Privy Council Office, Capital Case; L.W.B. Fisher, June 22, 1961.

15 "Fisher Hangs at Don Jail," *Toronto Star*, June 27, 1961, 2.

16 The definitive case insofar as drunkenness is concerned is *D.P.P. v Beard*, [1920] A.C. 479.

17 "Bill Davey" and all other names connected with this story are pseudonyms.

18 "Memorandum for the Honourable Minister of Justice," Ronald Turpin, *Capital Case Files, RG 13 Series*, National Archives, Ottawa, Canada, 8.

19 Minutes of Cabinet meetings, disclosed under *The Access to Information Act*, July 1987, Privy Council Office, *Ronald Turpin*, December 5, 1962.

Chapter Four

KILLING FOR MONEY

Rural life is part of the Canadian heritage. The windswept Canadian plain is too cold in winter and too hot in summer, with its surreal landscape of waving wheatfields. The Prairies are often referred to as Canada's heartland, home of all that is good and decent about our country. Tommy Douglas and John Diefenbaker, men of principle and vision, have been the ambassadors for this small pocket of our population.

Rural ideology stresses self-reliance, decentralized decision-making, and, in many parts of the Prairies, religious commitment. For Don Monarch, religious commitment was a problem. He wasn't under the influence himself, but he couldn't really get away from it either.

He was released from penitentiary in the mid-Seventies, after serving close to five years of a long sentence. He had met his wife while he was inside; it was a "jailhouse romance." She visited him regularly and they married after he got out. Within a year they had a child.

Within a couple of years, however, "the marriage started going for hell." Monarch's wife became committed to God, and more and more annoyed by his drinking and cigarette smoking. "She used to be a real party girl and then she started getting religion, so naturally that affected my drinking. On a hot summer's day you stop at the bar and you have a beer or two and you go home. Before, that was fine. Saturday nights, everybody would go out and party with the girls and wives, whatever. But then gradually it got to the point where she didn't want me stopping for the beer anymore."

"Pretty soon that wasn't good enough," he continues, "then I had to stop drinking. And in between there, she stops smoking. So eventually the house was down to one ashtray, which was a subtle hint that I should quit too."

Monarch's marriage started to evaporate; his wife left him several times and ultimately he left his wife. The couple tried again at several points to live together, but it just didn't work. Eventually he moved in with a friend of one of his co-workers, and his wife remained at home with their child. He says in retrospect, "So far as jailhouse romances and marriages go, I've seen quite a few of them and not too many work. Some of them do, sure, the odd one, but for God's sake, don't get married while you're in jail or right after. Get to know each other first. She had been on her own for six years. She wanted things the way she'd been doing it for six years. I had my idea of how I wanted our lives to be run. Maybe it was a lack of communication, I don't know. A difference in personality, I think, is more."

On the night before the killings, Monarch was out partying with his new roommate, Dave Judd[1]. The men had been to a few nightclubs and bars in the city, and then on to a couple of house parties. They drove home to get some sleep, at about four or five in the morning. Monarch sets the scene of the following day. "Sunday morning we get up, don't know what we're going to do. We had a couple of beers and we're sitting there watching TV and an advertisement came on TV for a fowl supper."

Monarch explains, "This one was a turkey supper. All the women in that church will put it on; they'll cook the turkeys and you come down and buy a ticket for $2.50 or whatever it is, and it's all you can eat." He and Judd decided that they would drive out into the country and go to the supper. The woman who lived in the apartment above the two men also went along.

Soon after they'd arrived at the supper in the church basement, they realized that there would be a two-hour wait in line for turkey. They cashed in their tickets and started to drive back to the city. Monarch picks up the story, "Halfway back,

Dave's driving; I'm sitting in the back seat, the girl's in the front seat. Dave said, 'Don, did you see how much money was in the cashbox? I said, 'No, I wasn't there, *you* were there.' He said, 'Don, they're using a big toolbox and it's full of money.' ''

Monarch continues, ''And nobody said anything. But we looked at each other in the rearview mirror and as soon as our eyes met, I knew what he was going to do. We were going back.''

The young woman didn't want to have anything to do with the robbery; she was screaming at them and begging them to forget about it. They told her that if she didn't keep quiet they'd throw her out of the car. There was a revolver in the glove box, often used for target shooting, and as they drove back to the church supper Monarch loaded the gun. The men discussed the robbery and agreed that Monarch should be the person to go in with the weapon. ''I said, I'll go in. You drive the car, have it pointed that way with the door open, and when I come out, hit it.''

It was a brick church, serving a rural community. Two local farmers were giving tickets and taking cash in an area set off from the main hall. Monarch demanded the money in the cashbox and ran out of the church with it. He and Judd and their less-than-willing female partner then drove off at 90 miles an hour down a gravel road.

They didn't have much time to celebrate their heist, though. Some headlights appeared in the rearview mirror; two cars were coming after them at top speed. At first they thought it was the police, but there were no sirens and no flashing lights. Driving the cars were the two farmers from the church supper, out to reclaim what was rightfully theirs. One of them drove right up to the back of the getaway car and bumped it. Monarch turned and fired off a few rounds at the car. The farmers dropped back — they were unarmed.

But they didn't give up the chase. A couple of miles further down the road one of the two farmers came up again and bumped the car. Monarch describes the scene, ''I told Dave, stop the car. If he hits us wrong, we're gonna flip this car, we'll roll, everybody's gonna get killed here. My idea was, stop him, take the car keys, throw them in a ditch, leave them there and take off."

The getaway car screeched to a stop and the two pursuers followed suit. The minute that Judd stopped the car Monarch was out the door, running over to the closest driver. The man rolled up his windows and locked his car door. Monarch took his revolver and shot out the window, ordering him to get out and walk over to the side of the road.

The frightened farmer dove out the passenger door and was followed by Monarch as he walked to the side of the gravel highway. Monarch had his cocked and loaded revolver pointing at the man's back. He describes what happened next, "So he started walking and I'm walking behind him. But I look to see what this other guy in the car in front of us is doing. While I'm looking over there, the guy in front of me gets to the side of the road and stops like I told him to. But I ran into him. I wasn't looking at him. I walked into him, my thumb went off the hammer and bang! down he went."

"I said, holy shit! This wasn't supposed to happen. And when he fell, everything...I don't know. I can't say. I guess I panicked in a way, because this was not in the books. This wasn't supposed to happen." Monarch ran over to the other farmer. He told him to pull his car over to the side of the road, and to go and lie face down on the gravel beside his dying friend.

The bullet entered the second farmer's skull near the ear; he was killed instantly. Monarch claims the second killing was also an accident. "I turned to go to the car on the gravel road, I was wearing leather-soled shoes, I slipped, I fell, I heard the gun go off, jumped up, got in the car and we were gone."

There were more headlights coming over the hills when Monarch fired his gun. He and Judd and the woman drove home. The next morning they heard on the radio that both men were dead. Monarch recalls, "We were arrested a day and a half later. Apparently the girl went to the cops. Tried, a 10-day trial, and found guilty of first degree murder, both of us."

Monarch argues that he may be guilty of second degree murder, but not first, "I have never ever once tried to say that I was framed or that I did not commit a crime. I admit that my gun in my hand took two lives. I admit that. But it was not planned and deliberate. And I'll say that until the day I die."

Monarch has served over 11 years of his 25-year minimum; he is looking forward to the judicial review of his sentence in 1991. "We were so bloody stupid," he says now of that evening in 1976. He believes that the circumstances of the killings produced the first degree conviction, "They were two well known farmers in the community, a small town, a small area. And because the whole thing started at a church, there was the religion angle."

Monarch also believes that his victims increased the likelihood of tragedy. "So why in the name of heaven did they chase us? Even if they wanted to chase us, when they got close enough to get the licence number and the description of the car, why didn't they drop back, stop in at the nearest farmhouse and then phone it in? The police couldn't understand it either, the way they kept pursuing us for something like 12 miles and trying to run us off the road."

A few years ago Monarch heard through a close friend that the brother of one of his victims wanted to meet him. He "didn't quite know how to handle that," and turned down the request. That Christmas a leather-bound black Bible arrived at the prison. It had his name engraved in gold on the front and inside was written "A gift from John and Thelma."

"I'm not afraid of reconciliation," Monarch says, "I think I've got over that; now I would meet them. But I don't want to get in touch with them now because people, not them, but the administration and the parole board, are liable to look at it as well, I'm getting close to that 15-year review and starting to look for brownie points. And I don't want that to be misunderstood."

"How do you think it will be when you get out on the street?" he is asked.

"Strange. I don't know. That's hard to answer. There's

going to be a lot of adjustment to get used to, a lot of changes. I'd be a way different person. I don't know if so much of that comes from being in the penitentiary as it does from being 15 years older. You gain a little more wisdom with age. Oh, Christ, I've seen myself come in so many times, and other guys that I've known. It's a revolving-door syndrome. It's the same guys coming back. You look at some of these young guys and you see yourself in the mirror 15, 20 years ago. And you look at them and you say, how could I have been so stupid? Why didn't I listen to somebody?''

Don Monarch is fairly typical of a person who kills during the course of a robbery. Murder, first or second degree, was not really planned or deliberate, but it could not have been totally unexpected. When a person carries a gun and uses it to take property from other people, it is very likely that sooner or later someone will die. That person could be a bystander, a man or woman who is simply in the wrong place at the wrong time. This is what differentiates killing for money from killing family or acquaintances — the chilling randomness in selection of the potential targets.

Over the past decade about 10% of all criminal homicides can be classified as killings for money. The average number of murders in Canada over the past decade has been 660 per year; of these, the average number of killings during the course of robbery, theft, or break and entry has been 66 per year.[2] This is a relatively small percentage of the total of all such violent deaths, but here we enter the realm of the more unpredictable and frightening of killings. We encounter people who, if only for a passing moment, are willing to kill to further their own economic ends.

In this category of violence we find a small number of contract killers, those who have taken on the job of ending human life. Peter Demeter and Helmuth Buxbaum are the best known for this kind of murder, men who either killed their wives for financial gain, or hired "hit men" to do the job for them. These two were wealthy and powerful, accustomed to ordering the world to suit their own tastes and desires.

But this duo of Demeter and Buxbaum does not adequately

represent the reality of Canada's contract killers. Most contract killings are related either to gang warfare or to the internal discipline of illegal businesses. These unsolved "probable gangland" murders appear to represent the overwhelming majority of contract killings, and it is understandably difficult to arrive at any precise figure as to the numbers of such killings in Canada over the past 25 years. We do know, however, that as the percentage of unsolved murders increased from 1968 to 1974, from 7 to 15% of all homicides, so too did the number of unsolved "probable gangland" murders increase from 22 in 1961-1967 to 123 in 1968-74.

As the unregulated economy of illegal drug distribution expanded, the need for enforcement of the internal rules of these businesses became more pronounced. Execution, the ultimate sanction, became more common. My best guess from the data available is that we now have about 20 to 30 contract killings each year in Canada. Most of these flow from the underground economies of organized crime and from the discipline imposed by the groups of people involved in this kind of crime.[3] In Montreal, for example, during the Sixties and Seventies, rival motorcycle gangs had contracts out on each other. There was a reward of approximately $10,000 for the president, slightly less for the sergeant-at-arms, and $5,000 for the execution of any member.

I am going to tell you about two contract killers, one from the work of organized crime, the other unconnected to that lifestyle. Arthur Lucas of Detroit made a living out of gambling and prostitution. He was born in Georgia in 1907, and moved north, ultimately settling in Detroit. He had a number of convictions for forgery, theft, armed robbery, and living off the avails of prostitution. His friends were men who drank too much, distributed heroin and lived off the incomes of their prostitute wives and girlfriends. They had names like Checkerboard Thomas and Kid Knox.

The scene of the crime was the Spadina-College area of Toronto. The landmarks that figure in the killing are still there, the Waverley Hotel and the Silver Dollar. East of Spadina in this distinctive section of the city is the venerable University of Toronto. Just down the street on the west side is the El Mocambo, the small club which has served up musicians from Johnny Winter to the Rolling Stones. A little further south is the diversity of Kensington Market, with its tempting bakeries, and stands of fresh fruits and vegetables. This was mid-town Toronto, rich and poor, black and white, Jew and Christian.

In mid-November 1961 Arthur Lucas drove up to Toronto from Detroit and checked into the Waverley Hotel in the late afternoon; he was travelling with a man by the name of White. The manager of the hotel recalled that Lucas was ''very jolly and pleasant'' when he registered and that White was small and nervous. The two men went to the hotel bar and then on to the Silver Dollar for a couple of drinks of rye.

Lucas went back to his room and at about 3 a.m. he phoned Therland Crater; he left the Waverley alone shortly afterward, and drove the mile and a half to Crater's apartment on Kendal Avenue. It was one of four apartments in a three-storey brick house; Crater and his girlfriend had a two-storey unit.

For the next few hours Lucas sat and drank rye with Crater and his girlfriend, Carolyn Ann Newman. Crater, who was a pimp with Newman as his source of income, was scheduled to testify against Detroit businessman Gus Saunders in his up-coming narcotics trial. Lucas knew both Saunders and Crater; he was driving Saunders' car and was talking to Crater about a possible prostitution business in Toronto.

Lucas left the house a little before six a.m. and drove back to the Waverley Hotel. The night manager recalled that Lucas asked him for the house phone and then called White. ''Come along, we are checking out,'' he said.

At about 6:30 a.m., Harold King and his wife awoke to the sound of scuffling in the apartment above them on Kendal Avenue. ''Okay you don't have to hold me,'' King heard a male voice say; he then heard shots. His wife Margaret recalled a voice saying ''Let me go,'' the sound of a thud on the floor, and a woman's scream. She also remembered hearing two people on the stairs, one with light feet and the other much heavier.

Carolyn Ann Newman had called the operator and when the operator heard her screaming, she patched the call through to the Metro Toronto Police. Jemima McCabe, the police operator, heard further scuffling and Newman saying, "Oh, my throat" or "Not my throat."

The police were at the scene about 30 minutes after the killings. The apartment was empty, except for the two victims. Forty-three-year-old Therland Crater was found in his underwear; he had been shot four times and his throat was slit from ear to ear. Twenty-one-year-old Carolyn Ann Newman was found naked on the couple's bed, her throat also slit from ear to ear.

The next day Detroit police picked up Art Lucas and Gus Saunders on suspicion of murder and conspiracy to commit murder. The newspaper headlines wee quick to report the underworld context of these killings — "Hold Two Suspects in Gangland Murder of Drug Trial Witness," and "Link Double Slaying and U.S. Vice Ring." In Detroit a prosecuting attorney told a U.S. District Court that Gus Saunders had offered $5,000 for knowledge of Crater's whereabouts, just a few days before his death.[4]

Another news item noted that the trail of evidence led to Chicago. "Police said Tuesday," the story began, "that a man named White, registered at a downtown Toronto hotel along with murder suspect Arthur Lucas, may have been a Willie White of Chicago. Police in the Illinois city have been asked to trace him."

Only Arthur Lucas was extradited to Toronto to face the charge of capital murder. In April 1962 he was committed to trial, and in May he was found guilty and sentenced to hang. The evidence at trial was circumstantial. Blood was found under his fingernails, diluted blood was found in a bucket at his wife's home in Detroit, gunpowder was found on his hand, and his ring — one that was too big for his finger — was found under Carolyn Ann Newman's body.

The most damaging evidence was not put before the jury, however. Two police officers had interviewed Mrs. Delores Lucas in Detroit about a week after the killings. The transcript was inadmissible, barred by the status of Delores Lucas as the wife of the accused.

Mrs. Lucas spoke of the violence that her husband had shown her. "He never did cut me, but I've been hit with chairs, baseball bats, and anything he could get his hands on. Most of these scars under my eyes are from rings. He hit me when he had his ring on and it cut me."

Delores Lucas had bought her husband a small diamond ring after he came home from a stint in jail, but he soon lost it and bought himself another larger ring. She recalls, "He never hit me with that one, but he wore that large ring on his little finger."

Delores Lucas described her husband's confession. "Well, he seemed to be nervous and he was winded. And I asked him, I said, 'What is wrong?', and he said, 'You sit down and don't say nothin.' He said, 'I just, I just killed two people.'"

The jury at the Lucas murder trial did not recommend mercy, and on December 4, the Diefenbaker Cabinet met to decide whether they would allow him to die. Some members of Cabinet said they were not concerned with the details of capital murder cases, and that with the new murder law, those convicted of capital murder should be hanged as a matter of course. This, after all, had been the rationale in 1961 for dividing murder into categories of capital and non-capital. The minutes noted, "The Cabinet should not re-try these cases. Ministers [are] not more competent than the courts in such matters."[5]

But Diefenbaker could not be silent. The Cabinet has a clear responsibility to determine whether there has been a miscarriage of justice, he argued. "In the Lucas case," he continued, "if Lucas was the murderer there was no ground for clemency, but Ministers should satisfy themselves on whether or not he was the guilty party. If the wrong man had in fact been accused, the Cabinet would be exercising its highest responsibility by so concluding."

At the final vote, however, there was not enough doubt to lead the Cabinet to commute the sentence of death. Arthur Lucas died in the Don Jail on December 11, 1962, with Ronald

Turpin, the last contract of death paid for by the Canadian state.

Doris James, unlike Arthur Lucas, did not live on the proceeds of organized criminal enterprises.[6] She is a contract killer in the mold of Peter Demeter and Helmuth Buxbaum; she didn't have as much money as either of these men, but she had the same idea.

James married her husband in the late Seventies, but after about a year the couple drifted apart and she headed out of the city. Her husband had abused her emotionally and physically. They stayed apart for over two years, while she spent some time in jail and thought about a relationship with another man. "There was a guy in AA that I met in January of '80; I was staying in a halfway house that he owned. He wanted me to live with him."

"Naturally," she continues, "I was just getting over being hurt [by my husband] so I got cold feet and I took off to B.C. Then, after I was in B.C. I went back to the city [Calgary]. I should have just kept on going."

The city was where her life went over the edge. It hadn't been easy at any time; her life had been spent in bars, first experimenting with illegal drugs, and then focusing on legal drugs. "In '74 until the summer of '77 I was using drugs. Marijuana, hash, I tried cocaine a couple of times. I tried MDA once. In '74 I was using marijuana quite a bit. That's [also] when I started drinking heavy. I had some prescription drugs, valium and something else, but they were for my nerves." By the time of the killing in 1981, James had narrowed her focus. "It was legal drugs only. The illegal drugs I quite in '77."

She had moved in with her husband again, and was working part-time as a receptionist and secretary in her apartment block. He still physically abused her, however, and she finally decided that she couldn't take any more of it. When she was out drinking one night she asked a friend "if she knew of anyone that I could get to take care of my husband for me."

The young woman agreed to look into the matter, and ultimately came up with a former boyfriend who was willing to help out. He reported to James that he had found a man who would do the killing for $1,000. She picks up the story, "There was no way I could afford that much money because I was on social assistance, and all I could afford was $100. So anyways, this guy says okay. He agreed to the $100."

"So on Sunday I met them for coffee," James continues, "I gave her the money and she gave it to him later on that night. Meanwhile my husband and I had gone out for supper and we had a fight. And I was pissed off at him anyways. So about 7:30 this guy comes strutting upstairs, [asking] my husband to go for coffee. So they went out."

The men went for coffee and then on to Princess Island. Princess Island is a civic park in the city, a small oasis in the middle of the Bow River, just a few minutes walk from downtown. On a hot summer day families from the bluffs above descend on the cultivated landscape, its red gravel paths alive with joggers and walkers, and its sunny open areas a temporary home for picnickers and frisbee players.

There are only a few lights on Princess Island, though. On a January night you wouldn't expect to see many people around. A person could be stabbed to death without any witnesses. Doris James recalls that evening, "So the guy says to [my husband], you're going in the wrong direction. When he turned around to face him, he kneed him and stabbed him 19 times. He came back to my apartment, and he says, well, what kind of flowers would you like for your birthday? So I says, everything's okay? He said, yeah."

James continues, "So anyways, I said roses." She recalls that while the killer told her he had slit her husband's throat, he had not actually done this. "It was just a little bit here and a little bit there. But I didn't know this until after I seen the pictures at my preliminary. And, ah...then we went out for coffee."

James then reported to police that her husband was missing. They told her that they couldn't do anything until he had been gone for 24 hours. A few days after the murder, they came looking for her, taking her down to the police station for intensive questioning. She recalls her arrest. "About five o'clock they came and told me that I may as well tell them everything, that my girlfriend had told them everything. I found out afterwards that she made a deal with them, to tell them everything and they'd make sure that she didn't get 25 years. Plus the stupid jerk was taking the cops out to the murder scene.''

She recalls a phone conversation, after arrest, with the man who had once asked her to live with him. ''And when I phoned him he says to me, oh, where are you now? I says, I'm in the remand centre in the city. He says, jail, what are you in there for? I said, remember what you told me you were in for a long time ago? He said, the armed robbery? I said, no, the other one. He said, you're charged with that? And I said, yeah. He said, who were you supposed to murder? I said my husband. He said, you stupid fool, why didn't you just stay away? You could have had it better. I said, believe me, I'm kicking myself for that now.''

At trial Doris James was convicted of first degree murder and sentenced to the minimum term of 25 years in prison. She feels that she was improperly convicted of the offence, that she should have been sentenced to 10 years. ''I wasn't at the scene and I didn't have nothing actually to do with the murder other than I paid the money. I was never around the murder scene.''

Paying for another person's death does usually fall, however, within the legal definition of first degree murder. In all of her various appeals against conviction, James has not met with any courtroom success.

Ultimately she is similar, at least in one sense, to her more celebrated brother in crime, Colin Thatcher. He was convicted in 1984 on the premise that he either killed his wife or had someone else do the job for him. James wasn't economically, politically and socially successful in the way that Thatcher was. But like him, she just couldn't walk away from a relationship that was becoming increasingly ugly and sour. ''If I went to see Legal Aid I could have got my divorce for $400 instead of doing this stupid thing that I did. Sure, I have a little remorse over that. I wish there had been something different done. Actually, what I should have done was just stayed away instead of going back. I think things would have been better that way."

Doris James and Arthur Lucas were different types of contract killers; Lucas was responsible for carrying out an order of execution and Doris James was responsible for creating an order of execution. In both instances, though, human life was destroyed through the cold business of giving cash for violent death.

At the same time, however, these killings can also be categorized in one instance as the murder of family, and in the other as the murder of an acquaintance. There is little doubt that the three victims of these acts were killed for money. But these victims were also otherwise connected to their killers, in the case of Doris James, by marriage and, in the case of Arthur Lucas, by a shared business interest.

Nonetheless, one does not find that the majority of murderers who killed for money are in the business of contract murder. When wealthy men like Peter Demeter and Helmuth Buxbaum are involved, their sensational crimes become front-page news. But the vast majority of those who kill for cash do so during a robbery. In the midst of using force or threats to extract money, a victim is shot, beaten or stabbed to death. Murder during a robbery is a frightening prospect; we tend to think of the innocent bystander bleeding to death on the floor of a bank, a person left holding a losing ticket in the lottery of violent death. We see the man who commits such a murder as cold, callous and calculating, more concerned with bank notes than human life. In truth, there is a continuum of murder during robbery, ranging from a heroin-sick junkie killing a friend who will not give him money, to a man who executes a jeweller in an underground parking garage. I will work from an example of a less premeditated robbery killing to one of the most calculated and callous, beginning with the story of Thomas Hanen, a man now serving a life sentence for second degree murder.[7]

Hanen was in his mid-twenties when he killed another man. He was living something of a nomadic life, "just crisscrossing the country, you know, aimlessly really. I'd hold the odd job here and there but wouldn't work for more than a couple of months at a time." Hanen had been introduced to heroin at the age of 16; a friend encouraged him to try the drug and he found that he enjoyed its effects.

It wasn't until years later, however, that his habit became overwhelming. Hanen describes his lifestyle prior to the killing. "When my habit got serious, my attitude got serious too. So during this period of time I suppose in a way I was living well. I had clean clothes, I suppose, and that was about it. My outlook was pretty narrow."

He was living with a woman and the relationship was relatively sound. But as Hanen describes it now, "we were both in the same headspace, in the same frame of mind. And then it came to where, you know, the glitterdome collapsed and we had to really struggle. That's when I became more aggressive than I ever thought I could be."

Hanen began to combine various prescription drugs with heroin. "Back then [about the time of his killing], I really didn't care from one day to the next. I had no drive, no desire for anything, and now [after years of prison] I realize, after you witness a lot of violence, mindless acts, real psychological torture, massive depressions that you can really hardly pull yourself out of, I mean, life is too short to waste on that kind of garbage."

One evening Hanen went over to a friend's place, looking for either illegal drugs or money to buy them. He recalls the evening, "I realized that this guy had a certain amount of money. My intention was just to go in and take it and leave, but the party was there and I was just not in the mood to be diplomatic about it. I wanted it and that was it."

The friend refused his demand and Hanen became furious. He told the man that he didn't want to discuss the money; he just wanted it. The next thing I know, it's, ah...I've killed him."

"How did you kill him?"

"Just through physical violence. Like, my fists and boots and that."

"So you beat him to death?"

"Yeah. And I got the money and I left. And after that I realized what I'd done. It really didn't dawn on me at the time. I mean, like, okay, now what do I do, you know. Well, obviously I've got to hide out or get out of the country or something."

Hanen didn't have any judgement at all; his mind was tied in knots by his dependence on heroin, and a hostile view of the world. As he says now, "I was just sick, irrational; I suppose, emotionally, I was on overload. I mean, a normal man would never do that. But I wanted something and I wanted it now."

About a month later he was arrested; a handprint at the scene of the crime implicated him in the violence. Within a year he was tried, found guilty of second degree murder and sentenced to life imprisonment, with a 15-year minimum term. He escaped from prison twice, once before sentencing, and once after. His second escape came about a year into his sentence: "I'm thinking I don't want to spend the next 15 or 20 years in a dump like this, you know, dirty grimy place, cold food all the time. So I decided, either you do it or you leave, and I decided I wanted to leave."

He broke out of maximum security with four other lifers, but all the men were quickly recaptured. He laughs, "We had it planned how to get out but we didn't have it planned how to stay out. It was, like I say, very bad planning. I don't think any of us believed we were going to make it to begin with; we were all lifers, figured we had nothing to lose."

Hanen's escapes led to time in solitary confinement and then in the Special Handling Unit. He was now classified as one of the most dangerous men in the country. "Well, it was pretty wild, but for me it was like a homecoming 'cause I knew just about everybody on the range. We were from the same prison. We all knew who we were."

While Hanen was in the Special Handling Unit, his mother died. He was told about it three days after her death. "Well, she passed away from cancer. And it's really difficult, like she's already passed away and nobody told me, like they wouldn't tell me anything. Three days after. I told them that was really great of them. I was really bitter about that."

At about the same time, though, Hanen's attitudes began to change. He started to write letters to a person outside prison and to take a much closer look at what was going on around him. He began to read extensively, and he stopped thinking about escape. "You just don't change overnight. Like it kept building and building all the time. And then you'd start seeing people in a different light, and like I say, start thinking there's got to be more to life than this, just sitting around and talking about the same old robbery that the guy's pulled for the last 20 years."

A little over a year ago Hanen married a woman he had been corresponding with for some time. He found that he enjoyed letter writing, losing himself in the task for hours at a time; he also found that putting pen to paper helped him to be more open emotionally. The relationship has changed his outlook considerably. "It's excellent. I mean, a lot of people say that all prison romances will only last a little time, but this is one person I can talk to realistically. There's no ego trips between the two of us. When it gets down to the nitty gritty of discussing something, we can sit and discuss it."

For the present, Thomas Hanen remains imprisoned in a federal penitentiary, looking at the possibility of release in the early 1990s. He recognizes that, for many lifers, return to the street is a difficult process. "Some people, after so many years, are burnt out. And the longer you keep them in, then they're total burnouts. They have no function on the street other than maybe going drinking in a bar or something. They have no drive or desire to do anything. So when life gets too tough for them there, they do something frivolous to be sent back. Then that's another statistic saying murderers can't stay out."

With any luck, Thomas Hanen will not fall into this trap. He does seem to have some sense of when and why his life fell apart. "Like I say, I wasn't really disturbed about things, whether I should stop at a stoplight or not. I just went the way I went. If I'd been, I suppose, exposed to different cultural settings, you know, maybe I would have adapted to them and started saying, hey, this is all right. I don't mind this. But I never really did. I lived a very narrow life. And at the time, it was an exciting life too. To me, it doesn't seem that exciting now, but at the time it was.''

Marcel Lowe's crime was not as brutal as Thomas Hanen's — Lowe didn't actually kill anyone. He claims that he was present when a plainclothes police officer was shot to death, but that his co-accused was the one who fired the gun.

The circumstances of this killing are, in virtually all respects, more frightening than Thomas Hanen's. A police officer died because he had the arbitrary misfortune of bursting through the wrong door at the wrong time.

Marcel Lowe was familiar with police and prisons. He'd started breaking and entering and stealing weapons when he was a juvenile. He was committed for treatment, but ran away. A few months later he was sent to training school for car theft.

From there he went to the reformatory, and then on to the penitentiary. By the time of the killing he had been convicted of a number of break, entry and theft offences, a weapons offence and robbery while armed with a knife. He recalls the robbery, ''This guy was sleeping in his car. So we walked over and asked him to tow us to the next gas station or something, lend us five bucks and he told us, don't bother me, I'm sleeping. Like he might have been 22 at the time, I was about 16 and I just pulled a knife and said, okay give me the money. So it was armed robbery.''

He was out on parole during the mid-Seventies when the killing occurred, while he was living in an apartment in Montreal. His friend Guy Black had just escaped from a medium-security penitentiary and came over to see him. ''We had known each other as juveniles and he felt comfortable coming to my place. He was into armed robberies.''

Lowe was more interested in distributing illegal drugs. ''I was trying to draw him away from the hold-up scene because I said, there's more money to be made here. There's less risk.'' They had made contact with a couple of men, given them $1200 for a pound of hashish and arranged to come back later to pick up the drug. The hashish itself was destined for a third party.

"We were dealing with people who we weren't really confident with," Lowe recalls, "We knew they had guns in the house." When he and Black went back to the house at about six o'clock, they were told that there wasn't any hash for them. "We caught the play, like it was a small house. You could see right down the hall; we could see the guy sliding into the room. So we kicked the door in, you know, it was a game. And we were in the house and we had one guy so we said, okay, where's the money?"

Within minutes a plainclothes police officer burst through the door. "I'm sure they were surveilling the house. They say they weren't. They say they were called, but we were in the house about five minutes at the most and one of them came busting through the door. The other one came around the back of the house and the one that came through the door got shot. Boom! They didn't identify themselves. They claimed to have identified themselves at the trial. They claimed that I was the gunman. But I wasn't the gunman."

Lowe and Black were arrested and charged with capital murder. Black died during an escape attempt just after the coroner's inquest, and Lowe was left to fend for himself in court. "The two men in the house turned Crown's evidence against me and said I was the gunman, because my co-accused was dead. I guess they had a dead cop, so they wanted somebody to go down on it. And these two guys walked free, 'cause they needed somebody to corroborate the evidence of the other police officer."

Lowe was convicted of non-capital murder in 1975 and is not eligible for parole until 1995. He doesn't think that he should have been charged with capital murder, but he feels that he deserves some penalty. "I can't say that I'm innocent. I was guilty in being there and I knew the consequences of what might happen. I didn't expect the cops to come busting through."

Lowe knew that his partner was carrying a gun but he doesn't believe that murder is the appropriate label for his role in the crime. "There is actually too broad a spectrum for murder to be put into that one section of the *Criminal Code*. I don't think life should be mandatory for murder. Maybe in my case it might be justified, but I'm saying it's not.''

For the present Lowe looks forward to completing his university degree and to helping out his 17-year-old son. "I've been taking courses off and on since I came in and I've accumulated maybe six, seven credits. Now I'm just going to focus on this library science course and complete the B.A. here." He says of his son, "I'm glad that I have a good relationship with my son because I give him direction in that sense. And he listens, or he seems to listen. He's been through the same training school as me now, but he went for placement rather than juvenile delinquent acts. He didn't have no place to stay. Now he's in independent living at 17. He's living on his own, which is difficult."

Marcel Lowe's crime is, again, one of those that cuts across the boundaries imposed by the chapters of this book. There is a sense in which it is the killing of an acquaintance, and a sense in which it is motivated by factors other than money. But it was ultimately $1200 and a pound of hashish that led to this death and so it fits best here — a killing for money.

There are a lot of men like Marcel Lowe in Canadian prisons, serving time for murder that they either watched or knew about. This kind of conviction is particularly prevalent in cases of killing for money; co-conspirators in a robbery can all be classified as murderers if a death results from their crime. From 1867 to 1962 Canada hanged dozens of men who fell into this category; my own survey of 96 cases turned up five — Tony Arosha, 1909; William McFadden, 1921; Tony Frank, 1924; Donald Perreault, 1948; and George Hamilton, 1949. Given the total of just over 900 capital convictions between 1867 and 1962, one could expect about 50 hangings of this kind, men who did not pull a trigger, thrust a knife or throw a punch, but were dropped to their death for lending some kind of support to a killing.

The case of Yvan Vaillancourt, discussed in the first chapter, has changed this doctrine of constructive murder, narrowing the scope of the label of murderer. Would Marcel Lowe's crime now be described as something other than murder? Or would the fact that Lowe knew his partner had a loaded gun make him as guilty as the one who fired the fatal shot?

In some cases, all the participants in a crime can be described as murderers with clear justification. If one man holds a woman down while his friend stabs her to death, both of the participants are guilty of the same crime. But if your accomplice in a robbery unexpectedly fires a shot that kills, are you a murderer? Where should we draw the line?

Drew Allen's lifestyle was more like Thomas Hanen's than Marcel Lowe's. Allen was a heroin addict who had served time for property offences — efforts in support of his expensive habit.[8] He was in and out of a major provincial institution through the 1970s, winning a lot of acquittals, but spending no more than nine months at a time on the street.

Allen started using heroin in high school, and found that the price of the drug in the late Sixties allowed him to work and still pay for his dependence; a $15 capsule would last him three days. But in the early Seventies the heroin market changed. "I think about '72 or something like that, the price went up and the quality went down, so instead of paying, say, $15 for one cap, you were paying $30 for a cap but the cap was only like half a cap. So it was like 400% interest. I really didn't have any money. For the habit I'd acquired over six years, I turned to illegal activities."

Allen was one of many who suffered from the restructuring of the West Coast heroin market in the early Seventies. It's not clear whether heroin distributors or law enforcement officers or both, acting independently, were responsible for the increased price and diminished quality of the product. It is clear, however, that reducing the supply for this group of drug addicts made some of them more desperate, and ultimately, more likely to be violent. Drug store robberies in Canada have increased dramatically over the past 15 years.

In the late Seventies Allen put himself through a voluntary heroin treatment program, motivated by some pending charges for break and entry. He left after three months, determined to stay away from heroin. But he drifted back into the city and within a month he was back into the drug. He married for a second time. "We were both downtown people. There was no qualms. I would make the money today; we would split it. She would make the money tomorrow; we would split it. It was a partnership, more than a marriage. Partnership of crime, I guess.''

Allen generally made his living by stealing property, and his wife rented out her body on the street. One night in early May when it was her turn to raise the family income, she was having no success. He had been sitting in the bar, and was angry that no money was coming in. "Now I guess the macho trip comes in and I said, well, fuck, here...and I give her some money. I said, you go sit in the bar, I'll go make some money.''

"I had not one iota of an idea what I was going to do," he continues. He had already had a lot to drink and taken some pills, and as he walked through the downtown streets he was looking for a way to get some cash. He saw a man in a second-floor window, counting business receipts in the early hours of the morning.

He quickly came up with a plan that he thought at the time was very intelligent: "The way the office was set up, he would have been sitting at a desk there, I'd come in over here and I thought well, I'd just hit him and knock him unconscious. He'll wake up in a half hour and I'll have the money and I'll be gone and he'll have a headache, but that's all.''

But the robbery didn't work out that way. Allen hit the man with a brick, but he wasn't knocked out. "To my surprise, he started getting out of his chair. He was a larger man than myself. I think I weighed about 120 pounds. Now, I guess shock, fear, survival, to name a few, started setting in, hazed over by the drugs. I hit him again. He was, I guess, also in a state of shock.''

Allen continues, "We were wrestling around and all I'm trying to do now is get away. The money, just forget that. We struggled, knocked over I don't know how many machines. Struggled my way to the doorway...I could not get away. I had come to a point where he wasn't just holding on to me like this, he had a hold of my hair. I just go black when somebody starts hanging on to my hair and pulling. At that point I pulled the knife out. I thought right up to the time of the trial that I had stabbed him once. It was a paring knife...it went in, and it happened to slip between the rib cage and unfortunately hit his heart. I found out later at the trial that he had been stabbed four times, twice in the chest, twice in the neck.''

Allen describes the time prior to his arrest as the worst two weeks of his life. He fled from the scene of the crime, and continued running. ''I was daily going out and breaking into a drug store or a doctor's office. I was not concerned about going downtown and getting heroin, I was just eating barbiturates, valiums, whatever pill I could eat that would take it out of my memory and I could forget about it. Until tomorrow, then wake up and eat more.''

He was coming back home from the store one afternoon when he saw police cars. He waited until they were out of sight before approaching his home. What he hadn't counted on, though, was that the police were still at his home — only their cars had disappeared. Allen was captured after a short chase, and charged with second degree murder.

During the trial he kept himself under the influence of various drugs. ''I stayed, again, as high as possible. I just did not want to face reality, the reality of what I'd done. That was the only way I'd ever really learned to deal with pressures like that.''

He was convicted of second degree murder, with a minimum term of 10 years, and sent to a maximum-security institution. He stayed there for almost four years, and then was sent down to an institution with somewhat less security. He became active in this prison's drug trade. ''The last three months I picked up a number of charges, five or six, for a syringe, for being under the influence. The last one, they caught me in the kitchen and I had about 30 valiums in my pocket and a hundred down my shirt. I was trafficking valiums.''

He was sent back to maximum security, and soon afterward, he began to question the way he was living his life. ''I started sitting down and doing some writing as to what I wanted, whether or not I seriously wanted out again and how to go about doing it.'' Within a few months he was transferred to the same lower-security institution, and for the past year and a half he has stopped using pills, narcotics, and bombs; he hasn't smoked any hash in almost a year. In one sense, at least, he is not comfortable with this change. ''Morally, inside myself, I don't think I'll ever be able to repay it. Going back to the ironic...I murder somebody and I'm the one that's rescued. I've had a hard time dealing with that fact.''

Family support has been critical for Drew Allen. About six years ago he made contact with his uncle, "I read the classified ads section and there was an article, 'Allen, Drew. Please contact Uncle Art.' And I'm thinking, holy, I haven't seen my uncle in 15, 20 years? The letter I got back,...being a pessimist from in here, it goes with the territory, so you expect the worst. I thought, oh Christ, he's passed on, it's his lawyer and...it was my uncle. He was getting old and he wanted to wrap up loose ends.''

His uncle soon responded to the initial letter. He wanted to know "everything that's happened since 1958.'' Allen recalls, "Well, my God, what a hard letter to write. I, again, went through chronological order. I told him basically that I had turned into a juvenile delinquent, turned to drugs; it got control of my life. I says, 'I'm in jail. I have been since 1980 on the same sentence.' '' Allen carefully avoided any mention of the murder conviction; the response from his uncle and aunt was an offering of help.

Allen continues, "There was one night a couple of months later, I was up all goddamn night, it was tearing me apart. I sat down and I wrote him a letter and somehow I started, "I haven't lied to you. Everything I've told you is the truth. But I haven't told you everything.''

His uncle told him that he had guessed his conviction was for "something quite serious,'' but to Allen's surprise and pleasure, the old man was still committed to helping his nephew. "The bottom line, by then, was, 'Drew, everybody's got skeletons in their closet. Just work towards the future.' ''

There are times when Allen would like to meet the parents of his victim, "trying to explain to them that my past led up to my attitude, which led to the ultimate crime and what I've done since. I don't know whether I would just be regurgitating their bad memories again. I'm trying to weigh and I don't know. I'd hate to take the chance of....''

If Allen had the chance he'd probably tell the family and

friends of the man he killed something similar to what he said in the summer of 1987, "An apology is not near enough to offer them...if there's anything, regardless of what it is, please call, please ask. I'll do whatever I can. I've taken something very dear to them away from them. I hope they don't ever think that it was...it was easy when it happened, because there was no thought put into it, but it is not easy for me. I live with it every day too."

For Reid Lander, religion has helped to ease this pain of recollection. He developed an interest in Christianity while awaiting trial, and has maintained it. But religion is not really a factor in his brief episode of violence. It was the cold logic of the "perfect" criminal that lay behind Lander's plan of robbery — eliminate the witness, and detection will be more difficult.

Reid Lander is not typical of men who serve time for murder in Canada's prisons.[9] He comes from the ranks of the upper middle class. "We were your average typical North American family. My mom was just a housewife, all three kids went through high school. My sister went on and graduated [university]; my brother graduated with a commerce degree; my dad's a professor in accounting. So you'd think that everything was great, hunky dory."

"But," Lander continues, "we never really learned how to deal with emotions, especially negative ones. I really got a strong impression from my dad, who's a very emotionally controlled person...I've never seen him lose it or really get angry, he controlled everything, he's not a very expressive person. My mom, on the other hand, is kind of the opposite. She's very flighty, very emotional...she's really sweet, she really is, she's very expressive."

Lander went from high school to college to university. He was living at home during his second year at university, and having problems in both places. He was going out with an honour student in her final year, a popular sorority president whom he "really admired." As he recalls, "My insecurity really started hitting me hard. I didn't feel worthwhile. I wasn't getting the attention, and I didn't know how to express myself to her or let her know what I felt my needs were or anything like that. So, I remember very succinctly all that pain and suppressing it. At that point I started going quite callous.''

Life at home was also difficult. He felt his mother was pressing him too hard about his schoolwork and he would drive away from the house on his motorcycle in a silent rage. He dropped out of university and began to earn a living as a milkman.

Lander spent about a year at the job and found it enjoyable, but he felt that there was no future in it; he wanted to make a lot more money, and the oil rigs beckoned. After graduating from a training course with the highest marks in the class, he quickly became a derrickman on a rig. ''Well, on my first job out the drillers said, 'Hey, why don't you try going up the stick? That's derrickman.' And so, well, I loved it. I love heights, I love challenge, I love daring. You see, I was a real excitement fiend.''

He was making very good money and wanted more, ''I just kept wanting more and more excitement, more money to get to where I wanted to. I was never big into drugs.'' But the oil and gas recession of the early Eighties hit hard, and his oil rig was ultimately shut down. Lander, with his new car and his very fast motorcycle, was not patient with his reduced standard of living.

He bought a brand new Volvo from a scruffy man in a parking lot, knowing the car to be stolen. He paid $1,500 for what was a $19,000 car and planned to drive it into the U.S. to sell it. But his suspicious behaviour while crossing the border alerted customs officers; he was later convicted of possession of stolen property and given a year of probation and a $1,000 fine.

His parents didn't hear of the conviction. In about six months he was broke; he'd moved out of his penthouse apartment, and sold his car and his motorcycle. But he still wanted a life in the fast lane, and more crime seemed at the time to be a logical and attractive route to the good life. He stole a car and committed a couple of break, entry and theft offences.

Lander was not, however, the clever crook that he imagined himself to be. The city police force picked him up; he was convicted of the crimes and sentenced to a year in jail. He spent the time at a wilderness camp for young offenders. At 22 he was the oldest person there. "I kind of ran that camp...I could do anything. You know, I was getting in really good shape and everything that was needed I could do. I still wanted to get some money fast...I didn't care about people. So I decided, well, I can go into robbery, but then I decided I'm still after thrills. Everything was so glamorous on TV with hit men, you know. You don't have to worry about a thing as long you do your job well and don't leave any witnesses. I found I had all the skills and capabilities for it and I just didn't care any more."

On his way out of the prison system, Lander came into contact with fences — men who sell stolen property. He was told by one man of a jeweller who took all his merchandise out of his store at night, the perfect target for a robbery. This fence would be happy to sell the proceeds of Lander's crime.

Lander scouted the job, found that the man carried a pistol in his car and decided that he would need to kill him in order to get the goods. He describes the murder: "So in the underground parking lot, he got out of his car. I'd already plotted everybody coming and going who lived there. I popped out and shot him. And I killed him. No witness, right. So then I got into his car and drove away into another underground parking lot a few blocks away where I had my car. It was like a picture perfect crime. Nobody saw me, you know; I even wore a good disguise. There was no evidence leading to me. The police had given up their investigation and just hoped that their $10,000 reward might bring somebody forward with some information."

The one person who could foil Lander's perfect crime was his fence, and both Lander and his fence knew it. He began to make preparations for this second killing. "Since he was the only guy who knew about it, he was a liability. As soon as I made some connections, and I had made the connections...I was starting to look at some other contracts. Thank God I was picked up before that happened."

His fence set him up for his arrest: "I was sitting in his place and he said he'd be right back. Well, all of a sudden in through the back door and in through the front door come all these men. I didn't know who they were, they were in plain clothes. All of a sudden I had four .38s pointing at my head and I was not too pleased. It was funny because I figured, obviously I'm not going to make a move, that's suicide. So either I'm going to die here or I'm being busted."

He was being busted. He went to trial on a charge of first degree murder and was convicted; he is not eligible for parole until early in the next century. Prior to his trial he was reunited with his family. A friend had read about his arrest in a local newspaper and passed the information on to his family, who were living in a city several hundred miles away. His parents came out to see him, while he was awaiting trial, unaware that he had ever been in any trouble with the law. "That was an incredibly tough time. And that's when I really started letting things out and really starting to see the pain that I'd caused. I started to realize, I'm sitting here causing this pain in my dad and my mom and the rest of my family and friends, and I think, well hey, I'm still alive! How would I feel about somebody who did that to my dad, what I had done to this guy? 'Cause I knew he had a son; he was divorced. Like I knew this, right; I had seen his son and girlfriend. And then I started really realizing what had happened. I was worried and I started to do some heavy praying."

Lander's commitment to Christianity has remained during the five years that he has been in federal prisons. He has already spent two years in a program for violent offenders. "It opened my eyes to a lot of people, and that's why I say to you it's sad, how some people cannot look at anything beyond because they've had such rough lives and they've had really horrible sufferings. Like you can't almost really blame them for being hostile and bitter."

Lander knows that he has not suffered in the same way. He feels that although he benefitted substantially from the two years in the program, he did not gain as much as he might have. The Violent Offender program requires that prisoners confront each other about their violence, but Lander felt intimidated. "I could only go to a point...you kind of worry about the repercussions 'cause there were a couple of guys who were totally unpredictable. And you couldn't trust them with retribution down the line, whether it would be direct or indirect. It could be a very sure possibility, if I did a lot of confrontation that would actually have benefitted myself and them.''

He says of the possibility of release, ''I wouldn't trust me right off the bat, but at the same time I would give chances to get out so I can prove myself and so that I can reestablish that trust. And that's all I ask. To be able to reestablish the trust so society can say, okay, he has changed, he's not going to do it again. 'Cause the only way I can prove that I'm not going to do it again is by gradually reestablishing that trust.''

He looks back on his crime, by any standard a chilling act: ''It had a lot to do with all the bottled emotions I had inside of me. It was just to the point where I couldn't let any cracks start because then everything would come out, right. So I had to put such a forced lid on my feelings. I wouldn't allow myself to feel anything, good or bad. It was just, like I'd become very cold. Now I was still very polite, I was still very easy to get along with, because logically it's not in my best interest to get people offended; you know, I had to manipulate people.''

In over 120 years the phenomenon of killing for money hasn't changed very much. It is not becoming more common, relative to other types of murder, and its contemporary character and range are similar to past killings of this type. In considering a number of men convicted recently of murder, we saw something of the diversity of this category — from Thomas Hanen's desperate beating of a friend who wouldn't give him money to Marcel Lowe's involvement in a drug deal that led to death; from Drew Allen's frenzied stabbing of a man he had confronted to Reid Lander's calculated killing of a jeweller in an underground parking lot. Allen Robinson, George Hamilton, and Roger Trudel present a similar diversity, linking us with our past. These men were convicted of killing for money, all were hanged for their crimes, and yet they are not easily comparable with each other.

Roger Trudel was, like Thomas Hanen, a man who killed an acquaintance for money, but this is where the similarity ends.[10] Trudel was a 34-year-old theatre usher in Montreal in 1948. A bachelor who had grown up in nearby St. Jerome, he moved into the city to make a living. He had a mistress, a married woman from St. Jerome who came to Montreal to visit him on a fairly regular basis.

In late November of 1948 Trudel was working at the Bijou Theatre; one of the theatre's regular clients was a 49-year-old married woman named Angelina Desjardins. She was physically handicapped, having one leg several inches shorter than the other, and she wore a shoe that had a four-inch iron brace as part of its construction. Mrs. Desjardins became quite attracted to Trudel and asked him to invest some of her money. She told Trudel on one occasion that she was carrying $150 in her bag, and on another occasion, more than $500.

On November 30 Trudel told his mistress from St. Jerome that he did not want to be disturbed the following evening. He explained that there was a woman visiting the threatre who made a nuisance of herself, but who was insisting that he invest her money. Trudel arranged to meet Mrs. Desjardins at 11:30 the next evening, after he finished work at the theatre.

Trudel and Mrs. Desjardins took a bus together, going to Montreal South, via the Jacques Cartier Bridge. They left the bus at the stop on St. Helene's Island, and began walking in the dark along the sidewalk across the bridge. According to what Trudel said later that evening to his mistress, Mrs. Desjardins scolded him for "being with another woman the night before." She struck him across the face, telling him that he was not going to get her money to go and spend with his mistress.

Trudel's response was to strike back. As he told his mistress later, he lost his head and beat the woman's face and head against the iron railing of the bridge. Her bag fell to the ground at the same time that she did. Trudel grabbed the bag, opened it and removed the money, and then threw the bag over the bridge. He left Mrs. Desjardins in a pool of blood, and took a taxi back to Montreal and his mistress.

Two police officers on St. Helene's Island heard a woman crying out from the sidewalk of the Jacques Cartier Bridge. They proceeded as quickly as they could, but when they arrived they found Mrs. Desjardins unconscious in a pool of blood, her face covered with cuts and bruises. She died the following afternoon in hospital.

The police did not have much difficulty arresting Roger Trudel. He had quit his job at the Bijou Theatre the night before the killing, and the victim's handbag, found in the river below the bridge, contained a card with his name, address and telephone number. A few days later he was arrested in St. Jerome as he stepped off a bus with his mistress. Both he and his mistress then provided the police with a complete statement of the facts of the case.

At trial his lawyer, Lucien Gendron, argued for a verdict of manslaughter, suggesting that Trudel had been provoked by Mrs. Desjardins. "It was a matter of jealousy on the part of Mrs. Desjardins," he said, "[the evening rendezvous] was her plan. All he would have had to give in return was the passion she wanted."[11]

While Gendron was addressing the jury, Trudel began sobbing and covered his face to hide his tears. Gendron asked the court to break for a 10-minute recess, and the request was granted. When ultimately convicted of the murder and asked if he had anything to say, Trudel said nothing. His eyes were shut and his head hung low. The *Montreal Gazette* of January 23, 1950, reported the outcome of the trial in its headline, "Movie Usher Sentenced to Death for Murder of Crippled Woman."

At the same time, though, the jury had recommended clemency, suggesting that the Cabinet commute the sentence of death to one of life imprisonment. Trudel had no criminal record, and showed great remorse during the trial. He had also co-operated with police, and had been subjected to the "depraved solicitations" of Mrs. Desjardins.

But the decision to commute did not rest with a jury of Trudel's peers; the Cabinet of Louis St. Laurent would have to choose either hanging or commutation. The memorandum prepared for Solicitor General Hughes Lapointe explained the jury's recommendation for clemency by reference to four points: "1) The accused had no criminal record and was never up against the law; 2) The accused is a somewhat abnormal individual with a neurotic temperament, unable to stand contradiction, and having always been spoiled by his mother; 3) On account of this inability to adaptation and because of his nervousness, the doctors found him fit for discharge after spending a year with the Army; 4) I think they also took into account the behaviour of Mrs. Desjardins towards Trudel and her depraved solicitations as revealed in evidence.''

But, M.F. Gallagher continued, ''It was noteworthy that the trial judge made no recommendation of his own in his report.'' Gallagher had travelled to Montreal to speak with Justice Wilfrid Lazure about the crime. He was told by Lazure that there was ''no clement feature'' that could be distilled from what was ''a most abominable crime,'' and that while Trudel may have ''mental peculiarities,'' he was not ''mentally affected to any considerable degree.'' A psychiatrist who was commissioned to examine Trudel came to a similar conclusion, writing, ''Trudel is not insane in any sense of the word and in my opinion, he was fully responsible for his crime.''

Gallagher concluded his memorandum for the Solicitor General with the comment, ''Considering the facts and circumstances of this case, the undersigned is of the opinion the law may well be allowed to take its course.'' A few weeks prior to the execution, Trudel's brother Henri sent a petition to Solicitor General Lapointe, urging commutation of the death sentence. He argued that his brother was not in possession of all his faculties at the time of the crime and begged that his life be spared.

But the sentiments of the jury and Henri Trudel were no match for the trial judge, the civil servant M.F. Gallagher and the Cabinet of Louis St. Laurent. Roger Trudel had killed a handicapped woman with the apparent motive of financial gain, and in the summer of 1950 he paid for this crime with his life.

George Hamilton also died on the gallows, alongside his brother Rufus. The Hamilton brothers, among the most marginal of New Brunswick's citizens, lived in Barker's Point, a suburb of Fredericton. The brothers had been abandoned by their parents when they were two and three years old, dumped in their grandparents' backyard in the winter of 1928.

When they were older, they had been sentenced to jail terms on a number of occasions.

George Hamilton described his upbringing in an appeal against his sentence of death: "My grandmother brought me up until I was nine years old; they would not let me go to school like my brother...they would beat and pound me all around, and make me do without food half of the time...then when I was 10 years old my mother came home, she was in prison at the time, she took me to Halifax and it was not fit for me to live in the house she had, she was running a fast house and she beat and pound me around because I woulden take liquor that she had and sell it for her...."[12]

George Hamilton's criminal record dated back to 1944, always for the same kind of crime — auto theft, attempted break, entry and theft, and possession of burglary tools. He was, by all accounts, a thief, but not a man of violence. On the evening of January 7, 1949, his wife was in hospital, having just given birth to their second child. He and his brother Rufus wanted to get some money; there was no food in the house and there would be bills to pay when his wife was sent home with their new baby. They had even been stealing firewood in order to keep their house warm. Rufus had a prior conviction for robbery, and he suggested that they travel into Fredericton in order to find an opportunity to commit another crime.

The brothers were refused admission at the Canadian Legion in Fredericton. George called a taxi to take them to a friend's house on the opposite side of the city. The robbery plan was now in motion. George sat in the back seat and his brother in the front beside the taxi driver. George had a hammer in his possession and he was to knock the driver out when the taxi arrived at its destination on Wilsey Road.

But George Hamilton recognized the taxi driver, a man by the name of Norman Burgoyne, and gave up the idea of hitting him. Rufus asked Burgoyne to drive to one location and then on to another; the plan of robbery appeared to be unravelling. Finally the three men returned to Wilsey Road, the intended site of the crime. The two brothers got out of the car and Rufus asked George if he had developed "cold feet.'' George responded that he simply could not hit Burgoyne; he was a man he had known for some time.

Burgoyne was ultimately asked to drive to the home of a man by the name of Nat McIntyre; Rufus had suggested that they might be able to buy some homebrew from McIntyre. When the three men arrived at the house, George Hamilton went in for a visit and Rufus stayed outside with Burgoyne, sharing a beer that Burgoyne had taken from his trunk.

George Hamilton returned to the taxi to find Burgoyne bloody and unconscious on the front seat. As he wrote later, ''I new Rufus was a bad man to leave alone with a hammer in his site or in his hands, but now I was scared of my brother, so when I came back and found the taxi driver knock out, I should of left every thing and went to the plece, but now I help my brother.''

Rufus Hamilton had not used the hammer to kill Norman Burgoyne, but the empty beer bottle. Burgoyne's body was wrapped in a blanket and locked in the trunk of the taxi, his skull fractured, and his death caused by a brain hemorrhage. Rufus and George Hamilton divided the proceeds of the robbery between them and drove off in Burgoyne's taxi; the loot amounted to $166, a wristwatch and a ring.

The police did not have a great deal of difficulty tracing Burgoyne's murder to the Hamilton brothers. The two men were seen by several people while driving Burgoyne's taxi, and at least one of these individuals notified police. Rufus and George Hamilton had left a trail of evidence all over the Fredericton area — blood-stained coins, and blood stains in particles of snow; Burgoyne's watch and ring were also found in a pile of ashes outside the Hamilton home.

At trial, counsel for George Hamilton argued that there was no common intention to rob and kill Norman Burgoyne. Lawyer Leo Cain suggested that while the brothers had originally embarked on a joint mission to rob Burgoyne, George Hamilton had abandoned this common purpose when he went into Nat McIntyre's house. He had left his brother Rufus standing by the taxi, sharing a beer with Burgoyne.

The judge and jury were not convinced; they convicted both Rufus and George Hamilton of murder. The memorandum prepared for Solicitor General Hughes Lapointe was unsympathetic. M.F. Gallagher quoted approvingly from trial judge J.E. Michaud, "Evidently the jury didn't believe that George had given up the intention and had sufficiently communicated it to his brother, as they found him guilty after deliberating for one hour and 23 minutes."

In late May of 1949, George Hamilton wrote a letter — "To the Wright Honarble Govner General of Canada."

"Dear Sir," he began, "I am a married man with a wife and two young children and since being comited to goal I have found my Lord and have been converted in March, 1949...if it wood be your plasure to grant me a pardon and spear my life I wood love to go out and tell my fellow friends and the hole world what you have done for me and what my saviour has done for me...."

Hamilton concluded his unsuccessful 18-page plea, "Thank you sir and I beg sir, please have mercy on me and my wife and children, thank God and Bless the King and the Queen and you, Sir, amen, amen, it lies in your hands, my life now, Sir, your truely slave, George Albert Hamilton, I thank you, Sir, with all my Heart and Soul...."

This kind of desperate begging would not have been Allen Robinson's style; he was, like George Hamilton, something of a career criminal. Unlike Hamilton, however, he was prepared to take property from people with the aid of a weapon.[13]

Robinson's crime occurred early in the evening on Vancouver's Georgia Street, in April 1921. Georgia has long been one of the main arteries of the city, like Toronto's Yonge Street, Winnipeg's Portage Avenue or Montreal's St. Catherine Street. In 1921, the scene of the crime, the corner of Burrard and Georgia, was being readied for a major development.

Canadian National's Hotel Vancouver was about to be constructed on the east side of Burrard. It was finally opened to the public in 1939, and still stands as one of the area's major landmarks, a companion piece to Ottawa's Château Laurier or Quebec's Château Frontenac. In 1988, this stretch of the city is the home of money in Vancouver. The Stock Exchange is only a few blocks away; corporations and their lawyers dominate the skyscrapers that now tower above Georgia Street's six lanes of busy traffic. An elegant stone church is one of the few reminders of the past, its appeal to an omnipotent deity dwarfed by more imposing visions of secular progress.

In 1921 there were tall shade trees on Georgia Street. This was still a residential part of the city, and as is the case today, it was home to the economically advantaged. Allen "Slim" Robinson and his friend Alex "Frenchy" Paulson were a couple of young men from the downtown east side, then and now the home of the economically disadvantaged.

Robinson and Paulson were apparently opiate users. Robinson carried a gun at 19 years old. Paulson, his accomplice in robbery, was a 25-year-old Russian emigré who spoke only a few words of English. On the evening of April 12, 1921, as they were walking through the city, they had already demanded — and received — money from one man.

At a little before nine Robinson noticed William Salsbury walking along Georgia Street, a short distance from Burrard. Robinson and Paulson left the shadows of the shade trees. Robinson confronted Salsbury with his handgun, telling him to stick his hands in the air. Salsbury refused. A second demand was made that he stick up his hands, but he resisted with his umbrella. Robinson fired the gun.

The bullet pierced Salsbury's heart and he fell to the ground. He lay on the street, groaning loudly, whereupon a few people who had seen the shooting ran to his assistance. Robinson and Paulson ran west on Georgia Street, disappearing into the night. Salsbury was carried into a nearby house where he died a few minutes later, never regaining consciousness.

William Salsbury, Jr., was a man of social and political stature in Vancouver. He was a 43-year-old accountant and the son of W.F. Salsbury, a pioneering member of Vancouver's Board of Trade and a former city councillor. The news of his murder was the lead story on page one of the *Vancouver Sun* the following day. The younger Salsbury was referred to as "one of the best known residents of Vancouver";

he was also a member of the Royal Vancouver Yacht Club and an avid horseman.

The police had very few clues at their disposal, and it was not until June that they were able to arrest Robinson nd Paulson. Robinson had been under suspicion shortly after the killing, and police moved to lay a vagrancy charge against him. There was a conviction, but the sentence was suspended and Robinson travelled to Lethbridge to work on a farm. Within days, however, he returned voluntarily to Vancouver, and within weeks he was arrested on a second vagrancy charge. This time he was sentenced to two months in Oakalla, the provincial jail.

He was in Oakalla when Frenchy Paulson confessed his guilt to Vancouver City Police. Paulson's roommate, a man by the name of Arthur Simpson, had apparently first given information to the police about Paulson's actions on the night of the killing. The arrest of Robinson and Paulson was front page news on Saturday June 11, 1921. "Police Get Confession From Slayer," read the *Vancouver Sun's* headline.

There were two trials and at least four more page one headlines before the drama was over. At the first trial Frenchy Paulson had given testimony against Allen Robinson on the understanding that he would not be hanged if he did so. As Robinson's accomplice, he would still be guilty of murder, but his sentence would be commuted to life imprisonment. The trial judge agreed to bring this issue to the attention of the Minister of Justice.

The Court of Appeal ordered a new trial, rejecting the deal of commutation for testimony. Paulson had made no bargain with them, and in April 1922 the two men were tried for a second time. The result was no different; both were again convicted of murder and sentenced to hang.

"Goodbye, boys," Slim Robinson said as he was led from court by police. He asked for a cigarette before getting into the van to be taken to Oakalla's death row, and was given it. A few minutes later, after being handcuffed, he turned to the officers and said, "All right, let's go."[14]

The memorandum prepared for the Minister of Justice was

not sympathetic to Robinson, concluding, "So far as I am concerned, I am of the opinion that Robinson and Paulson his accomplice have been both proven guilty of murder." The sentence was underlined.

But the memorandum also noted, "There seems to be some feeling in the community that he is too young to be hanged. On the other hand, there is a very strong feeling on the part of a large portion of the community that the murderers should suffer the extreme penalty."

The *Vancouver Sun* ran a number of editorials urging death for Robinson and Paulson, variously titled, "Scales of Justice Rusty," "Justice — Speedy and True," and "Mocking Justice."

The newspaper's editors were particularly upset by the Vancouver Council of Women's 106-13 vote in favour of a plea for commutation. "These 106 women...are being made the instruments of mawkish and maudlin sentimentality," they wrote.

"Women's new sphere [they had just been given the right to vote] gives scope for constructive work. [But] attempting to interfere with the machinery of justice by outbursts of ill-timed gush is neither constructive nor profitable to women or to civilization," the paper concluded.

These sentiments did not sit well with Mrs. D.D. Mackenzie, the wife of Canada's Solicitor General of the day. Three days before the date of the double execution she told a Vancouver meeting of a visit with Robinson at Oakalla Prison. The *Toronto Star* reported her talk to a packed hall, "As Mrs. Mackenzie began, she could scarcely be heard, but as she continued, a stillness took hold of the meeting so that every syllable reached through the hall. She told of...his story to her of repentance, of his request that she buy something that his brothers could wear that would forever keep them from sin and remind them of his death. She spoke also of his desire that she should visit his mother in Nova Scotia and comfort her with the news that he was not afraid to die."

As Mrs. Mackenzie spoke, the federal government had already delayed its decision on commutation once. On the morning of July 28, they delayed again, postponing the executions from 8 a.m. to 7 p.m. — this particular life and death struggle was not easily resolved.

At the end of the day, the *Vancouver Sun* and its supporters prevailed; the "mawkish and maudlin sentimentality" of Canada's early feminists was ruled out of order. A more powerful collective of men decreed that the death of William Salsbury would be avenged, and Alex Paulson and Allen Robinson were dropped to their deaths in Oakalla Prison.

Like many men who kill for money, Paulson and Robinson did not realize any proceeds from their crime; they fled from the scene just after the shot was fired. As we have seen, even when killings for money are "successful"; the amount taken is virtually always negligible. The property involved couldn't change a person's life in any meaningful way. These are depressing scenarios — tales of innocent victims killed by desperate strangers, of cold-blooded executions for cash and of killings of friends and acquaintances for money.

Consider, finally, the case of Jessie Taylor, who lived in London, Ontario, in 1939.[15] Mrs. Taylor, a 50-year-old woman, killed an older widow who was living with her. The murder weapon was a piece of firewood and the cause of death, several blows to the head. The killing was apparently carried out while the widow Templeton was asleep. After Mrs. Templeton died, Jessie Taylor put a number of items of clothing on the dead woman, over her nightgown — a sweater, a house dress, stockings and shoes. Taylor then dragged the body onto the highway to make it appear that Mrs. Templeton had been the victim of a hit-and-run driver. Unfortunately for Mrs. Taylor, however, the scenario that she constructed was not at all convincing. The clothing had not been put on properly, and police doubted the explanation that she offered.

The motive for this crime was money, the proceeds of a will that Mrs. Templeton had recently had drawn up at the instigation of Jessie Taylor. Mrs. Templeton had named Mrs. Taylor the executrix of her estate. Two days before the killing Taylor called the lawyers who had drafted the document to make sure that nothing had been changed.

What Jessie Taylor never fully understood — at least not until her arrest — was that the executrix of a will is not the same as the beneficiary. The police report noted her surprise. "Mrs. Taylor evidently did not realize that being an executrix did not make her a beneficiary, for she told her friends prior to and immediately after the death of Mrs. Templeton that she was to receive money from the estate."

And so it goes.

[1] "Don Monarch," and all other names connected with this story, are pseudonyms.

[2] See *Homicide in Canada, 1976-1985: An Historical Perspective*, Statistics Canada, Canadian Centre for Justice Statistics, Ministry of Supply and Services, Ottawa, 1987, 37 and 138.

[3] See *Homicide in Canada: A Statistical Synopsis*, Statistics Canada, Ottawa, 1976, Table 4.1 and Table 4.26.

[4] "Newspaper clippings," *Arthur Lucas, Capital Case Files, RG 13 Series*, National Archives, Ottawa, Canada, 1962.

[5] "Minutes of Cabinet Meeting, December 4, 1962," *Disclosed under the Canadian Access to Information Act*, July 1987, 4-6.

[6] "Doris James," and all other names connected with this story, are pseudonyms.

[7] "Thomas Hanen," and all other names connected with this story, are pseudonyms.

[8] "Drew Allen," and all other names connected with this story, are pseudonyms.

[9] "Reid Lander," and all other names connected with this story, are pseudonyms.

[10] Roger Trudel, *Capital Case Files, RG 13 Series*, National Archives, Ottawa, Canada, 1950.

[11] "Trudel Convicted of Bridge Murder," *The Montreal Standard*, January 23, 1950, 1.

[12] "Letter to the Governor-General," *George Hamilton, Capital Case Files*, RG 13 Series, National Archives, Ottawa 3.

[13] *Allen Robinson, Capital Case Files*, RG 13 Series, National Archives, Ottawa 1921.

[14] "Found Guilty of Murder, The Slayer of W.F. Salsbury Jr. Is Again Sentenced to Death," *The Vancouver Sun*, 1.

[15] *Jessie Taylor, Capital Case Files*, RG 13 Series, National Archives, Ottawa, Mrs. Taylor's sentence of death was commuted to one of life imprisonment.

Chapter
Five

KILLING FOR SEX

Most of us enjoy sexual arousal. We associate sex with pleasure, and if we're lucky, with trust and intimacy. As we wander through adolescence and adulthood we try to sort out the context in which the act occurs — our own rules for sexual life. Among Canadians there is a range of sexual lifestyles: monogamous heterosexuality, polygamous heterosexuality, monogamous homosexuality, polygamous homosexuality and bisexuality.

But some of us become excited by violence and violation — sex with animals, sex with children, and sex without the consent of a partner. This is the world of sex offences and sex offenders. The victims are usually women or children and the wrongdoers are almost always men. Canadian culture, not unlike most Western cultures, holds out a lot of possibilities for male sexual arousal. We sell cars, furniture, clothing and alcohol with the promise of male sexual conquest. If you buy the product, you also buy, at least implicitly, the attractive woman who is selling it.

Our culture endorses images of women as sexual commodities and, in a more extreme form, images of women as victims of male urges. There is a sense in which women and their body parts have become commercial property, bought and sold in the marketplace of male desire. In one sense, the sex offender is a person who takes property that he cannot attain through socially legitimate means. When he can't have the blonde behind door Number Three, he steals her. Like the thief who can't otherwise easily acquire a television or a compact disc, the sex offender takes something that does not belong to him.

And yet it is both too simplistic and ultimately misleading to suggest that sexual assault can only be understood as a type of property crime. While sex offenders may regard their prey as property, we can be sure that Canadian women (and we can hope that most Canadian men) do not share this perception. One problem that we face, however, is that judges sitting in Canadian criminal courts do tend to treat men who rape as less threatening than men who rob. The best known Canadian sentencing text documents a range of one to 12 years for those who commit rape and a range of one to 20 years for those who commit robbery.[1] Current practice suggests that sexually assaulting a woman is a less serious crime than taking property by force. We may really believe that raping a woman is more fundamentally damaging than taking money from a till, but one finds weak evidence for this assertion in the current workings of the Canadian criminal justice system. To the contrary, we find that, in spite of what are probably good intentions, Canadian judges are tacitly encouraging the notion that women are to be regarded as property — and not altogether valuable property at that.

In the case of prostitution — the purchase of sexual services — women rent their bodies to men. But prostitution does not necessarily involve violence, and the subject of this chapter is killing for sex. We move away from the unregulated transaction of the marketplace to come to terms with the range of our sexual criminals — the incest offenders, the violent pedophiles, the passive pedophiles, and the rapists. Rapists tend to be young men between the ages of 16 and 30; pedophiles and incest offenders tend to be men in their thirties and forties. Like most other people convicted of serious criminal offences, they have usually been poorly educated, economically disadvantaged, and exposed to aggressive and alcoholic parents.

It is the sexual aggressives, the rapists and the violent pedophiles, who go so far as to kill in pursuit of sex. One Canadian researcher concludes of these men, "Rapists and child molesters are unconcerned about others and are inept in their efforts to relate to other people. They have poor personal relationships, suffer from boredom, and use alcohol to excess. All in all, these men are ill-equipped to deal with life and it is little wonder they constitute a disruptive and dangerous force in society."[2]

At the time of John Borman's offence, he was certainly a "disruptive and dangerous force."[3] He is quite typical of men who kill during a sexual assault, having experienced poor personal relationships, set against a backdrop of physical abuse and emotional neglect. Borman lived in a suburb of a large Canadian city; he figures that his difficulties began when he was about six years old. "When [a] man came into my mom's life and became my stepfather I had some major reactions to the guy. He was, as I saw it, a brute...he was big, he scared me a lot. He interfered with my relationship with my mother. And he was also a very harsh man. Not physically, he probably only struck me about three or four times [in seven years]...once very severely, though. His trip is mind games."

Borman recalls two other "significant experiences" of his early childhood. "When I was a kid I happened to view my mother and her friend having sex and it scared the shit out of me. I think I was about four or five...it seemed like a pretty scary thing. Also I remember at the age of seven being told that if I masturbated I would never be able to have children."

"Who told you that?"

"Some kid. I don't remember. I took him quite seriously. He was older than me, and so I never masturbated until I was around 17, 18 years old."

When Borman was about 10 he tried to poison his stepfather and a year later he tried to kill himself by taking a handful of pills from every bottle in his parents' medicine cabinet. He became very sick and threw up. "I was actually quite happy about it all because suddenly I had loads of attention, okay, and so that was pretty good."

As he approached puberty, Borman's fantasies of killing his stepfather started changing. "They became a mixture of curiosity, sexual curiosity, what is a woman all about, what is a man all about...everywhere from neat, appropriate, cute fantasies to violent rapes, murders, and often at the same time. I didn't really distinguish between what was right or what was wrong. Again, it wasn't something that I did — questioning myself. It was just not the way it was.''

When he was 12 he decided that he would kill a woman so that he could look at her body. ''I was at the point of having a knife in my hand, watching somebody, and then just wasn't able to do it. Couldn't carry it out, and so ran, ran away home. A scared little boy.''

His sexual relationships with women were very difficult. ''I remember actually trying one girl I was with who had approached me...she started out with spin the bottle, so we both wound up nude. And I'm sitting there, and she's beside me and she's very developed. And so I go through the motion that I remember on TV or in the movies, and of course, I don't even have an erection, right, I'm scared shit. And she's saying, not now...[I] got out of that situation, ran home, and I think I never approached her again. Just hid.''

When he was about 15, Borman became involved in a series of robberies with an acquaintance. He describes the experience: ''Met a kid and we talked to each other and somehow it got into the idea of armed robbery. I don't know if I manipulated him. It was about a four-month cycle. At first it was one armed robbery and another armed robbery, and another armed robbery — and then he said he'd had enough.

But Borman still craved the excitement. He went to a motel to commit another robbery and abducted the motel clerk. ''It wasn't like my fantasy. I attempted it. I told her to take her clothes off; she took her clothes off. I think I tried to, well, no, I did...I tried to penetrate her, right. I don't even think I had an erection. I climaxed, right out in the air, as far as I know, and at that point I ran.''

''When I was doing it,'' he continues, ''I played like I was a real creep about it. I threatened her, you know. Threatened her to the point where she didn't admit [being sexually assaulted]. She admitted to the robbery but she didn't admit to the rape or attempted rape until a day or two later.''

Within about a month, Borman was back out in the community, "having spilled the beans for everything," the robbery and the sexual assault. Because he was a juvenile offender, his sentence was not comparable to the time that he would have received in jail from an adult court. As Borman recognizes now, he should not have been back in the community. He sexually assaulted another woman — and then, on a third occasion, he killed.

He scouted his victim for about a month, "fantasizing about her and wondering what it was all like and things like that...I focussed in on one person. And then built up whatever it was that I needed to finally go over and attack her."

He describes the killing itself, "She couldn't speak English. I was telling her what to do...wound up with a fight, we both got cut with a knife. At that point I seemed to gain control, okay, and attempted to rape her...the adrenalin was going, that was true. I was playing out my role as I had envisioned it. And every time something would alter that, I would panic even more."

"I'm wrestling with her," he continues, "...and in the process, through the contact, I get excited and I climax with my pants on. And we wound up fighting and at some point I got her above the throat and I held on until she stopped and I kept holding on until she was dead." Borman had also tied a rope around the woman's neck and "explored" her body after death. "I saw her breasts and then I checked out her vagina, like touching it...like that took all of about two minutes. A lot of my fantasies had to do with exploring a woman's body and to do so, for instance all the pictures in the magazines you know, have the pubic hairs, so I was going to shave off the pubic hairs so that I could see what the hell's going on...but I did none of that. All my ideas and thoughts went down the drain."

He had committed the offence in his own neighbourhood and police came into contact with him during house-to-house interviews. They eventually asked him to come down to the police station, "and they did a checkout and I saw them take my prints on a glass. And as I left, I saw them scooting off with the glass, so I knew they knew what was going on.''

Borman was arrested at his school, called to the principal's office on the public address system. He was 16 years old, and at the time he felt that he was actually being rewarded for his crime. ''I didn't think about running away. I was getting all of the attention. That was great. I didn't really think this was wrong or anything like that. I didn't really have much of a value system. It started a process of having all these people who were professionals coming out of the cracks in the wall to come see me. I was special. And I loved it. There was no way that I could feel bad about it all, you know, it was perfect.''

Borman's life was so lacking in any kind of positive feedback that the creation of his identity as a major criminal came as a welcome transition; he was finally an important person. He was convicted of second degree murder a little over 10 years ago and will soon be released on parole. He says of his time in prison, ''I lived in terror for years. It was a process...but I learned how to live with men. And I actually adopted a father...an outside sense father.''

''An outside...?''

''Not your dad inside. You know, your dad inside is someone who looks after you for special favours.''

When asked if jail has been a help or a hindrance, Borman responds, ''I have to say a help, because I am actually quite pleased with who I am right now. I have a lot of fun... overall I'm pretty happy with who I am and where I fit in the world...that's a fucking lie. I am not very happy with where I fit in the world right now. I'm on the bottom end of the stick and I have reams of people, including a whole system, that wishes to keep me there. But right now I'm their little toy and their little toy is being wound up and is doing very well right now. And so they treat me very well. Once in a while I get really pissed off about it and I say a few things to them and they get all in a fluster, but I have this knack for fixing it all up.''

It is an understatement to suggest that John Borman's life prospects are somewhat bleak. As one of Canada's sex killers, he occupies the bottom rung of the social order and the prison subculture. The stigma of his offence — or of any sexual offence — is not easily erased, inside or outside the penitentiary. Men who use their physical strength over women and children for the purpose of sexual excitement are universally reviled. In Canada's prisons they are the "rapos," "skinners" and "diddlers," invariably held in a separate part of the institution for their own protection. The general population of the prison has let it be known that the penalty for sex offenders shall be either death or serious injury.

Borman argues that both his crime and his punishment were sick and perverted. "I think that the correctional system is an extremely sick system...it's a bureaucracy that is made up of a bunch of people who are invested in their jobs and their money and job stability. And quite literally, they're confused. They're not quite sure if they want to deal with the system in terms of punishment or in terms of rehabilitation, and so they're Jekyll and Hyde. And if you come in, like me, doing a life sentence, they have you by the balls all the time. If you're extremely lucky, extremely talented, and have a couple of friends, you can get through. But I know some people who don't look good, don't talk good...and they're going to stay in a lot longer than I am, simply because they can't talk well."

He continues, "I think the only reason that I've done well in it is because I happened to meet some people who actually cared for me...and allowed me to go through jealousy, love with them, you know, allowed me to go through the whole spectrum and then blew my lights by telling me that they had fantasies about me too, right."

Borman argues that he is no longer a danger to the public, though he may be a danger to himself. "I think I went through a burnout period. If I go on a rage now, I'll just kill myself...like it would be because I've decided the world is, like I'm just tired of dealing with the world. That would be it."

Borman recognizes that his crime was particularly repugnant, and when asked how he would explain himself to the "regular Joes" on the street, he responds, "Hello, normal people. This is from somebody who you have deemed to be abnormal. I question why you love reading through the papers finding the most gruesome details and most gruesome books, and why you decide to focus on the most gruesome things that you can find. Ah, you're appalled, you say. Great. I say that you're just denying something about yourselves.''

Borman argues that Canadian society is still "fairly barbaric," and that most people just go through the paces of life. "Maybe you love to get through the day by drinking some alcohol or smoking a little pot or doing some other drugs, or maybe you don't need the drugs. Maybe you just go through like a gerbil on a treadmill. You go to work, you go home, you watch TV — the great babysitter of mankind who conditions you to look at violence....''

"But if you can't get through life just ducking out," he continues, "someday you're going to lash out. Look at how many people are showing up in Canadian society who are molesting people. It's not just the guy down the street with the trench-coat, flashing his prick all around. It happens to be doctors, it happens to be lawyers, it happens to be psychologists, psychiatrists. I've met a few social workers, I've met lots of teachers, ah, members of parliaments — like these people aren't something out of your closet. They happen to belong to the same species.''

Borman concludes, ''So, maybe if you decide to deal with that and maybe decide to deal with an oppressive society which loves to condition you to believe that this is a great free land, you'll figure out what the hell life is all about. And then,'' Borman chuckles, ''you'll probably commit suicide, because it's all shit.''

The prognosis for John Borman is, by definition, uncertain. When he says that life is ''all shit,'' it seems that he is approaching his release with an alarming carelessness. And yet he also says that he is determined not to hurt again, apart from the possibility of hurting himself. Neither I, nor any other informed professional who deals with the subject of violence, can give any guarantees about John Borman, or make entirely accurate predictions about his future behaviour. We know only probabilities, that about 99% of murderers will not kill again, for example, and that the overwhelming majority will not commit another violent crime. Will John Borman hurt again? The best answer, as imperfect and as worrying as it may be, is probably not.

Men who kill during a sexual assault — men like John Borman — form the tip of the iceberg as far as sex offences are concerned. There are about 40,000 sexual assaults in Canada each year — over 100 on any given day — and only half of these attacks are reported to police.[4] Only one in every 1,000 sexual assaults results in the death of the victim, but this must provide little relief to Canadian women. Rapists who kill are not necessarily different from "normal" rapists. In many instances, they intend only to take sex from a woman, but ultimately feel compelled to "cover their tracks." Many of the stories that are presented in this chapter will make this point clear.

Canadian police forces knew of a little over 20,000 sexual assaults in 1986. Over the past decade the number of reported incidents has doubled, and since 1962 there has been almost a tripling in the annual number of recorded offences per 100,000 population. What lies behind these data is unclear. The most obvious explanation is that women are being victimized more often in 1988 than they were a generation ago.

But, as said above, reported assaults amount to less than half of all cases. The Canadian Victimization Survey of 1982 revealed that over 60% of all incidents of sexual assault are not reported to police. It is quite possible that there is no more victimization of women today than there was 25 years ago; we may be seeing a tripling of the offence rate only because more women, with the assistance of the women's movement, are now prepared to go to police. There may well have been a time in recent history when less than 10% of all sexual offences were reported to the police.

In 1988, data suggest that about 40% of women will report their victimization. Research reveals that the most common reason for not reporting a sexual assault stems from the perception that the police cannot do anything to help. Other motives for not reporting include a negative attitude towards the police, a fear of revenge, the fact that no property was taken and a feeling that the violation was either a personal matter or too minor. Finally, for about 15% of assaulted women, there is a desire to protect the offender from court action.[5]

The man who kills during a sexual assault is a rapist who has slipped over the edge of control. The most common method of killing is strangulation, followed by stabbing, beating and suffocation; a firearm is involved in less than five per cent of all such deaths.[6] Killing during a sexual assault is a very personal and physically brutal kind of violent death. The characteristics of men convicted of killing for sex are very similar to those of men convicted of rape or sexual assault; these individuals are typically economically disadvantaged, without any sense of family and likely to abuse alcohol or other drugs.

In this pool of men who take sex by force we also find the most reviled of all criminal offenders, the man who kills children in pursuit of his sexual pleasure. The sexual killing of a child — a person under the age of 16 — is a little less common than the sexual killing of an adult. The best evidence available suggests that about 40% of all sexual assault-murder victims are between the ages of one and 15.[7] These are typically the most upsetting cases of killing for sex; they represent every parent's nightmare, the innocent child as a trusting victim of male sexual violence.

Canada's child sex killers receive a significant amount of media attention, despite representing only about one per cent of all persons charged with murder. Clifford Olson has probably become the prototype of the category. He now lives in solitary confinement in Kingston Penitentiary, having sexually abused and brutally murdered more than a dozen children in British Columbia. The monstrosity of his crimes provided fuel to those who have argued for the reinstatement of capital punishment. One Member of Parliament went so far as to introduce a private member's bill, calling for Olson's execution.

Olson, an informer for the RCMP, was once nicknamed "Ollie the Parolee," by fellow prisoners at the British Columbia Penitentiary. As one convict explained, Olson always seemed to be able to get himself an early parole. He is, of course, no longer "Ollie the Parolee," but a reviled man in his mid-forties, likely to spend the rest of his life in prison. No longer able to live among the general population of Canada's prisons, Clifford Olson is the epitome of the protective custody prisoner, an informer, a child molester, and a rapist.

I did not try to arrange an interview with Olson. Too much has already been written about him. By focussing on his crimes we have neglected study of the range of men who kill children for sex, not to mention study of the range of killing itself. There have been other well-publicized convictions for child sex killings, and for actions that are similar in cruelty. Newspapers, magazines and television have told us of Saul Betesh, convicted of first degree murder in the late Seventies sex slaying of Toronto shoeshine boy Emmanuel Jacques, and of David Shearing, convicted in the early Eighties of killing the Johnston and Bentley families in British Columbia's Wells Gray Provincial Park.

I could not find a man, outside of the discarded possibility of Clifford Olson, who was willing to talk, even under a pseudonym, about having committed this kind of crime. In order to give you a picture of a man who killed a child for sex, I have to take you back to British Columbia in the year 1956.

Gerald Eaton was 25 years old when he left his working-class home in London, England, and emigrated to Canada. He came to Saskatchewan in the spring of 1929 and worked as a labourer on various farms. In the winter of 1933, at the age of 28, he became "very friendly" with a girl under the age of 16, and travelled to the north of the province with her.

The girl's mother was less than impressed with her prospective son-in-law and laid a charge of seduction against him. Eaton was convicted later that year of seduction under promise of marriage and served eight months in Regina Gaol for the offence.

Not long after his release, and now in his early thirties, Eaton married. In the spring of 1941 the family moved to British Columbia with their baby boy. Eaton managed to find work as a deckhand on a ferry boat operating on the Fraser River and eventually became a skipper, having passed an exam that earned him his captain's papers for inland waters.

He remained out of trouble until 1954. In this year, it was the child welfare authorities who became concerned about his behaviour. In 1952, two girls, aged 11 and 12, who were wards of the child welfare system, were placed in the Eatons' home. An investigation in 1954 revealed that Eaton, now a man of 50, had begun to have sexual intercourse with the older girl a few months after the two moved in. Between 1952 and 1954 he also used both girls as prostitutes, bringing interested men over to the house to be serviced. It was only when suspicious neighbours contacted the child welfare agency that this behaviour came to public attention.[8]

Charges were still pending when Gerald Eaton committed his most serious offence in April 1956. Eight-year-old Caroline Moore left Langley Elementary School just after 3 o'clock on the 26th of the month, and was walking towards the local Anglican Church to meet her mother. She was particularly excited that afternoon because her father was coming home from a three-week business trip in the interior of British Columbia. She had dressed in her best clothing for the occasion, a blue nylon dress, blue coat, and a red summer hat decorated with a cluster of white daisy-like flowers.

Caroline Moore never arrived at St. Andrew's Anglican Church. By the early evening her family was becoming very worried. Lawrence Moore, afraid that his daughter had been abducted, notified the police. Early the next morning police and volunteers began to search in earnest for the little girl. Langley residents — businessmen, civic leaders, and high school students — dropped their usual daily routines in order to help out. There were about 150 volunteers, police cars, planes and a tracking dog covering the heavy bush around the Langley Elementary School.

Police questioned Caroline's Grade Three classmates, anxious to uncover any clues that might lead them to find her.

The driver of a milk truck was questioned with no success; a piece of a child's underwear was found in the bush, but it did not belong to the missing child. The *Vancouver Sun* reported on the day's activities, "Neighbours who went to the comfort of the distraught parents served coffee and sandwiches to the searchers as they returned from the bush. Caroline's new little brown dog, Taffy, seemed to sense something was wrong, as he raced around the yard barking.... In every cafe on Langley's main street the search for little Caroline was the only subject of conversation. 'Have they found her yet?' or 'Any word yet?,' were the queries put to every customer...."9

The teenage brothers of Caroline Moore were still searching for her after dark, looking through dense bush with their flashlights. Their sister had been missing for almost 36 hours, and the family was desperate. The day's search had covered an estimated 10 square miles, and as darkness fell, searchers returned to Langley and began another scan of the city itself.

Early the following morning a clergyman came to the front door of the Moore's home. "I knew what it was as soon as he came to the door," said 15-year-old Darryl Moore, "We all had known she was not alive yesterday afternoon, but we had just hoped for the best." The young boy later explained to reporters that his parents were "badly broken up" by news of their daughter's death.

Caroline Moore's body had been discovered about 6 a.m., dumped in dense bush about eight miles north of the city of Langley. The front page of that day's *Vancouver Sun* was covered with news of the little girl's death. "Child Victim of Savage Beating," "Peaceful Langley Stunned by Murder," the headlines read. The paper noted that a suspect had been arrested, 51-year-old Gerald Edward Eaton.

The *Vancouver Sun* reported, some 40 hours after the killing, "Police would not disclose what led them to the suspect, other than that an investigation of another crime against a woman by a man other than the suspect gave them the all-important lead."

During the 40 hours between Caroline Moore's disappearance and Gerald Eaton's arrest, the RCMP received information that a five-year-old child had been sexually molested while attending a show with other children in Langley. A 14-year-old youth who fitted the description of the attacker was picked up for questioning. This young man indicated that he had had "indecent relations" with a Mr. Eaton, and that this Mr. Eaton had encouraged him to commit such acts with other children.

Police stopped Gerald Eaton while he was driving along the highway, just before midnight. He was asked to follow the police car to the local detachment and complied. Another police car then proceeded to Eaton's home, and searched the premises. Found inside the house was a quantity of nudist literature and nude photographs. Eaton later indicated that he was president of the nudist colony known as "The Border Tans."

Early the next morning, during a search of Eaton's car, a small flower petal was found, similar in shape and texture to the flower petals on Caroline Moore's summer hat. "Where is the little girl?", police asked Eaton.

"She's dead," he replied.

After being given the usual statutory warning, police told Eaton, "For God's sake, tell us where she is. Think of her parents."

While initially reluctant, Eaton ultimately directed police to Caroline Moore's body, and then explained what had happened some 40 hours before.

Eaton had seen the little girl walking along the road and offered her a drive. He took her back to his house, telling her that he would take her home afterwards. She went indoors with him and he started to fondle her genitals, his excitement rising. "I did not try to have sexual intercourse with her, I just played with her private organs," he told his interrogators.

Caroline Moore started to cry, and then to scream. Eaton began to punch her in the head with his fist, hitting her again and again. She started to bleed from the mouth and nose, and fell unconscious on the floor.

Eaton went to get some water to wash up the blood. He piled some old newspapers on the floor and cleaned up the mess that he had made. He went to his car, got a sack, and wrapped it around the little girl's head. He then carried her out to his car and locked her body in the trunk.

Eaton drove to the local Elks Hall where his son and a friend were taking music lessons. With the body still in his trunk, Eaton drove the boys over to Mabel's Inn, a local restaurant, for a milk-shake. His son's friend stated at trial that Gerald Eaton was not behaving unusually when he saw him that afternoon.

At about 6 p.m., Eaton left the boys and drove out of the city to dump Caroline Moore's body. He described the sequence of events to police, "I drove down there; I didn't know where I was going. I just took her out of the car then and that's when I took her into the bush and then I got the tire iron out of the car and hit her quite a number of blows." A pathologist testified at trial that the blows from the tire iron had been so severe as to cause portions of brain to ooze out of the cuts that had been made.

There were two trials, one in December 1956, and a second in April 1957. Through all of his court appearances, Gerald Eaton maintained his innocence. He claimed that he had accidentally run over Caroline Moore and then covered up her death, in a moment of panic. When asked why he did not report the "accident" to authorities, he responded, "Well, at that time, I don't know why I didn't — I just seemed to lose my head, but I knew I had killed her, and afterwards when I did start to think about it, I knew it was too late...."

The story was, of course, a fabrication and the jury did not believe it. At the conclusion of the first trial they found Eaton guilty, with a recommendation for mercy. The trial judge explained this final judgement, "There are two possible explanations for their recommendation for mercy, one being the aversion to capital punishment, the other a feeling of sympathy because of a mentally disturbed mind, although there was no attempt to show insanity within the meaning of the *Code*."

The British Columbia Court of Appeal ordered a new trial, on the ground that some statements made by the accused to the police were not entirely voluntary. At one point, prior to Eaton giving information about the location of the body, a police officer had said to him, "I would like to throw you out that window."

The second trial led to the same conclusion as the first; the evidence against Eaton was overwhelming, the admissibility of certain statements notwithstanding. The second jury did not recommend mercy and the trial judge concluded, "I have no slightest doubt that the jury reached the proper verdict, and I have no recommendation to make."

Attempts then began to save Eaton from his midsummer date with Canada's hangman. The memorandum prepared for Cabinet concluded with the words of the trial judge, set out above. A letter from Eaton's lawyer noted that he had provided considerable assistance to other prisoners on Oakalla's Death Row. Norman Mullins wrote, "In the time Eaton has spent in condemned row, he has endeavoured with all of his fellow prisoners, to talk to them, to console them, to encourage them and to reconcile them to their situation."

A letter from Eaton's wife pleaded, "He always lived a good life.... He would drive miles for others too old to go to the store, etc. and taking children home from entertainments. He was really good to me. I am nearly blind and he did everything for me.... Most of the men that get into this kind of trouble have been in trouble all their lives or are alcoholics or drug addicts. My husband has never been any of these."

Gerald Eaton's letter to Prime Minister John Diefenbaker was written a few weeks before he was scheduled to hang. He did not speak directly of his offence, concluding, "I feel that given the chance, I can help others more unfortunate than myself in the penitentiary and so make at least a partial contribution towards repaying for the harm I have done. I am also asking you to show this mercy towards me, so that the innocent will not suffer too much, such as my wife who has nothing left, and my son who hopes to grow into a useful citizen."

On the morning of his execution, Gerald Eaton finally confessed his crime publicly, and wrote of his upcoming death, "Society has decreed that a few minutes after midnight tonight I shall die. After 14 months of facing death, I cannot say that I am sorry. It is a release from mental torture that at times is almost unbearable."[10]

Lawrence Moore, the father of Eaton's young victim, was present for the hanging. He explained his desire to watch the execution, "I have had two choices in the matter. One was to continue through life with the mental picture of this man beating my daughter to death. The other was to see him hang for the crime. Only the latter can obliterate from my memory the former picture."

After the execution Lawrence Moore walked down a stairwell to look at Gerald Eaton's uncovered face in death. Asked if he could now forgive the man, Moore shook his head.

A few hours before he died, Gerald Eaton noted that he could not explain why he had committed such a terrible crime. "I keep asking myself that over and over," he wrote. "Why, why?"

"It was an urge, and once I started beating her I could not stop. It seems to me now as a dream that happened in the long ago.... I must have been in a haze of some sort."

Canada now experiences about 10 sexual assault killings of children annually. The men who commit the crime share the characteristics of most men who kill; they are economically disadvantaged, and almost always come from family backgrounds of physical and emotional abuse.

What distinguishes the child sex killer from other killers is to be found in the crime itself, finding sexual satisfaction in, and then killing the most powerless human beings. Gerald Eaton, Saul Betesh, David Shearing and Clifford Olson are not demographically, psychologically or neurologically distinct from other killers. They form a category that is based upon the horrible logic of the morality that they practiced.

Like Gerald Eaton, Leonard Peete practiced a horrifying morality. He raped and killed an elderly woman.[11] Unlike Gerald Eaton, however, Peete was not put to death, and now, some 17 years later, he is on the verge of release from prison.

In the fall of 1970, Leonard Peete had just been released

from a penitentiary in western Canada, after serving most of a two-year sentence for breaking and entering. He was 19 years old and quite an unhappy human being. Peete's mother was a Métis who became an alcoholic when he was very young; his father was a white Catholic, a strict disciplinarian who was physically violent towards his children.

When he was "just barely old enough to understand," Peete's parents separated and his father received custody of him and his three brothers. He describes himself as an adolescent: "I was an intelligent individual but I had a whole lot of emotional problems, problems with sexuality, problems with lack of communication with the family, background of physical abuse."

By the time he was 14, Peete was well over six feet tall and weighed about 200 pounds; he was drinking in the local hotels, and skipping school. But he did have some achievements. He was a very good athlete, invited to the 1968 Canadian Olympic trials on the strength of his performance in the shot-put and discus. He was also a successful army cadet. "I became involved when I was 14...and it just so happened that I joined the best organization for cadets at that particular time in the entire city. We were second within the country in shooting, that's target shooting. I believe I was the first one selected in western Canada in '67 for the Expo exchange."

But these accomplishments were overshadowed by his continuing sequence of crimes and his increasingly frequent prison terms. "These were all great individual performances but they didn't make me feel better as a human being. They certainly never repaired my relationships with my family. I very seldom spoke with my parents and whenever we did speak it was very restrained conversations. I had initiated leaving my father when I was 14 years old because I got tired of physical abuse. But I missed my brothers."

His offence occurred in the spring of 1971. "It was probably that breaking point between winter and spring where there are still lots of opportunities for snowfalls and storms. And there was lots of snow on the ground."

Peete's relationship with his girlfriend had broken down and he had been travelling about the country, looking for a better opportunity. He came home to the western plains, began to drink more and was "only looking temporarily at different jobs." He wasn't really interested in working and he was associating with a group of individuals who were "real party animals."

On the night of the killing Peete was dropped off at his apartment in the early hours of the morning. "I recall drinking over 24 bottles of beer that evening. My particular brand at that time was Old Stock, malt liquor...I had also taken some benzedrine — speed. I recall getting into an argument with my mother on the phone and blaming her for a lot of my misfortune...rightly or wrongly, I'm not sure. What I'm trying to give you is the perspective."

Peete broke into the apartment of his next-door neighbour. "I didn't know the woman. I had only seen her, brief encounters in passing. I didn't know her name. I didn't know her background. I didn't know her age. I didn't know anything."

He describes the killing, "During the process I had, in the initial contact, in the initial struggle, I guess in order to inhibit her movement I inadvertently ended up placing my knee on her chest and ended up breaking 12 of her ribs."

"Because you're a big man?"

"Yeah. I didn't even realize that I had done it. I mean, at that particular time I had no indication of what I'd done. I guess I was too wrapped up on the inside of myself to be external. External events weren't registering a whole lot. I've been accused of hitting the woman in the face with a clock. I don't think I did that, but there was a broken clock. I took my pleasures and I left."

"My intent," he continues, "was the assault. I don't know...sexuality, the experience of sex was some kind of a release...the release mechanism involved. And I was a very subjective individual. I was punishing the world. I couldn't express myself emotionally to people. I couldn't sit down and talk. I couldn't talk about what was going on inside of me. I couldn't put together the pieces of my life, to understand. I just knew the hurt and...I just kept hurting...."

Peete figures that he wanted to be caught; he was out of control, and he quickly emerged as the prime suspect. "I woke up the next morning not comprehending what I had done, blocking out the horror of that. I was taken down the next day to the police station and questioned and subsequently released, and then later rearrested."

He recalls that he slept for most of the first week that he was in prison, and then came down with pneumonia and pleurisy. "So in the period from March to my trial in October, it was all like...I don't know...a bad movie. It was a movie that you could see at nine o'clock of someone else's life, or someone else's story, a horror story. The testimonies, all of that...the coroner's report."

Peete was convicted of non-capital murder and sentenced to life imprisonment. He was very fortunate that he was convicted in the early Seventies. If his crime had taken place in 1962, he probably would have been hanged; if his crime had taken place after 1976, he would have been found guilty of first degree murder and subjected to a mandatory 25-year prison term.

As it is, he's served about 17 years for the offence, and, like most of us, he's quite a different person at age 36 than he was at 19. The first few years of his imprisonment were very difficult; his crime made him a walking target in the penitentiary. "There were a number of individuals who came in, because of crimes, who had to be segregated...separated from the rest of the population. We were put on display and we were treated in that way. And we were degraded. There were times when we used to have to worry about razor blades in the laundry. Sometimes I'd get my laundry back slashed."

Peete was condemned by both prisoners and guards. "There was a tremendous amount of time after my crime, because of the atrocity, the fact of her age. And all the threats against my own life, not only from inmate to inmate, but from staff to me as well. There were those threats."

Peete's own behaviour wasn't really changing: "After

the turn of the calendar I would always have some kind of build-up and in February, March, I would do something. And I would find myself in the hold. It was some kind of acting-out behavious. I was either involved with a skirmish in the kitchen or I was acting up to one of the officers...."

In the winter of 1976 Peete became involved with native culture. "From 1976 to 1980 I spent the better part of 16 hours a day from eight o'clock in the morning to 12 o'clock at night studying art, carving. I could carve anything in wood that I could set my mind to. I had developed a skill with not only wood but the tools and the machinery, the mythology, the stories. I could talk about the legends."

He began to develop pride in his skill as a carver and to immerse himself in native religion. "I discovered my spirituality in here...I've gone on four-day fasts, which is the native way. The elders of the community have given me a sacred pipe, a holy pipe to use, to carry for the rest of my life. I receive instruction in Indian medicine, in healing."

Leonard Peete regards himself at 36 as a very different man from the Leonard Peete who raped and killed an elderly woman some 17 years ago. "I thank God that I'm a Canadian and able to have done the kinds of things in my life that I've done, and yet to be able to sit here today on the verge of release, of going into the larger community and realistically being able to make a difference in life."

Peete concludes that he is no longer a dangerous man. "I don't believe in violence. Right now, as I am today, I don't support any form of violence, whether it be physical or verbal. But the thing that makes human beings what they are is that we are susceptible to a lot of factors. As human beings, we don't understand a lot of emotional things...what makes me, what makes you, what makes anyone else...there are so many things with our lives that we cannot explain, we cannot rationalize, we cannot justify."

What are the prospects for Leonard Peete? Will he present a danger when he is released? What of John Borman? To put the issue more directly, how changeable is male sexual aggression?

I want to show you a little more of the range of specific cases before I try to answer those questions. The most common kind of killing for sex is, like John Borman's crime, the rape-murder of an adult woman. I will tell you in a moment about a few other men who have committed this kind of crime — a little more data for the mill of social science.

During both the 1940s and 1950s there were only 14 reported convictions for murder during sexual assault in Canada. There were 73 killings for sex during the 1960s and 200 during the 1970s. There has been no significant change from this latter figure during the present decade.

Some of the rapid escalation in the number of sex killings can be explained by the more thorough reporting procedures implemented by Statistics Canada in 1961. Sexual assault-murder followed the same pattern as other kinds of killings in Canada during the late Sixties and early Seventies; its incidence more than doubled in the space of a decade. And these changes do ultimately represent real increases. Canadian women are more likely to be the victims of rape-murder in the Eighties than they were in the early Sixties.

I am going to give you some sense of the breadth of this category, killing women for sex, by telling you about two men who killed before the 1960s and about a man whose crime was committed just a few years ago. You will see that a sexual assault-murder from 50 years ago is not really all that different from the contemporary crime. I'll begin with Harry O'Donnell, a man who raped and killed a woman in a ravine in Toronto's East End in 1935.

On November 6, the headlines across the front page of Toronto's *Globe and Mail* told of a violent and unusual crime. "A criminal maniac was sought last night," the story began, "for the brutal slaying of pretty 20-year-old Ruth Taylor, business stenographer, whose battered body was found in a ravine off Gerrard Street East yesterday."[12]

The newspaper did not specifically state that the young woman had been sexually assaulted, but noted, "Her body was found at 1:30 Tuesday afternoon, slumped in the mud, her battered head covered with her own clothing, and various belongings scattered over a distance of 75 feet."

The rain was driving down when Ruth Taylor left her work in downtown Toronto at a little after 11 p.m. on Monday night. She boarded a streetcar for her home in the east end of the city. The conductor of the streetcar noticed that when he arrived at the intersection of Coxwell and Gerrard there were only two passengers, Ruth Taylor, a regular on his route, and a man whom he did not know. Both passengers left the streetcar at the same time.

On the day after Ruth Taylor's body had been discovered, the case was again featured on the front page of the *Globe and Mail*. "Man Charged with Girl Murder," the bold headlines proclaimed, "Harry O'Donnell, Age 25, Father of New Born Babe, Taken at Gas Station."

O'Donnell was a gas station attendant whose wife was in the hospital, recovering from the delivery of their first child, a boy born about 48 hours before Ruth Taylor's murder. O'Donnell was quoted as saying, "I'm absolutely not guilty — I know nothing about this." Police were suspicious of O'Donnell's statements; he had spent almost three years in Kingston Penitentiary on a conviction for attempted rape, and was considered to be a potential sex offender.

On November 8, 1935, the *Globe and Mail* again featured the Taylor murder as the most prominent story on its front page; for three days the brutal killing had occupied the space below the masthead, capturing the attention and imagination of Torontonians. "Scientific Data Held Important in Ravine Slaying," the paper claimed. The story noted that the police were in possession of several articles that would make "a solid case" against Harry O'Donnell. There was no direct evidence of the crime and O'Donnell was denying any involvement. The newspaper was serving notice that the prosecution would have to win its day in court on the basis of circumstantial evidence.

The trial took place in February 1936. The court heard that Ruth Taylor had left the streetcar on that rainy November night and been dragged into the Gainsborough Ravine, near

Coxwell and Gerrard. She was found lying on her back; her body and legs were naked up to her breasts. Her brassiere had been torn off; there were bruises and cuts all over her face, and her skull had been fractured. There was a lot of blood around her vagina, again from injuries inflicted by an assailant.

Police had taken the clothing that Harry O'Donnell was wearing on the night of the murder and had it analyzed. Blue hairs, similar to those on the sweater of the deceased, were found all over O'Donnell's apparel. There was mud on the front of his overcoat and his suit was damp and flecked with burrs similar to those found in the Gainsborough Ravine. There was a reddish stain on the fly of his trousers, and there were mud stains from the knees to the cuffs of the pants. It was after seeing the condition of this clothing that police decided to take Harry O'Donnell to headquarters for further questioning.

At the trial, O'Donnell continued to deny any involvement in Ruth Taylor's death, but the circumstantial evidence against him was overwhelming. He was convicted of murder and sentenced to be hanged in early May. The *Ottawa Journal* reported that O'Donnell was smiling as he left the courtroom. He leaned over to the men sitting at the press table and whispered, "Can I take it, boys?"

In late April the Ontario Court of Appeal rejected O'Donnell's bid for a new trial, in a unanimous decision. Sir William Mulock, the 92-year-old Chief Justice made a very brief statement to a crowded courtroom. "Rex versus O'Donnell," he said, "This is an appeal from a conviction for murder, and it is dismissed."

It was not until 10 days before he died that Harry O'Donnell admitted to the killing of Ruth Taylor. In a seven-page statement from Toronto's Don Jail, O'Donnell spoke of his "unnatural practices."[13] He wrote of his adolescence: "Now about this time I began to show a tendency to have my feelings gratified, whether the other party wanted to of its own free will or not...on several occasions I forced girls to submit to my wishes. This included actual sexual intercourse, or when not possible, to be satisfied with touching or looking at the exposed privates of the other person or have them touch or look at me, or look at me while I abused myself.''

O'Donnell was also a peeping Tom; he would walk for hours about the city, ''looking in windows to see the occupants bathing, going to bed or for any reason getting undressed.'' He added, ''This feeling of wanting to see a nude person was so strong that I actually carried a ladder for blocks to a window I knew would be open and knowing a person would undress there.'' With the prospective woman in view, O'Donnell would then proceed to masturbate to climax.

But unlike most peeping Toms, Harry O'Donnell was also violent. He described his killing of Ruth Taylor, ''I remember suddenly grabbing this unfortunate girl and throwing her to the ground, and after beating her with my fists and hitting her with a stone I proceeded to carry out my desire to disrobe her, and when she was quite nude I tried to satisfy my urge to touch and fondle her body in every way except natural sexual intercourse. My desires of touch and sight were completely satisfied without me actually having an erection or losing my seed, but in a most brutal way I explored the private parts of the girl's body with my hands only. Then I suddenly seemed to realize what I was doing to this girl and in a fright, hurried home.''

O'Donnell's wife had also noticed that he had some abnormal tendencies. In an affidavit prepared for his appeal she stated, ''...he would appear to be satisfied by simply using his hands on my body. This tendency developed to a point where I would say it formed 60% of his sexual marital activities — the other 40% being performed in the natural way, but this 40% was largely due to my insistence upon the act being performed in the natural way.''

Eda O'Donnell also recalled an occasion on which she had cut her hand quite badly with a knife. ''I called my husband to come out to the kitchen where I was and he came and looked at my hand and seemed to derive a great deal of pleasure over the sight of the blood. In fact he seemed to gloat over the sight of blood on my hand. Looking back, I can still see the look on his face. I paid no great attention to it at the time, although I had a funny sensation when I looked at him. But knowing what I do now, I can see that his actions on that occasion were not normal.''

Tom Hutchings was no more normal than Harry O'Donnell. Like his predecessor, he was married at the time of his offence and beat his victim to death with a rock. Unlike Harry O'Donnell, he wasn't a Canadian citizen; he was only visiting our country.

Hutchings was a 22-year-old sergeant in Britain's Royal Air Force, stationed near Black's Harbour, New Brunswick, during the Second World War. It was the summer of 1942, and the British were preparing Canadians for the war overseas. Hutchings had left a wife and child behind in England and was, like many of his friends, spending his evenings drinking cheap Canadian rum and trying to find sex with some of the local ''girls.''

Black's Harbour is set on a peninsula of land that juts into the Atlantic, just north of the Maine border. Hutchings came to the little town in 1941 with one black mark already against him. His military file contained several reprimands over his conduct towards women who had been travelling on the boat from England to Canada.

In late April of 1942 he assaulted a woman whom he was dating. She described the event to police, ''We decided to go down to the river and have a drink. We sat on Roy's tunic and drank a bottle of whiskey between us. The next thing I can recall was Roy wanting to go a little bit further than I did, and when I refused, he hit me on the right side of the face with his fist. I don't remember taking my clothes off and wanting to go in for a swim, although I may have, and although I know that Roy hit me, I am not certain as to whether I had my clothes on at the time or not.''

The young woman was embarrassed by the circumstances of her beating; she told her mother that she had been attacked by a man with a knife. When she confronted Hutchings a couple of days later about the condition of her face, he denied any role in the violence.

But another young woman, Bernice Connors, did not have the opportunity to complain about Tom Hutchings' contempt for women. She met the man with the jutting jaw and the vaguely Hitlerian mustache on a June night when the Women's Institute of Black's Harbour was putting on a dance in the community hall; the guests of honour were the men of the visiting Royal Air Force.

Hutchings left the hall about 11:30 that Friday night. He and Bernice Connors walked down Deadman's Harbour Road; they were spotted by another couple and exchanged a few words. Later, still another couple saw a man and a woman lying on the side of the road. The man was on top of the woman and she was naked from the waist down. The man called out, "Buzz off" in an English accent. The "intruders" then went on their way, presuming that the man and woman were having sex, but wondering why the woman was not moving.

Hutchings arrived back at the dance about half an hour after midnight. He had a lot of blood on his face and asked for the help of his friends in cleaning his face. They obliged and he explained that he had been in a fight. When asked why there were no cuts or marks on him, he responded, "it must have come from the other fellow."

Bernice Connors didn't go home that night, but that didn't alarm her mother; she often spent the night with relatives. The following day, however, her family began to panic. About 48 hours after her death, her body was discovered, buried under some moss about 50 yards from Deadman's Harbour Road. The RCMP report documents the condition of Ms. Connors, who was discovered lying on her back: "Face of victim was badly battered, both eyes were swollen, as were the lips — the right jaw also badly swollen...cut over left eye, back of left ear and top of head...a wide cut about two inches long under the chin. The victim had lost a lot of blood...the hymen had a deep laceration...complete spermatozoa present in vagina."[14]

Tom Hutchings was the first and only suspect, arrested shortly after the finding of the body. In the face of overwhelming circumstantial evidence, he denied that he was responsible, and in October he went to trial on a charge of murder. His lawyer argued that he might be guilty of manslaughter, but not murder; he suggested that Hutchings' intent had been clouded by alcohol.

But Hutchings had told an RCMP officer that he was not drunk on the night in question, just "merry"; his protest of provocation by drink was not believed. The jury convicted him of murder and he was sentenced to be hanged in mid-December of 1942.

The trial judge and the jury disagreed, however, with respect to the issue of commutation. The jury recommended mercy and the trial judge wrote, "This [verdict] was no doubt founded upon the position and domestic circumstances of the accused. I find myself unable to support this recommendation. The crime was of a brutal and revolting character. I am unable to see in the whole case any ameliorating circumstances."

There was some dispute about whether Tom Hutchings should die for this crime. Jury foreman W.W. Quartermain wrote to Minister of Justice Louis St. Laurent, "...in the District recently, where the crime was committed, I asked of several men, as to their opinion, 'What percentage of the people would favour the carrying out of the sentence?' Their reply in each case was, the number would be very small, and that almost 100% would feel that the sentence should be commuted."

Psychiatrist E.C. Menzies argued that Hutchings could be suffering from a treatable "mental disease." He wrote, "...the basis of this mental disease consists in the susceptibility of the patient to enter into a dream state when under the influence of alcohol. The amount of alcohol may be very small." Hutchings' father sent a cable from England to his son's lawyer, "Trust appeal will be successful. Please convey thanks to all interested. Regret lost elder son on active service on the 10th. Use own discretion about informing Tom — Captain Hutchings.''

The cable was used by the lawyer in his appeal for commutation, but the lobby against leniency would prevail. The prosecutor, the trial judge, Hutchings' commanding officer and the Premier of the province all favoured execution, and in December 1942 the prison officials of Charlotte County began to prepare for the hanging in the early hours of the 16th.

At this point the small communities of the district wanted to forget about the crime and about the young British sergeant. Sheriff C.W. Mallory wrote to Ottawa about 10 days before Hutchings died, ''In Capital Cases Procedure...it states...that the bell of the prison, or the bell of the Parish Church be tolled for 15 minutes before and after the execution. In a small community like this...it is desired to have the matter attended to with as little publicity as possible. I am writing at the suggestion of the Deputy Attorney General of New Brunswick to ask if this cannot be omitted.''

The response from Ottawa came two days later: Tom Hutchings was to be dropped quietly to his death behind prison walls. The 1200 people of St. Andrew's, New Brunswick, were not to hear the dirge of the hangman.

The letter from Ottawa allowed, ''The close application of the rules above mentioned has apparently not been observed in every case...it would appear that, in the event of the execution taking place on December 16th, 1942, the tolling of the bell could be dispensed with.''

No bell has been tolled for Wally Jansen,[15] but he's not sure about whether death would be better than his present sentence. He has more than 20 years still to serve on his first degree conviction for the murder of a businesswoman, attacked in her motel room and then raped and bludgeoned to death.

The murder occurred about seven years ago, but he has only recently admitted his guilt, his final appeal to the courts exhausted. Jansen was 21 at the time of the killing. He was working sporadically in a small city, hundreds of miles away from his home in the northern interior of the province. He quit one job because he "couldn't take working indoors," and in early June he was spending a lot of time drinking in the bars around town.

He describes the impetus for the crime, "I left the bar; somehow or other I ended up behind the bar, in a motel room. I figured I'd go and steal a wallet or whatever. I was walking along, just sliding glass windows all the way along, I was just walking along to see if I could see anything or whatever. I saw the purse and I went in to take the purse."

Jansen had been drinking whisky that night and says that he was "pretty loaded." He continues, "Well, I grabbed the purse and I went to run out and the purse was a little heavier than I thought because there was somebody attached to it. I yanked at the purse and she came with the purse and hit her head."

As Jansen recalls, the woman hit her head on a dresser and was knocked out. "I picked her up and put her on the bed...."

"Was she an older woman or a younger woman?"

"Well, I didn't really pay any attention; she was around my age or older."

"You find it difficult to talk about it?"

"Yeah, at that spot I seem to get stuck, same with the psychiatrist.... I believe there was a nightgown or something on the edge of the table, she was bleeding...and I put the nightgown...it started to stop the bleeding...at the time it didn't look to be too bad...and then the sexual assault took place."

She was talking to him while he was raping her. "It was just something that happened, I didn't really enjoy it...not sexually anyway...."

"I started getting a little scared," he continues, "but I packed everything up...and took her out...there were some trees just 50, 60 yards...I told her to get on the ground sort of thing...and, uh, she got on the ground, and then she started yelling and screaming...."

Jansen picked up a brick and struck the woman with it. "I'm not saying that I didn't have any other thoughts in my mind at the time but that was my intention at the time, to knock her out and leave her.''"Like, the thought went through my mind,'' he continues, "if I don't kill her or whatever I'd probably get caught — it just flashed — I was just intending on knocking her out...anyways I hit her once and took off, threw her suitcase in the river and went back to the apartment.''

The woman died, but Jansen didn't hear about it for a month. After the killing he had gone north to find work in a logging camp. His crime remained an unsolved murder for over two years, until he committed another brutal rape in his home town.

He recalls, "I was fairly drunk...stumbling around, I went outside to get sick. I thought no, I'm going home.'' He was given a ride by a young woman in a pickup truck and he encouraged her to drive him to a remote spot, where he raped her and knocked her out. This victim lived, however, and went to police. Jansen reflects, "I saw a pattern. Maybe I wanted to get caught. I don't know.''

Within two days of his arrest for the new offence in his home town, he was charged with the unresolved murder in the south of the province; his fingerprints matched those found at the scene. He recalls his trial, "I had no concept, no...I was, I don't know...kind of like sitting in a movie theatre...watching somebody else on trial...and being reminded halfway through that it was me on trial....''

This is a common theme with people who are convicted of murder. What goes on in court is a drama in which they are more observers than participants. This should not be surprising — the trial is, after all, a ritual for the community. The offender watches what is done to him, dependent on the outcome of the "movie,'' a version of his life that is unfolding in the courtroom.

It's about five years since Wally Jansen was convicted of first degree murder. He's experienced his share of violence in prison, targeted by his crime. He lives in protective custody in a maximum-security penitentiary, and remains angry, "My rages come...just like you stick a thermometer into boiling water...I can feel it.''

Asked if they come very often and if he understands them,

he responds, "I know how to stop them now...with pent up emotions, I don't let them out. I feel that if I let out my emotions, somehow or other I'm going to get into an altercation."

He has changed his views on capital punishment since his conviction. "I was out on the street when Clifford Olson was [arrested]. I figured they should kill him." With the shoe on the other foot, Jansen was quickly converted to the abolitionist cause. He argues now that he might prefer a lethal injection to his 25-year minimum: "I would probably take the injection. I have thought about that quite a bit. 25 years. There are so many guys doing 25 years in jail now. In 25 years, they'll have all these guys getting out. What could happen in 25 years is just incredible."

For the present, Jansen leads a life fraught with tension. "In here...just a simple argument can lead to a death. It gets to be a little crazy sometimes. Especially when there's, say, a fight or somebody gets killed, the whole population, we're all locked up in here. We're stuck for 10 days or whatever. We really get on each other's nerves." Jansen hopes for transfer to a lower-security institution that houses only protective-custody prisoners.

Asked for his philosophy of life, he chuckles, "I'm here. The way I deal with my sentence is...you gotta live your life, being here or being out there so...it's still life... experience...I don't want to go off the walls in here. I believe in an elsewhere...I don't believe in God or the Devil, but I believe in a different existence."

"After death...?"

"Yeah.... I don't know. I think I've read too many science fiction books." Jansen says, "It's just something — I'm a loner basically, in here, I enjoy myself alone, and I'm alone."

Wally Jansen will not be eligible for release for over 20 years, but for many Canadians this may seem a small comfort. Like the crimes of others profiled in this chapter, Jansen's violence is not easily explained.

As I noted earlier, the methods used to commit sexual assault murder are different from the methods used in other kinds of killings. Strangulation is the most common means of killing for sex, followed by stabbing, beating and suffocation. Men who kill women and children during a sexual assault use their own physical force to commit the crime; they rarely use the trigger of a gun to distance themselves from their prey.[16]

It is a very cruel death, and fortunately, it is a relatively rare occurrence. Over the past decade, only one in every 100,000 Canadians has been killed during a sexual assault. Victims of sexual attacks are much more common, however; over the past decade at least one in every 60 Canadians has been sexually assaulted. If adult males are taken out of this equation, the risk of victimization for women and children almost doubles, and even this figure is almost sure to underestimate the magnitude of the problem.

We have two sources of information for the conclusion that there are about 40,000 sexual assaults in Canada each year — offences reported to the police and information elicited during the National Victimization Survey of 1982. This survey of Canadians was conducted by telephone. While guarantees of anonymity were given to those who were called, many women who had been sexually victimized would probably have been unwilling to give this information to a stranger on the other end of the line.

At the same time that we acknowledge the magnitude of sexual assault in our culture, we need to recognize the heterogeneity of sex offenders. There are men who expose themselves, masturbating in public, and men and women who engage in what the law terms "gross indecency," typically performing sex acts in public. There are nonviolent pedophiles, that is, men who use children for sexual pleasure, but inflict no physical harm; there are violent pedophiles — men who hurt children. And there are men who sexually assault and rape adult women, inflicting harm in their pursuit of sex.

It is only violent pedophiles, those who sexually assault and rape, who could kill for sex. Within these categories, however, we are still speaking of at least tens of thousands of Canadian men. And the effects of a sexual assault are typically profound. Researchers have shown that women who have been assaulted tend to differ significantly from women who have not been assaulted. The survivors of sexual assault tend to be more depressed, have higher levels of fear, are more likely to have sexual problems and are more likely to report that they are dissatisfied with their present sexual relationships.[17]

A sexual assault is more than an act of violence. Most men who commit robbery, holding up banks, stores or pharmacies, do not inflict physical harm. Over 90% of the time, no one is hurt. With sexual assault, a person is always hurt and degraded. And it is the sexual character of this crime that is so distinctive. The men of this chapter were reluctant to talk about the actual sex involved in their crime — their unusual coupling of pleasure and pain.

A man who finds his erections in acts of violence or coercion is typically a dangerous man, likely to deny his crime and not easily treated. The leading judicial decisions suggest that Canada treats this group of criminals with relative leniency. In 1976, in one Manitoba case, a 22-year-old male, under the influence of alcohol, raped and beat a 75-year-old woman. He hit her several times and threatened her with death. The offender was sentenced to three years imprisonment, a sentence upheld by the Manitoba Court of Appeal. In another case, in 1974, the Ontario Court of Appeal upheld a one-year sentence for a 17-year-old male who raped and injured a 14-year-old girl.[18]

These sentences can be contrasted with sentences typically given in robbery cases. In one instance a man who had committed four bank robberies, with threats of violence but no weapon, was sentenced to five years imprisonment. The accused had a criminal record but there were no injuries. The sentence was upheld by the Ontario Court of Appeal. Criminal lawyer Clayton Ruby, in his text, *Sentencing*, writes of the approach of Canadian courts to small business or variety store robberies, "The range...is usually from one year to six years, where little or no violence is involved in the commission of the offence."[19]

The moral logic that underlies these distinctions between robbery and sexual assault is elusive. We have made some horrible mistakes in our collective judgements about sex offenders. Clifford Olson was probably our worst. A "good talker," and always able to get a parole, Olson was only discovered after more than a dozen murders.

We know that most men who kill for sex are between the ages of 16 and 40, and that their victims are about equally divided between women and children. The men who kill adult women are known to the victim in about 60% of all rape murders; the men who kill children for sex are known to the victim in only 20% of cases.

How should Canada respond to sexual aggression, and to its worst result, the death of the victim? When one compares sentences for robbery, thievery and distributing certain drugs with sentences for rape and sexual assault, one sees an unsettling disparity in the length of imprisonment ordered by the court. There are many circumstances in which the time given for property offences significantly exceeds the time given for the act of sexually penetrating and beating a weaker person.

The prognosis for the treatment of violent sex offenders is unclear. There is no consensus as to which form of treatment or reeducation offers the best hope for change. Those who work in this field are currently trying a number of strategies, using both competing and complementary techniques. For example, there is aversion therapy, learning theory, Freudian analysis, and modification of behaviour through drugs. The ultimate aim is always the same, a significant behaviour change.

But no researchers or clinicians, no matter what theory they espouse, have been able to show that any one method of treatment can systematically reduce sexual aggression. There are success stories, men who abandon sexual assault, but they cannot be explained by the treatment given. Psychologist Vernon Quinsey concludes cautiously, "The most important questions remain unresolved: What is the most effective treatment program for a given type of sex offender? How much does the most effective program actually reduce recidivism?"[20]

Others have been less restrained. Barry Ledwidge, a

psychologist with 23 years experience in treating Canadian sex offenders, writes, "...the social problem is frightening in its pervasiveness and scope, the offender in treatment cannot be believed, there are no reliable methods of assessing sexual deviance, there are no effective methods of treating it, there are no reliable predictors of re-offence."[21]

This is close to the truth about current treatment techniques. Thousands of Canadians are working 40 hours a week in Canada's jails, trying to change behaviour, but they don't really know how successful they are at what they're doing. What they do know is that sex offenders have a relatively low probability of being charged a second time for an act of interpersonal violence; a longitudinal study of convicted males indicates that 23% of the total will face another charge of violence or sexual assault, over a 22-year period.[22]

While this statistic might underestimate the real rate of assault, considering that only a minority of sexual attacks are reported, it also suggests that a significant number of sex offenders make real changes in their behaviour. Unfortunately, however, we have very little idea about what kinds of assistance and what kinds of control prompt these men to stop assaulting women and children.

Killing for sex is, perhaps, the most disturbing and brutal kind of killing. We may not always want to impose a mandatory 25-year term of imprisonment, existing *Criminal Code* provisions notwithstanding. But we need more community control of men convicted of crimes of sexual aggression, more surveillance and support in the "real world," not more surveillance and support behind prison walls. It seems doubtful that we will gain any measure of social safety by punishing these offenders with long jail terms, but we should not underestimate the horror and misery that these men can wreak. We cannot release them to the community without a carefully ordered network of both supervision and support.

The men who kill for sex are often similar to the men who rape and batter, not only in terms of shared demographic characteristics, but also in terms of intent. There are men, like

Harry O'Donnell and Wally Jansen, who do not intend to kill but to beat their victims into submission. The victims die and the men face first degree murder charges. A misplaced blow is the difference between the label of rapist and the label of sex murderer, the difference between two years in prison and 25.

And there are, at least occasionally, men who want to kill, but do not complete the task. I want to conclude this chapter by telling you about Hollis Cooper, a young native Canadian who did not kill for sex, but whose intention was to leave a corpse at the scene of his crime.[23]

Cooper was born on an Indian reserve in northern Canada. He was brought up by his grandparents, "right from the hospital"; neither of his parents was able or willing to care for him. When he was about 13, he started to drink alcohol and smoke marijuana, going to school under the influence of both drugs.

Cooper's life revolved around partying, drinking a lot of alcohol, smoking a lot of marijuana and staying up to the early hours of the next day. When he was about 16, he left his grandparents and went to live with his uncle. "Like, my uncle partied all the time so every time he partied, I'd be right there too. And whenever he goes out to parties he calls me along and says, c'mon.... I guess that's where I started picking up the drinking habit." His life at school was deteriorating, "I got kicked out of school three months before the end of the year...I don't know the specific reason...."

Cooper was sent to an alternative school, but had difficulties there as well. "I lasted two months. I fought in a bus...I really hurt the guy. I broke his nose, knocked out a couple of his teeth and the bus driver had to grab me and pull me away, and that's why I got kicked out. I remember that now."

Cooper's uncle told him that he'd better find another place to live. A couple of months later, at 17, he was kicked out of the house and went to live in a small lean-to in the bush. "So I'm on my own again. I have my own bags. I'd made a little lean-to. I figured I might live out there. It's pretty cold, though, but that's got to do because I wasn't going to stay anywhere else.''

Cooper was wandering at the time of his offence; he was staying with his sister in town, still partying, but without any place to call home. ''My sister made some good soup and told me I'm welcome any time. I didn't feel right to go there and take their food away because they got a family too and they're just living on welfare.''

He and a friend were running out of alcohol and marijuana, and both of them were broke. They turned to break, entry and theft as a solution; they took a rifle and hunting knife from a truck and hoped to sell the goods to a local man to get some money for some beer. ''So anyways we go down to his place and it's getting pretty late. So the guy said, no, he didn't want to buy them because they were too hot.''

Cooper and his friend just threw the rifle away and went downtown. Cooper was carrying the knife in his back pocket. ''I forget who thought about robbing somebody, but both of us were going to do it...a person on the street. We were just going to grab them, beat the hell out of them and take [the] money 'cause we were in a desperate mood.''

But they saw a cab go by and decided that it would be easier to just call a taxi, take the driver out of town and rob him. When the cab arrived, it was being driven by a woman. The two young men got into the car and gave her directions.

A few minutes into the drive Cooper held a knife to the woman's throat, screaming instructions at her. She ultimately stopped the car in a dead end. ''I jumped out of the cab right away and I jumped into the front seat. I'm tearing the front seat apart, like I'm trying to look for the cash. She told me where the money was, so I picked up the wallet, took all the cash out of there...I gave it to my buddy, I told him, 'Hold on to this.' ''

Cooper continues, ''Then she started screaming and she said, 'I thought you weren't going to kill me, I thought you weren't going to kill me,' and I told her, 'Shut up, shut up.' Then it got to a point of where I had to grab her and told her to shut up. Now she's getting even more terrified because I'm grabbing her and I'm shaking her, saying 'Shut up.' Then I guess I told her to take down her pants, which she did. So we ended up raping her.''

Cooper explains the rape, "I'm not sure of what made me do that, but let's see…. No, I can't recall it…maybe it's just that I had a sex drive of screwing any lady that I meet.''

The taxi driver ran from the men as soon as she spotted the possibility of a getaway; she was half-naked but desperate, already the victim of two rapes. But her two young attackers turned around when she was only about 20 feet away. They ran after her, "My buddy's booting off towards her and I'm right behind him. So he grabs her and wrestles her down. At this point I'm still with the knife. I don't know what made me do it. I kind of blanked out there, eh, because this is the first time ever doing this kind of stuff.''

Cooper stabbed the woman at least seven times, "Like I blacked out. My conscience wasn't in control of my body. My mind wasn't in control of my body. My body was doing it by itself, I think, that's the way I figure my action was.''

After the stabbing, Cooper turned the taxi around. Away from the car, his partner was sexually assaulting the driver for a second time; the two men had dragged her off into the bush and were leaving her to die. "So we got in the car and we took off, and we knew the cops were going to be after us.''

Asked if he left the woman thinking she was dead, he responds, "I thought…I thought we did. I didn't have any remorse at that time. The only thing I was…I was thinking about…was the next drink, the next toke. And now that we have money, we're going to have a party. And that's what I was looking forward to.''

Cooper was driving at top speed and his friend was scared, asking to be let out of the car. There was a police car behind them. Cooper stopped quickly, ordered his friend out of the car, and drove off again at top speed.

The police found one of their two rapists standing by the side of the road, and a crime that might develop into first degree murder. The woman was in bad shape; it was not clear that she would survive. Cooper ditched the car and began crawling through the bush, "Crawling in the bush and it's raining like crazy and I'm just crawling away. So I crawled back to the highway and I see a cop car go flying by.... Then I heard the dogs, and I said, 'oh, oh.' "

He managed to evade the search, moving along railroad tracks. "I ran 10 miles on the tracks and I'm beat. I'm still burning. I'm figuring 'What am I going to do now?' First thing, I could go see my girlfriend; maybe she could let me in.' "

When his girlfriend wouldn't let him in, he gave himself up to face charges of robbery, kidnapping, sexual assault, attempted murder, and theft. He avoided conviction for the offence of first degree murder; after extensive surgery and hospitalization, his victim recovered physically. Cooper was convicted of attempted murder and sentenced to life imprisonment; his accomplice was convicted of crimes other than attempted murder, and sentenced to seven years imprisonment.

He claims that he has changed in the few years he has been in jail. "There's quite a bit of difference. Back then when I was 17, I was...a hoodlum, I guess you'd call me. Now a person would consider me a normal person that has a good attitude, has a big heart, pretty well can adjust to everything, adjust to people, realize how people are."

He also says that the memory of the stabbing has always been difficult for him. "Like I remember most of it, but when the stabbing happened...I remember after it happened, that's it. I remember all that, eh. It sends a horrible thought towards me...I just tighten all up. Why did I do that?"

As far as Hollis Cooper is concerned, jail has been more of a help than a hindrance. He may not be granted parole for a good many years but for the present he is not concerned, "I was living one day to the next, trying to survive. Like I had to steal my own clothes, steal my own cigarettes. I didn't have no money, I didn't have anything."

The victim of the crime also "didn't have anything" when she was raped and beaten. Not enough to matter, anyway, just enough to provide her attackers with a few cases of beer and a few nights of partying. She wasn't getting rich by driving a taxi.

A couple of years ago, she went back to work in the same town, driving a taxi again. It's a small northern place with high unemployment, muscle cars, lots of alcohol and other drugs. Resource extraction is the name of the game — hewers of wood and drawers of water, the bounty of the north shipped to the wealth of the south.

Driving taxi again in the wilderness, it seems an appropriate note on which to end this unhappy chapter.

Hats off to you, ma'am. Long may you run.

[1] See Clayton C. Ruby, *Sentencing, Second Edition*, Butterworths, Toronto, 1980, Chapter 19.

[2] W.L. Marshall, "The classification of sexual aggressives and their associated demographic, social developmental and psychological features," in Verdun-Jones and Keltner, *Sexual Aggression and the Law*, Simon Fraser University, Criminology Research Centre, 1983, 10.

[3] "John Borman" is a pseudonym.

[4] See John Evans and Alexander Himelfarb, "Counting Crime," in Rick Linden, *Criminology: A Canadian Perspective*, Holt, Rinehart and Winston, Toronto, 1987, 43-73.

[5] Ministry of the Solicitor General, Canada, *The Canadian Victimization Survey*, 1982, cited in Evans and Himelfarb, note 3, *above*, 66.

[6] Statistics Canada, *Homicide in Canada, 1976-1985: An Historical Perspective* Canadian Centre for Justice Statistics, Ottawa, 1987, 64.

[7] Statistics Canada, *Homicide in Canada: A Statistical Synopsis*, Statistics Canada, Ottawa, 1976, 39.

[8] "R.C.M.P., Division File 56E 681-4, Dated 15-1-57," Gerald Eaton, *Capital Case Files, RG 13 Series*, 1957, National Archives, Ottawa.

[9] *The Vancouver Sun*, April 28, 1956, 2.

[10] "It Was An Urge," *The Ottawa Citizen*, July 17, 1957, 16.

[11] "Leonard Peete" is a pseudonym.

[12] *The Globe and Mail*, November 6, 1935, 1.

[13] "Statement of Harry O'Donnell," Harry O'Donnell, *Capital Case Files, RG 13 Series*, Ottawa, National Archives, April 26, 1936.

[14] RCMP Division File No. 42 J-636-4-1, October 9, 1942," Tom Hutchings, *Capital Case Files, RG 13 Series*, National Archives,

Ottawa, 1-2.

[15] "Wally Jansen" is a pseudonym.

[16] See note 6, *above*, 64.

[17] J.V. Becker, L.J. Skinner and G.G. Abel, "Sequelae of Sexual Assault: The Survivor's Perspective" in J. Greer and I. Stuart, eds., *The Sexual Aggressor; Current Perspectives on Treatment*, Van Nostrand Reinhold, New York, 1983, 240-266.

[18] See, respectively, *R. v. Andrejczuk* (1976), 19 *Criminal Law Quarterly 152* (Manitoba Court of Appeal), and *R. v. Shonias* (1974), 21 C.C.C., (2d) 301 (Ontario Court of Appeal).

[19] See note 1, *above*, 451. See particularly, 423-500.

[20] V. Quinsey, "Prediction of Recidivism and the Evaluation of Treatment Programs for Sex Offenders, in *Sexual Aggression and the Law*, note 2, *above*, 37.

[21] Barry Ledwidge, "The Treatment of Sexual Deviances: Some Observations," *B.C. Psychologist*, Fall, 1987, 42.

[22] K. Soothill *et al.*, "Rape: a 22 year cohort study," *Medical Science and the Law*, 16 (1) (1976). See also K. Christiansen *et al.*, "Recidivism among Sexual Offenders" in K. Christiansen ed., *Scandinavian Studies in Criminology*, Vol. 1, Oslo, 1965.

[23] "Hollis Cooper" is a pseudonym.

Chapter Six

EMOTIONALLY DISTURBED AND MENTALLY HANDICAPPED KILLING

When do we say that a killer is insane? What combination of acts and circumstances do we need before we say that a person is not responsible for his or her actions?

The answer to the first question is simple enough — we do it rarely. Fewer than five per cent of all murders are committed by men or women legally defined as insane.

The answer to the second question is, however, a lot more difficult to find. There is no easy way of determining whether a person is responsible, no sure way of knowing if a person will or should be committed to a mental hospital or to a prison. There is a continuum of emotional and mental disturbance attached to the offence of murder. While there is a sense in which all killings can be seen as the consequence of either emotional disturbance or mental breakdown, there are also some killings that one can only describe as "mad," flirting with the borders of what we call "insanity."

The mental state of the accused is always an issue in cases of culpable homicide. From the early years of the twentieth century to the present, psychiatrists have been providing Canadian courts with information about "diseases of the mind." The issue that both they and the courts have to grapple with is that of diminished responsibility, the extent to which a human being is to be held accountable for the damage that he or she has inflicted.[1]

To be blunt, psychiatrists have not had, and do not now have much concrete information to contribute to this discussion, in large part because the question asked is not medical or scientific, but political, social and cultural. When we transform a killer's emotional trauma or mental handicap into a claim of diminished responsibility, we lessen the evil of his assault. He's not bad; he's just sick, potentially amenable to the treatments or teachings that a hospital or school might prescribe.

This would all be quite acceptable, if psychiatric diagnoses of a propensity for violence were shown to be either reliable or valid, and if being mentally disordered actually made a person either more or less likely to be violent. But psychiatrists are unable to predict future behaviour, unable to consistently separate the "psychopath" from the "disordered personality"and unable to demonstrate corrective success behind prison walls.[2] Yet they are empowered by faith and legislation to impose their treatments on prisoners, sane and insane — and to engage in what are appropriately termed scientific experiments.

With the cases of emotionally disturbed or mentally disordered killers, we confront the frontiers of normalcy: when does a man or woman commit an act of "madness"? I cannot argue, as have Thomas Szasz, R.D. Laing and others, that mental illness is nothing more than mythology or even tantamount to enlightenment.[3] The point that these critics make is well taken; mental illness is, in many senses, only representative of a deviant outlook or approach to life.

But the resulting behaviour still has to be dealt with. In everyday psychiatric practice one finds many people who cannot or will not cope, men and women who display behaviour that is upsetting and difficult to be around. There are also neurological diseases that prompt unpredictable responses in those afflicted. Some of the broader diagnostic categories employed by psychiatrists — schizophrenia, depression and paranoia — have a certain explanatory power. There are also some behaviour problems that respond to a wide range of psychotherapies. And, finally, there are men and women whose debilitating behaviour can be controlled using drug therapy, judiciously applied.

Psychiatrists do not understand any more about violence, however, than do social workers, psychologists, sociologists, lawyers or police. They can administer drugs and shocks, and prescribe various kinds of individual and group therapy, but they have no better understanding of who will be violent and who will remain violent than other informed individuals who are involved in criminal justice. The causes of interpersonal violence cannot be systematically delineated; no professional can really evaluate the mind of a violent offender.[4]

Consider the evaluation of Donnie Armand during the early Seventies at Ontario's Oak Ridge institution, a maximum-security hospital for the criminally insane.[5] Armand was convicted of several violent offences, the most serious being manslaughter. In that instance — a prison riot — he hadn't actually killed a man, but he had been there. His offences were usually the result of lashing out with his fists when drunk.

Armand had been given shock "therapy" at Kingston Penitentiary on seven different occasions, and was beginning to worry about the memory loss that increased with each "treatment." Two of the men he was serving time with were subjected to the same experience, and had committed suicide. On one occasion Armand complained to security about a pain in his chest and was told that it would be taken care of. "Don't you worry, Armand, we'll fix you up." The recipe for recovery was not what medical practice would ordinarily dictate — it was another session of shock treatments.

When he first arrived at Oak Ridge, Armand was placed in a cell, naked, and told that he would have to earn all his privileges. He realized that he could not fight back if he wanted to get out of this place and back to the pentitentiary; he figured that he had to conform.

Now on parole, he recently recalled some of his experiences of psychiatric evaluation, "You play their game, play the patient — they had absolute control; you couldn't take the chance of being locked up in a place like Penetang." On one occasion Armand was subjected to LSD therapy. "They put you in what they call a time capsule, naked, with some other offenders you never met before — all of you naked. And you're given LSD...and they're watching you, from outside the room, through the glass."

Armand's criminal history indicated that he became violent when he was under the influence of alcohol. At Oak Ridge he was given "alcohol treatment," that is, he was asked to drink alcohol, watched, and then provoked. Armand ultimately lost his temper. "That was what you would expect," he laughs, "That was what they wanted to see."

When Armand saw the film *One Flew Over the Cuckoo's Nest* in 1975, he didn't think it was a far-fetched remnant of a less enlightened era at all. Kesey's *Cuckoo's Nest* seemed rather a documentary about the practices of psychiatrists in Canada's correctional system during the late Sixties and early Seventies.

The scientific experiments performed on Donnie Armand and others some 15 years ago are no longer commonplace. Shock therapy is used in more restricted circumstances, and LSD evaluations have been discontinued. But psychiatrists remain involved in experiments — imposing treatments without any demonstration of their social utility. While the psychiatrist is only one of many professionals concerned with the emotional state of violent offenders, he is nonetheless given considerable powers of control and direction — in the absence of any sound evidence of therapeutic abilities. As I suggested earlier, social workers, psychologists, sociologists, police — and even lawyers — understand at least as much about violence as psychiatrists do.

I should note as I begin this chapter that the subject of insanity and its treatment is beyond the scope of this book. I did not attempt to interview men and women found not guilty by reason of insanity. These people are not defined as murderers, and, as the subtitle of this book indicates, my concern here is with murder. This chapter focusses rather on those murderers who seem on the *edges* of that very blurry line between sanity and insanity — the emotionally disturbed and the mentally disordered. I begin by telling you about a killing that leaves us with more questions than answers.

Vince Moro grew up in an armed forces family and led what he describes as a "nomadic military life."[6] As a child he had seen most of western Europe. During a posting back home in Canada during the mid-Seventies, the family began to fall apart. Moro's parents separated and he bounced back and forth between the two houses. Despite this difficulty, he remembers his adolescence as very pleasant. "It was great, you know, I had everything I needed. My parents, even today, like I never went one Christmas without my parents being together. My father came over to stay with us in the house and that, and my parents got along. Me and my brothers still can't understand that. They loved each other, but they stopped loving each other, you know, as husband and wife."

As he headed into his late teens Moro became involved with what he calls "a fast lifestyle." At one point he wound up in hospital after overdosing on alcohol. He wasn't using any injectable drugs: "I loathe people that use needles and stuff like that. It's a very filthy sort of scene." But he was experimenting with a wide range of psychoactive substances: valium, marijuana, cocaine, LSD and psilocybin mushrooms.

Moro's relationships with women were fairly superficial. "I had a few bad relationships. I [wasn't around town enough] to start a relationship with a lady. So I started on strippers. Not prostitutes, more like escorts, you know. And I took a relationship off of that...because it was less frequent, and with the exotic dancers, they were there for a week or two and then they're gone somewhere else. I didn't really have to carry on relationships from there."

It was through a stripper that Moro met the man he would kill. Tom Borden was a middle-aged male who wanted Moro to get him an ounce of cocaine. Borden was having a "social" and wanted to provide his guests with some party stimulants. Moro agreed to provide the drug, an act that was not at all out of character at the time. He had been acting as a courier

— or mule — for a biker club. "I would take packages from point A to point B. I didn't ask what. Anything from non-negotiable bonds and securities to drugs, whatever. The thing I liked about it was, high profit, low risk. They liked me because I was young, clean-cut, dressed well...like I wore jeans and stuff like that, but I pride myself on the way I dress. It's something I like to do. So they got off on it, right. I wasn't your typical [mule], you know."

The drug deal that Vince Moro struck with Tom Borden had Moro "fronting" Borden an ounce of cocaine, valued at about $2500. Borden had 30 days to pay. "So what happened is this month went by and he didn't have the money. So I extended it as well. That's what I was dropping by for."

The meeting between the two men was amicable enough. Moro needed a place to stay, and Borden agreed that he could sleep over, spending the night on his couch. Indeed, it was not the drug deal that would lead to violence between the two men; it was what happened while Moro was asleep that would lead to a killing.

Vince Moro awoke to find his pants down around his knees and Tom Borden's mouth around his penis. Moro recalls, "...the man was giving me head. I knew he was a homosexual. He was married before. I figured he was bisexual. He knew my trip. He knew I was straight, you know."

Moro's first response was to strike Borden with the back of his hand. He then got off the couch, did up his pants and "went after him." Borden took a knife from the kitchen table and Moro picked up a hammer in response. "It sort of snowballed after that. My original intent was, I was mad enough, I would have just hit him and left, you know. But he picked up the knife."

What followed was a lot of yelling and screaming, described by Moro as "verbal confrontation." Then Borden ran out of the living room with Moro after him. "He ran into his bedroom and I just waltzed up behind him. He was jumping on the bed, swinging his knife, screaming things at me. And I reached down and I grabbed the sheets and I pulled. He hit the bed and...I tried to strike him with the hammer. I hit him in the head quite a few times, actually. Seven or eight times. Seven or eight, I don't know.''

Moro then left Borden for dead, only to return a short time later: ''...at that point in time I was...he didn't really exist at that time. At that stage, I don't know. See, that's what I mean. It's weird, I don't really know where my head was at.''

When he came back the first time, Moro broke every bone in Borden's face with his fist. ''It's like, ah, you've got a person with a pistol and you've got to keep shooting it and shooting it, until there's no bullets left. I ran downstairs, and like there was grey matter all over the bed, right, and the smell of the brain cavity, it's hard to experience. It's a smell that's going to stay with me, you know. That smell really disturbs me....''

Moro also stabbed Borden, and slit his throat from ear to ear. When he came back the second time he cut off his penis and testicles and stuffed them in his mouth. ''I knew he was dead when I cut off his genitals...I was pretty sure he was dead, because there was nothing there. No chance of that. I thought, you know, it's like ''dick, suck your own.''

Moro saw some framed pictures of male genitals and some homosexual ''hump books''. ''He wasn't a very flamboyant homosexual. He didn't flaunt the stuff. But I went in there...he had framed pictures of male genitalia, yeah. I smashed those out with my fist. He had stacks and stacks of homosexual pocketbook material. I threw those around the room. I was just...I didn't know when to quit.''

Ultimately he threw up, and left the house, trying to make the crime look like a break and entry. He opened the back door, cut the telephone cable and drove off in the victim's car. ''I had all the time in the world to think of something more logical, right, but with the shock and that, it was just, you know, I was running around like a chicken with my head cut off.''

Moro drove off down the highway on an icy road, smoking hashish and cocaine cigarettes. ''I pull over to a rest stop and I have about 3/4 of an ounce of hashish on me and about two grams of cocaine and...I mix cocaine with the hashish and roll [it into a cigarette]. People say it's a waste, but you know, it counteraffects. Like cocaine is a 15-minute or less thing, depending on how much you use...and the marijuana...counteracts it. It keeps it there a little bit longer. So I roll about five or six of these things and I'm chain smoking these things on the way down.''

He turned on the radio, but all the songs seemed to remind him of the killing; he turned it off. He dropped his joint into his lap and reached down, losing control of the car. It swerved and fishtailed into some trees. He wasn't hurt and the car was only minimally damaged. He got back into the car and drove on towards his destination, a boat that would take him to the city, and a plane that would take him out of the country.

But he was stopped just near the dock at four in the morning. "With all these drugs in me, I'm trying to be evasive a bit. I guess [the police officer] had nothing to do, it was just Sunday, early morning. So he pulled me over and got out and asked me what I was doing. I said, I'm following those guys up there, right. There was some weird Paki, I don't know, who had something in burlap bags, so he figured it was marijuana or something like that, right.''

Moro's plan to distract attention from himself backfired rather quickly. The police officer called in other police cars to check out the man with the burlap bags; he remained with Moro. As Moro recalls, "So there was this poor guy who doesn't know what's going on, he's getting pulled over. He's getting arrested now...I think he had clams or something.'' Moro laughs, "He got arrested for that, too, 'cause he was poaching these things.''

The police officer asked Moro for his vehicle registration, and noticed that things didn't add up. "And he says, who does this car belong to? And I wasn't thinking too clearly at the time, so I said, oh, my uncle. He said, who's your uncle. I gave him my last name and it didn't match, so I blew it, right.''

Moro was then driven to the police station and shortly after police found the body of Tom Borden, he was charged with first degree murder. "So the police officer went in there and he found the body. I heard he quit two months ago. He was just a rookie, eh. It was a pretty gruesome scene. Afterwards, I seen some of the pictures that the police had taken...video, pictures...it just amazed me...after seeing the pictures at pretrial...I felt sick. I nearly threw up. To see that and to think of myself, how could I do that? I don't know. It was me. I realize that. I can't blame it on the drugs. I guess I did want to hurt him, but it...it just snowballed."

In court, Vince Moro pled guilty to second degree murder; he will be eligible for parole in the mid-1990s, 10 years after his date of sentence. Does he think that he'd respond the same way to a sexual advance today? "No. Because I've dealt with that now. Psychologists would have been a lot better before. If I had told someone about the previous incident and dealt with that, maybe this wouldn't have come about. Obviously it wouldn't have. But I didn't...."

The "previous incident" occurred when Moro was 17. He accepted an offer to stay overnight at the home of some men who had picked him up when he was hitchhiking. "They seemed like fairly all right people. Well, we get there and we start drinking a bit, and they slip me a Mickey Finn. I didn't know what was in it, right, but it just knocked me unconscious. I woke up and they sort of, ah...they raped me, more or less. And that was that."

The incident didn't come out at his trial, but Moro still remembers it clearly: "It really hurt me, you know, something like this would happen to me. And there was nothing I could do about it. Like I flew into that bedroom, [after I woke up], and I tried beating all of them. They just punched the shit out of me, tossed me out of the house and threw my stuff out. I was naked, right. And there was semen on me and stuff like that. I felt filthy; I felt really small."

Moro got dressed and flew back to his home. He wanted to tell his girlfriend about being violated, but ultimately felt that he couldn't. "I waited till she got off work, and that, and we drove up to her apartment and I jammed out. That's all. Like maybe it was my actions or maybe something I said."

Vince Moro was a victim of male sexual aggression. This first assault does give some understanding of his later violence.

He feels remorse for his crime. "I'm sorry for my actions; [it] is...his family who lost him, lost his presence. And that's just killing them, you know. Like I know if I lost a family [member]...if I lost my brother, and we're very close, it would just destroy me." And yet the dimensions of this crime continue to be incomprehensible. These acts were overwhelming violations of the boundaries of revenge.

For the present, Vince Moro leads what he calls an "unpredictable" existence in one of Canada's maximum-security penitentiaries. "It's like you never know. And it's not confrontation. I may die here. But I'm willing to accept that. But if someone stabs me who's going to take my life, I surely will do something about it, such as anybody or any animal — let's put it that way. 'Cause we're all, the human species is an animal...and it's just nature, I'd say."

"I wanted to mention something else," he concludes, "It was said by a man by the name of Dr. Johnson...a prisoner...'He who makes a beast of himself gets rid of the pain of being a man'...that really sunk deep with me."

Vince Moro did "make a beast of himself" and is probably still sorting out "the pain of being a man." Is he emotionally disturbed today? Probably not. Was he emotionally disturbed at the time of his crime? Probably, at least if we're using this term, "emotional disturbance" in the sense which attaches to it in the language of popular culture. Revenge in delirium might be another appropriate label.

These possibilities seem at least as useful as the current labels of forensic psychiatry. The doctors with the shocks, the needles and the pills are in many senses the shamans of our tribe. Emotional disturbance and its extreme form, "insanity," are only vague concepts, given content in the context of a mechanism of social control. The person found not guilty by reason of insanity is siphoned off to a hospital and the person found guilty is sent to a prison.

The line between the hospital and the jail is arbitrary; the question of who is "insane" or "emotionally disturbed" is not medical, but social.[7] A recent report from Statistics Canada suggests that about half of all Canadian murderers who are found "insane" have killed members of their family. A further 30% have killed acquaintances. The final 20% of insane killers kill for money, sex or undisclosed reasons.[8] The likelihood of insanity is constant across all the types of killings discussed so far, from killing family to killing for sex. In absolute terms, there are more insane killers of family than insane killers for money or sex, but in relative terms, insanity is just as likely to be a factor in one category of killing as the next.

How do we understand the boundaries of normalcy? What separates a mentally disordered killer from an insane killer? Is the legal issue of whether the accused has the capacity for "appreciating the nature and quality of an act" one that can be decided in Canadian courts, with a reliable measure of validity?

I want to tell you about Dirk Rochester, convicted of second degree murder about seven years ago and now serving a life sentence in maximum security.[9] I use this example, not because a single case can in itself prove that our capacity to judge insanity is flawed, but because this man's crime is symbolic of our problem of definition. I will return later to the question of psychiatric contributions to our understanding of murder.

Dirk Rochester has not coped well with the realities of his life. Born to a poor family in a rural part of eastern Canada, he grew up with physical and sexual abuse. His mother was disabled by a brain tumor and his father was an alcoholic. "My dad molested us first three kids, my two older sisters and me. There was a lot of physical abuse too, but when I think back a bit, mostly on me. I had chairs broken over my back, wine bottles whipped at my head and broken on my back and things like this."

Rochester recalls a couple of sexual incidents involving his father, his sister and himself. "I can remember when I was 11 or 12 thinking, well, it must be great to grow up and have a couple of kids and you can sleep with them. You've got more variety — you've got your wife and you've got your kids. 'Cause I thought it was okay. No one ever told me it was wrong.'' He continues, ''And I can remember, thinking...well, I hope I have lots of girls when I have kids. You know, that's what I considered normal.''

He learned as a teenager in the city that incest was considered to be criminal behaviour, that a father doesn't go to bed with his daughter or his son. ''That really threw me for a spin because the first couple of people I told, they believed me. They didn't do nothing about it. One guy did something about it...he invited me up to his house and tried to do the same thing. So after awhile I couldn't tell anybody. I still had it inside of me. And I couldn't deal with it.''

As a teenager, Rochester began to use illegal drugs. ''For a couple of years I sniffed glue, when I was 13, 14, 15. Then we started doing some acid, and mescaline...hallucinogenics, mostly. I used to love them...your brain was blown for 12 hours. I mean, you're literally seeing walls fall down.'' He was also quite violent on at least a couple of occasions. In one instance he killed his father's dog and in another, smashed all the windows in the family home.

When he was 22, Rochester began to use a lot of alcohol: ''I used to take two [cases of] 24 to a party and I would put one in the fridge like everybody else does, and I would sit on one, 'cause when the fridge was empty, that one was mine....'' He was restricting his use of illegal drugs. ''I'd do a few chemicals so I could stay up and drink something. They'd just keep me awake so I could get drunker. It wasn't for the high or anything any more. It was just to keep my body up; I'd let the alcohol take care of my mind.'' Rochester would phone his father on occasion and scream at him, ''Okay, aren't you proud? I'm just like you, a no-good fucking drunk.''

Rochester's difficulties were well known in the community. Between the ages of 16 and 23 he was placed in a mental hospital on 11 separate occasions. He describes his last admission, three years before he would kill: ''I sat for three days, four days, five days...five days in a full catatonic state. And I was fully aware of everything that was going on and I just shut my mind down...I did not move on my own.''

He continues, ''No one asked me what was going through

my mind those five days. When I was sitting in a chair, pissing myself, sitting in corners, pissing myself. If someone left me in mid-stride...I stood there in mid-stride one day for about 10 minutes. I was ready to fall down, if someone didn't come and move me, because I had only one foot on the ground. But I had to stay there because I was right in the middle of the action, so I knew from the nurses' station they could see me.''

Rochester finally came out of his catatonic state after being provoked by a person at the hospital. "He said something and it just flashed in my mind. I was going to say, 'Dirk's not here.' That started out of my mouth and it got changed and I just said, 'I don't want to talk.' But it started coming out, 'Dirk's not here.'''

There was another development in Dirk Rochester's life, one that he never discussed with the people working in the hospital: "I had this thing for a lot of years, a fixation for murder, for whatever reasons, I don't know what they are. Mass murderers, single murderers, Ted Bundys...all these type of people. And that's what I was being in my mind...And a lot of time when I'd go out and I'd be drunk or whatever, I'd just go out prowling around just looking for somebody to kill...for no reasons other than that I was very demented in my own head."

He recalls one New Year's Eve, about eight years ago, walking around the city at four o'clock in the morning, very drunk. "I was just looking around for somebody to kill and it was just fortunate that I didn't see anybody that night. The people I'd seen...just weren't right."

He explains, "What was right was somebody that was much like me. It was somebody that was so afraid of everything and so scared and you can tell that in people when you encounter them at four o'clock in the morning on the street. You can tell if they're afraid, you can tell if they're scared, you can tell if they're emotionally unstable...and that's what I was looking for."

Rochester's most significant relationship was with a young woman that he lived with for over five years. "I came close to strangling her a couple of times, but I didn't really want to kill her. I did want to hurt her. I know a couple of times I had her by the throat, just squeezing the life out of her. Just coming back, getting into a fight, I'd just grab her by the throat and hold her up off the ground. She only weighed 98 pounds, wet. There wasn't a lot she could do.''

On the night on which he finally did kill, ''everything just clicked.'' Rochester strangled a girl from a party that he was at. ''I can remember going through a field towards the lake and it's like I knew exactly what was going on. I think that's kind of when I clicked in...this is what's going to happen.''

At this point Rochester had consumed over 30 bottles of beer and a jug of wine; he had been drinking at one party in the afternoon and moved on to an evening session. ''So I know I had at least...I had one jug of wine, I had 30-some odd beers in me, I was doing bennies, and I'd smoked a lot of dope. But that was just about the norm, except for the bennies.''

The girl Rochester strangled was 16 years old, unknown to him, and living a life like his own. ''She had been living on the streets for a few years and this and that. She'd had the same kind of sexual abuse at home as my sisters did.''

After the killing, he went home and lay down on his couch. ''I was trying to feel what I was supposed to feel. I was trying to feel that big charge...the ultimate control and all this. That's what all these guys felt in these books, [books about multiple murderers] this great control, the look in the eyes and all these things. But it wasn't there. Nothing was there, the feelings weren't there, none of it was there.''

At the same time Rochester suspects that he would have killed again, if he had not been caught, ''...I wanted it to be so much like in the book...there's no doubt I would have done it again and again, and the next thing you know I would have been another Clifford Olson...thank God for that.''

He was turned in by the woman that he was living with at the time. ''Now [my girlfriend] told me, I came home two or three times...and I told her that I'd just killed somebody. One time I was away for a couple of days and came back and told her I'd just killed somebody. The next day she was cleaning up the back porch...there was a little brown paper bag with holes in it. There's a pair of pants, there's a pair of panties, and there's a bra and there's a sweater, whatever. Whose are these? To this day, I don't think anybody knows how they got there. I know I got nothing to do with it.''

Rochester's girlfriend called the police about the killing, and later he was arrested. He describes the process, ''I left town and went to my lawyer's. Spent the night in a mental institution and the next morning we called the homicide detective on the city police force.''

He was charged with first degree murder, and his lawyer began the case for the defence with a claim of not guilty by reason of insanity. But a plea bargain was struck at trial, so that Rochester then pled guilty to second degree murder. The insanity defence, given the backdrop of incest, alcoholism and ''hunting humans,'' was an effective bargaining chip, but it did not carry the day.

Rochester describes the process of imprisonment for his crime: ''Waking up [in a penitentiary in Eastern Canada], which is a jungle...hey, I'm here for life. Waking up in Kingston Pen saying, wow, this is it for life. I mean, those two things had a lot of shock. I killed somebody and I'm here for life...this is my first sentence. Being in prison is the prison that you see in the movies. It's very...you look the wrong way, say the wrong thing, you can end up on the end of a bar or a knife or something.''

Rochester will not be eligible for parole until the mid-1990s, but says that he has changed over the past few years. ''All of a sudden nobody else is responsible for anything that would happen to me...just me. Dad was no longer responsible, all the things he'd done to me when Mom was sick. I was the only one that decided if I would die in this place, if I would get along or if I didn't get along, if I was respected or I wasn't respected...only me.''

Rochester also indicates that the taking of a life is what troubles him most. ''That's the hardest thing to deal with. I have to deal with myself and I took somebody's life. It's not an easy thing to look in the mirror and say...you couldn't say that and smile. You can't say that and feel good about you. You can't say that and feel anything.''

In the month of June, the anniversary of the date on which he killed, he usually has his greatest difficulty. ''This year was the worst. It took me four days to shake it. Twice I had to leave work; I had to just get up and walk out because I started to cry and this has never happened to me before.''

Rochester has joined a group at the penitentiary in order to promote what he terms ''personal reconciliation, spiritual reconciliation, and societal reconciliation.'' There are a number of prisoners who share a common trait, ''we all had at various times...what I call hunting humans. We went out with the express purpose to kill somebody.''

He continues, ''...we were just hunting humans. I guess because we thought they were the hardest things to hunt, but humans are the easiest things to hunt. Deer and birds and bears are much harder. Humans are easy. Sad to say, but it's true....''

Was Dirk Rochester emotionally disturbed or ''insane'' at the time that he strangled his young victim? The question of who is sane or insane is ultimately answered by a form of drama. The courtroom is a stage on which opposing psychiatrists duel, one implying psychosis and consequent insanity, the other urging simple neurosis and a designation of normalcy.

The case which may best illustrate this point is that of Wayne Rabey, decided by the Supreme Court of Canada in 1980.[10] Rabey was a 20-year-old geology student at the University of Toronto during the mid-Seventies. He was very attracted to another student but saw a letter in which she implied that he and another young man were ''nothings.'' ''I want to be alone or with just one good guy,'' she wrote.

Rabey had gone out with this young woman on a number of occasions and was very upset. He confronted her, asking what she thought of him. When she replied that she considered him a friend, he struck her on the head with a rock and choked her. He told police, ''I did it, I know I did it, I just couldn't stop hitting her. She said something about just as a friend, then I guess I hit her right then on the head, she was bleeding from the head and the next thing I remember it all happened so fast, she was on the floor and I was sitting on top of her choking her. I thought she was dead, there was blood everywhere, I just don't know what happened.''

The woman recovered from her injuries and Rabey was tried on a charge of assault causing bodily harm. The key issue at the trial, the one which propelled this case to the Supreme Court of Canada, was the mental state of the accused. The psychiatrist for the defence argued that Rabey was the victim of a ''severe dissociative state,'' a psychiatric abnormality which usually occurs among ''normal people.'' The contention was that Rabey must be acquitted on the ground of ''non-insane automatism,'' to walk free without treatment or punishment.

The psychiatrist summoned by the prosecution argued that the accused was not in a dissociative state, but that he was a rather controlled young man who went into a rage and struck a young woman who had rejected him. He argued that the accused should receive from six months to a year of psychiatric treatment on an outpatient basis, in order to face up to what he had done. He considered the prognosis for recovery to be ''excellent.''

Dr. Orchard, the psychiatrist for the defence, could not agree, saying, ''I think he has a pretty healthy personality and he will find a healthy way through all this. So I don't see [him] in need of any treatment. I don't see him as sick.''

Both Orchard and Rowsell, the psychiatrist for the prosecution, did agree that ''he is not in any way a criminal type of person.'' An honours student at the University of Toronto, Rabey departed significantly from the normal demographic profile of the habitué of the criminal court; his status made possible his claim of ''non-insane automatism.''

The Supreme Court, by a four to three margin, rejected Rabey's argument and directed a new trial. His acquittal on the ground of non-insane automatism was set aside. But the outcome of the case is less important than what it reveals about forensic psychiatry, a highly debatable medical label has been applied to an essentially social phenomenon.

Psychiatric involvement in Canadian murder cases began in the 1920s. Since the lobby for abolition of capital punishment was also in its early stages, the psychiatrist in capital cases assumed the role of a gatekeeper. After a man or woman had been condemned to death, the state would appoint a psychiatrist to undertake an evaluation of the convict's state of mind. A judgement of "mental disease" could save a man from the gallows; a judgement of sanity could seal his fate.

In the face of increasing public pressure over executions, judges were sharing responsibility for their sentences of death with forensic psychiatrists, those considered to be expert in understanding the mind of the criminal. Defence counsel were also bringing their own psychiatrists to court to claim various kinds of mental and physical abnormality for their clients, to counter the prosecution's claim of normalcy. Insanity can be a coveted status, when the penalty for murder is death.

It was a status coveted by 49-year-old Valentine Schmidt in Regina, back in 1927. Schmidt had emigrated from Russia in 1914 and was working as a blacksmith in the city; he was regarded as a first-class tradesman. In June 1926 his wife took him to court for threatening her. He was convicted and asked to provide $100 as a peace bond, to be held for 12 months. Unable to find any capital, he served three months in the city jail.

Schmidt was a heavy drinker who believed that his wife was cheating on him and that she had tried to poison him. The doctor who attended him found no evidence of poisoning; members of the community noted that Rosie Schmidt, a scrub woman employed at Regina's Parliament buildings, was hard working, pleasant and not "immoral."

When Valentine Schmidt got out of jail, his wife didn't want to have anything more to do with him. He kept asking friends to try to persuade her to take him back, and he also kept up an intensive surveillance of her comings and goings. In December 1926 he was served with a writ seeking a separation agreement and financial support. As the prosecutor suggested at trial, this seemed to annoy him.

Later in the month, Schmidt purchased a shotgun and, on the following day, confronted his wife on the steps of the Parliament buildings. According to the city police report, "Schmidt emerged from behind an automobile and pointed a gun at his wife, saying, 'Rosie, I will shoot you.'"[11] Rosie Schmidt was walking up into the Parliament buildings with two friends to begin an evening of cleaning. All three women were terrified and ran. Schmidt raised his shot gun and blasted his wife in the back, after she had run about 10 to 15 feet.

At trial, Valentine Schmidt was convicted of murder and sentenced to hang; the defence of insanity was not successful, though the jury did recommend mercy. The prosecutor wrote to the government of this recommendation, "In capital cases, you frequently find that some jurymen for some unknown reason are averse to the death sentence. In the present case, the verdict would indicate that possibly one or two jurymen were of this type and as a compromise to them, the jury appended its recommendation of mercy. There is no basis for the recommendation."

The trial judge wrote to the Department of Justice, "I have a suggestion to make which is out of the ordinary and that is, that you have this prisoner examined as to his sanity by a mental expert from outside the province, and then you will have something definite to go upon. If the man was not insane it seems to me that the death penalty should be carried out, as it was a cold-blooded brutal murder. If the man was insane...then he should get the benefit of the law for such persons."

The Ministry of Justice went along with this request, despite its break with existing criminal procedure, and a protest from Schmidt's lawyer. The lawyer argued that there would be no right to cross examine this new evidence and that some five months after the crime, Schmidt's insanity might not be readily apparent to a medical examiner.

But the Ministry of Justice did not agree. It commissioned

"eminent alienist" Dr. Harvey Clare to look into the sanity of the condemned man to second-guess the first diagnosis of normalcy. Clare wrote to the government in June 1927, concluding his memorandum, "I would have no hesitation in certifying that the man is mentally diseased and committing him to an asylum if he came to me as a civilian case for a medical examination." Clare referred to Schmidt's "fixed delusions concerning [his wife's] immorality" and said that he was "the victim of a mental condition due to his environment and habits of living."

The memorandum prepared for Cabinet did not mention the conclusions of Dr. Clare's memorandum, and itself concluded, "After a careful analysis of all of the evidence adduced at the trial, and considering all relevant material now on record, the undersigned is of opinion that the law may well be allowed to take its course."

Two days before Valentine Schmidt was to hang, Dr. Harvey Clare sent a second memorandum to the Acting Minister of Justice. He was changing his opinion on the question of Schmidt's sanity, having been urged to reconsider the weight he was attaching to some of the evidence. He concluded his statement to the government of Mackenzie King, "...one must have very definite information...previous to the commission of the act. As we have not got this, I can only say that he knew what he was doing.... Having found out that I cannot make the letters [documenting his previous mental state]...the foundation of my opinion, I must say that I have not sufficient evidence to show that this man has any mental disease."[12]

With all the key players now onside, Valentine Schmidt's hanging went off without a hitch. It wasn't the first or last time that a person would be hanged, in the face of psychiatric debate about insanity. What made Schmidt's case unusual was the government's apparent manipulation of the psychiatrist's initial judgement of the condemned man. The Ministry of Justice had gone along with the trial judge's irregular request for a second psychiatric examination on the question of sanity. But when the eminent Dr. Harvey Clare suggested that he would have had the man civilly committed, irrespective of his criminal record, the government recoiled. Dr. Clare was asked to reconsider his diagnosis and Valentine Schmidt was ultimately dropped to his death.

There is a sense in which the forensic psychiatrist was a pawn in this game of power, albeit a very privileged pawn. The federal Cabinet was the court of last resort on mental disorder in murder cases, commuting if treatment was thought possible and ordering execution if the medical men were not as optimistic. The psychiatrist was a strategic ally, one who could share responsibility for the execution, or alternatively, for commutation. And psychiatrists were not always pawns or allies. In the last years of capital punishment they often argued for the lives of condemned men, committing themselves to a commutation of sentence that was not always granted.

The minutes of federal Cabinet meetings from 1959 to 1962 reveal that the Diefenbaker government's relationship with psychiatry was one of strategic accommodation, using the various notions of the developing profession to suit political ends. The Cabinet was deeply divided on capital punishment during the Diefenbaker years, and the doctor who could offer a positive prognosis for treatment was often looked to for advice.

Consider, for example, the case of John Vollman. On February 12, 1959, the Cabinet met to consider the case of this 20-year-old American who had killed in pursuit of sex, and been labelled a sexual psychopath. Vollman had been discharged from the U.S. Air Force and was living in Madawaska, Maine, just below the New Brunswick border, at the time of the offence.[13]

He had stabbed a local 16-year-old girl to death in a gravel pit near Edmunston, New Brunswick. The Cabinet minutes explain that Vollman "was subject to overpowering sexual desires when with women." He had apparently attacked other women, and had sought treatment for his behaviour. A psychiatrist from New Brunswick argued that "people of Vollman's type [are] usually driven harder by primitive drives than the average individual."

But the Cabinet could not agree on a solution for Vollman's case. Those arguing for commutation said that the jury's recommendation for mercy should be given great weight, and noted that Vollman had made an effort to obtain treatment, but "society had done nothing about him."

Those arguing for execution said that the man had been judged sane and that it was a "clear case of murder." Further, they said, "even with the special treatment given to sexual psychopaths, there was the chance that, if his sentence were commuted, [he] would be free again in 12 or 15 years time and would commit another serious offence."

On February 13, the Cabinet met again to try to resolve the deadlock of the previous day. The Solicitor General reported that the Parole Board would be looking into procedures for dealing with sexual psychopaths. Again, the meeting ended without resolution, neither side willing to bend.

On February 14, the argument resumed. Two members of Cabinet announced that they had changed their opinions overnight and several others indicated that they were prepared to accept a position contrary to their own views. The crisis was over, but the arguments went on, revealing an almost even split on the issue. At the end of the day, a slim majority vote for commutation emerged and John Vollman was sent to prison.

There was no special treatment for sexual psychopaths, no good evidence in male biology of "overwhelming sexual desires," and no formula that could guarantee the future safety of the community. But the court's dependence on psychiatric understanding of violence persisted and persists today. Forensic psychiatrists have always been as likely to engage in perpetuating cultural beliefs as they have been to reliably help the deviant.

The category we have discussed, of the emotionally disturbed or "insane" killer, has some meaning, nonetheless. But it is ultimately no more profound than the meaning conveyed by the language of popular culture. Words like "emotionally disturbed," "mentally disordered," "bizarre," "weird," "crazy" and even "nutty" can capture the essence of these

crimes as well or better than words like "sane" or "insane."
I am going to relate three killings that make this point in differ-
ent ways, beginning in 1936 with A. W. Bannister and New
Brunswick's Doll Baby murders.

Arthur William Bannister was a 19-year-old man living in
rural New Brunswick with his mother, brother and two sisters. He had a Grade Five education and earned his living by
working occasionally as a lumberjack. His mother, 43-year-
old May Bannister, was a widow, described by one observer
as "heavy set, ignorant [and] rather primitive."

In the fall of 1935 May Bannister was blackmailing two local
men, a neighbour by the name of Milton Trite and a Salvation Army officer by the name of Albert Powell. Mrs. Bannister had had sexual relations with both Trite and Powell and
told both of them that she was pregnant and would need "hush
money."

Both men, unknown to each other, had paid Bannister the
required hush money. By December of that year they were
both becoming curious about their new baby. It was a difficult
time for May Bannister; she had not become pregnant at all,
but needed to produce a baby in order to justify her ongoing
blackmail.

For a month or so, she used a plastic doll, bundling it in
baby's clothing. But she knew that her blackmail money was
in jeopardy if either of her lovers were to get a close look at
the contents of her baby carriage. Her sons, Arthur and
Daniel, tried to help their mother out by approaching a local
man named Philip Lake and attempting to purchase his newborn daughter.

Lake laughingly related this request to a fellow trapper,
amused by the thought that he and his wife would be willing
to sell their baby to the Bannister family. In early January
1936, unable to purchase the product that they wanted, the
Bannister boys moved to abduct young Betty Lake, the only
newborn child in the area. They apparently decided that if
they couldn't buy a child for their mother they would have
to steal one.

The Lake cabin was a few miles from the Bannister home;

Lake and his wife lived there with their two young children, aged 18 months and four months respectively. The RCMP report said of the Lakes, "They were a well-respected and popular family — living in harmony with all — Lake was known for his quiet disposition."[14]

Arthur Bannister walked over to the Lake cabin with his older brother Daniel and his 15-year-old sister Frances; he carried a rifle. It was January in rural New Brunswick, with deep snow and temperatures well below freezing. When the trio arrived at the cabin door, Frances and Daniel waited outside while Arthur went in to get the baby for his mother. Frances Bannister noted at trial that she then heard a shot, followed by Arthur running out of the cabin with the baby, handing it to her and telling her to take it home.

Bannister had shot 32-year-old Philip Lake in the head while he lay in bed; he then went back into the house, after giving the baby to his sister, and struck Lake's wife Bertha with a club. The woman fled into the sub-zero temperatures, and was clubbed again some 70 feet from the cabin, the force of the blow crushing her skull.

As Frances Bannister walked back home with her mother's new baby, Arthur Bannister took one small step towards covering his tracks. He poured the contents of an oil lamp onto the floor of the Lake cabin and set the liquid on fire. Arthur and Daniel Bannister then caught up with their sister and the three continued their long walk back home, across the frozen landscape. They heard a dog barking, and fearing that they might be seen, headed off the road into the woods. Arthur handed his rifle to brother Daniel and took baby Betty from his sister. Frances recalled at trial that as the three of them walked through the snow, they could hear the dying screams of Bertha Lake and see the bright light of the burning cabin from more than a mile away.

A local trapper discovered the bodies early the following day. In the smouldering ruins of the Lake home he noticed a body, with the legs and arms burnt off and the remaining torso badly charred. About 70 feet from the house was the naked body of Lake's wife, frozen in the January night. A little closer to the house was the frozen body of 18-month-old Jackie Lake. The little boy had not been assaulted, but left by the Bannisters to fend for himself in the bitter cold.

It was not difficult for the police to put this gruesome jig-saw puzzle together. They found four-month-old Betty Lake with Mrs. Bannister and charged her with kidnapping. Further investigation turned up Arthur Bannister's rifle, and ballistics tests matched the fatal bullet with the gun. Frances Bannister agreed to give testimony at trial, and all charges against her were ultimately dropped.

Many people in rural New Brunswick travelled great distances to Dorchester to attend the trial, making their way through the deep snow by horse-drawn sleigh. The case also aroused interest in the New York city newspapers, one journalist referring to it as "the weird doll baby murder." The same story described Arthur as "stolid and dull, ceaselessly toying with his teeth with a stubby forefinger." While the jury was being selected, he apparently sat in the prisoner's dock, giggling and sucking his thumb. And when his lawyer raised his voice during his final address to the jury, Arthur appeared frightened and sucked his thumb furiously. New York's *Sunday Mirror* magazine concluded of the case, "Strangely suited to that gaunt country was this amazing crime."[15]

Frances Bannister's testimony established the guilt of the accused beyond any reasonable doubt. Daniel Bannister had also been charged with murder and was convicted in a separate trial. Arthur smiled broadly when found guilty. Sentenced to death, he said only, "It could have gone either way." The memorandum prepared for the Minister of Justice regarding commutation was not favourable to either Arthur or Daniel Bannister, in spite of the jury's recommendation for mercy in Daniel's case. The memorandum quoted approvingly from the trial judge, "The crime for which they were convicted was a brutal and callous one.... It was fully established at both trials that the abduction of the baby was the motive behind the crime...I cannot conscientiously join with the jury in their recommendation for the exercise of the Royal Prerogative [in the case of Daniel Bannister]''.

The memorandum to Cabinet made no mention of either Arthur or Daniel Bannister's mental state, simply concluding, ''Upon consideration of the facts of this case, the undersigned is of opinion that the law may well be allowed to take its course.'' On September 23, 1936, Arthur and Daniel Bannister were hanged. The crime, its motive and its perpetrators, continue to seem, as the *Sunday Mirror* suggested at the time, ''weird — the work of primitives.''

The Bannister case points to the difficulties in determining responsibility for killing. When do we say that a killer is either emotionally disturbed or mentally handicapped? Arthur Bannister had only a Grade Five eduation, but he was not suffering from any neurological disorder. There is a sense in which this killing can be seen as one committed by a mentally disordered or emotionally disturbed offender. Yet these terms are more the product of social negotiation over time than the consequence of readily identifiable individual pathology. There can be no static and enduring sense of what it means to be insane, mentally disordered or emotionally disturbed.

And yet mental handicaps or disabilities do exist and are quite distinct from mental disorders. Disabilities can often be traced to the effects of genetic accidents, such as Downs' syndrome, or brain injury. The most recognized measure of human intelligence, the Stanford-Binet test, was first developed in the 1890s by French psychologist Alfred Binet. The test provides a numerical measure of intelligence quotient or I.Q. by assessing a person's grasp of vocabulary, comprehension of relationships between words, numbers and pictures, and by posing problems to be solved or rules to be interpreted and applied.

By the standards of the Stanford-Binet test, Mickey Feener was a ''moron.'' Feener, like Arthur Bannister, had less than a grade school education. And like Bannister, he grew up in a disadvantaged environment on the east coast of Canada. His I.Q. was calculated once as 64 and on another occasion as 69; these numbers were said by psychiatrists and psychologists of the day to conform to the intellectual range of the "moron."

Mickey (Owen) Feener was born in Bridgewater, Nova Scotia, in 1937. His father was an alcoholic and his parents separated when he was eight. Neither parent wanted or could be responsible for him. He was boarded at one home for about a year and then sent to another for three years. Both of the women caring for him in these homes had difficulties with him and he was ridiculed at school — "an easy target for the pranks of other children." When he was 11, he was sent to the Nova Scotia Training School near Truro. He was committed as a mentally retarded boy under the province's Children's Protection Act. The report prepared by the Children's Aid Society at this time noted, "Owen is commonly called "Mikey" and apparently likes to be called this. He has an amenable and affectionate disposition. He likes to sit in his foster mother's lap and be treated as a much younger child would be."

When he left the Truro Training School, Mickey Feener was 16. His teacher recalled that he never progressed beyond Grade Three and had a habit of taking things that did not belong to him. He was advised to remain in the institution until he was 16 because his mother did not have any room for him. He desperately wanted to be with her, and when she decided to get married again, he became very unhappy. At the time that Feener left the school he was lonesome and miserable. He had run away from the institution several times and on one occasion started to cry when told that he had to leave his mother and go back. A 16-year-old boy from the training school, he was left to fend for himself in the city, too much for his mother to deal with.

Before long he drifted into conflict with the criminal law, again by taking things that didn't belong to him. He was convicted in Bridgewater, Nova Scotia, of the theft of a rifle and hunting knife and sentenced to three months in jail. A couple of years later in eastern Ontario, he was convicted of two car thefts and sentenced to a year in the Guelph Reformatory.

The report from Guelph noted that Feener was subject to

epileptic seizures, said to be the possible result of a gunshot wound that he had suffered when he was eight. He had apparently been accidentally shot in the head and was hospitalized for three months.

When Mickey Feener got out of the Guelph reformatory in 1956, he bought himself a car. He was sent money for the train fare home to Nova Scotia but decided upon his own means of transportation. He didn't get a driver's license until 1959, because he was afraid that he would fail the test. He worked as a hard rock miner in the western United States, in western Canada and the Yukon. In 1957 he married a young woman from Halifax and had a child. She was also socially disadvantaged, and had been in and out of jail. The marriage lasted a little less than two years.

The couple was living in Kirkland Lake in late 1959 when Feener decided to leave town. He quit work at the mine and bought a convertible, in which he and his wife and child went to Nova Scotia. While there, he apparently had an affair with his wife's sister. "My wife accused me of shacking up with her sister. I tried to explain, but no good. That's when our marriage broke up. I then accepted her sister.... Well, that didn't last either — well, my wife wanted me back but from then on she got herself in one mess after another. Yes — other men. I then left her for good."[16]

Feener described his marriage in an interview with psychiatrist J.P.S. Cathcart, "Well, we split up — just cats and dogs — one of us just as bad as the other — but she ran out on me while I was on night shift." He continued to drift about the country, first back to Toronto, and later, up to northern Ontario.

In late August of 1960, he was working on a relationship with a 34-year-old Toronto woman named Cathie Essars. Feener later told the RCMP that he knew Essars from Halifax, specifically, from a bar in the Acadia Hotel. Feener and Essars apparently decided to take a trip through the United States together in Essars' red sports car, stopping in Cleveland, Toledo and Detroit and going to bars and dances. They had a fight on the way back and Feener rented his own car in Windsor to drive to Toronto. He followed Essars to Toronto, but then went on to Montreal. On arrival, he left the rented car parked in the street and took the train back to Toronto.

In late September Essars and Feener set out again in her sports car, this time for New Glasgow, Nova Scotia, the city to which Ms. Essars had emigrated from Belgium some two years before. Feener told police that they signed into a Fredericton hotel as man and wife. "When I came back from paying the bill she had a drink poured for me. We drank several drinks; after that I had intercourse with her. After that we drank heavy and she started to act funny and said, let's be on our way to Nova Scotia."

The next day, on the road, Essars and Feener apparently got into another argument over whether Essars could drive her car. Feener told police, "[she] wanted to drive and I didn't want to let her. She hit me over the head with a full bottle of beer. I was out like a light, almost. I stopped the car and grabbed her by the throat and almost before I realized it, she was dead."[17]

Feener threw Essars' body over a bank and into a roadside ditch. He took her cash from her purse and her electric iron from her suitcase and drove on to Nova Scotia. Two weeks later he was back up in Kirkland Lake, when he was noticed by city detective Ozzie Wright. Wright knew nothing of Essars' death but he recognized the blond young man with the stubbled beard. Mickey Feener wasn't easily missed. He was six feet tall and over 200 pounds. Moreover, Detective Wright knew that he had skipped out of town a year before on a reckless driving charge.

Feener was driving the red sports car, with "Mickey" now spelled out in adhesive tape across its hood. Taped to the dash of the Austin Healey were the photos of eight young women, one of whom was Cathie Essars. Feener dug into his pocket to find money for the reckless driving offence, all the while smiling and telling the officer that he had a good memory for an offence now a year old. The detective was curious about the car, however, and about Feener generally. He asked him to come to police headquarters and Feener obliged.[18]

The Kirkland Lake police then got in touch with the New Glasgow police in order to find out more about the registration of the red sports car, and its owner, Cathie Essars. Feener had told them that she was a former girlfriend who had simply given him her car. New Glasgow police told the Kirkland Lake detachment that Essars had been found dead and asked them to hold Feener in custody.

What neither force knew was that Feener had been out on a date with another young woman from Timmins just a couple of nights before he was arrested. Her picture was also taped to the dash of his newly acquired sports car. Kay Chouinor, a housekeeper for a city surgeon, had been reported missing the day before Detective Wright encountered Feener in Kirkland Lake.

Timmins police decided that they would drive down to Kirkland Lake to talk to Feener; he might know something about Ms. Chouinor's disappearance. He immediately admitted to them that he knew the young woman, saying, "She gave me her picture — See?"

Feener told police that he had been out on a date with Kay Chouinor. As her employers would later confirm, she had gone out with him on at least a couple of occasions over the past year. Feener told Chief Beacock and his detective that he had dropped Chouinor off near a bus stop, quite alive. But, Beacock noted, Feener was in possession of her ring and her watch and kept referring to her in the past tense. More to the point, the officer noted, it seemed likely that Feener was responsible for her disappearance.

"You think I killed her, don't you," Feener is reported to have said.

"Yes, I do," responded Chief Beacock.

"Okay, I will show you where she is."

A statement was then taken from Feener at the Kirkland Lake police station. He had been telling Kay Chouinor about "the other girl I killed," when she became scared. She tried to get out of the car but he grabbed her and told her to "hear me out." They were still sitting in the red sports car when Feener struck, "I hit her three times on the back of the head with my flashlight and she passed out. We were still sitting in the car...when she came to. I then took a hunting knife and struck her on the back of the neck. I don't know how many times."

She told him that she was not afraid to die and asked, "Why, Mickey?"

He didn't answer, but drove her, dying, some 20 miles out of town in order to dispose of her body. When taking her out of the car he realized that she still wasn't dead and threw her against a bank three times. The force of the blows broke her hip and blood splattered all over Feener's suit.

He left her out in the country. "It was an awful sight. I got stuck with my car and I cried. I pushed it to the road and drove to Kirkland Lake. My suit was full of blood and I burned it. I don't remember where I was when I burned it."

Asked to explain why he killed Kay Chouinor, he told police on the night that he was arrested, "Not for her money, or sex, but because of the other thing. My nerves were shot. I didn't plan it."

Feener's arrest for Kay Chouinor's killing inflamed the communities of Timmins and Kirkland Lake. Here was a man, apparently responsible for the brutal killings of two young women, who would shake his fist at an angered crowd of 1,000 outside the Timmins jail, a group of citizens gathered there to condemn the man local newspapers had described as a monster.

Feener's dress and demeanour in court were no more endearing. His gray pants were tucked into high-heeled boots and his striped shirt was open almost to his waist, a gold cross hanging from a chain around his neck — another boy for Jesus. His sleeves were rolled up to his elbows and one observer noted "the ghost of a smile [that] lurked beneath a three-day growth of blond beard."

Feener was ultimately represented by Toronto lawyer Hugh Latimer; local lawyers all refused to take the case. When he was committed to trial, he was without legal representation. *The Toronto Telegram* reported that at the preliminary hearing, "Feener shambled to his feet after each Crown witness testified and was asked if he wished to cross-examine. The first time he didn't appear to understand the question. The other times he said 'No' and sat down. He laughed softly, then covered his head with his one unshackled hand during much of the police evidence.''

A month after his arrest, he was still without legal representation. When Hugh Latimer arrived in Timmins, willing to represent this "monster," he must not have been very welcome. Latimer immediately went to work for his client, seeking a change of venue from northern Ontario to Toronto, on the ground that a fair trial could be prejudiced by local feelings, and more specifically, by published reports in the *Timmins Press* and the *Kirkland Lake Northern Daily News*. The court agreed that the newspaper reports were in contempt and that the two culprits should be proceeded against, but declined to move the trial from Cochrane. In return, the prosecutor gave an assurance that jurors from the Timmins area would not be called when this case went to trial.

Latimer's defence of Feener was thorough and consistent, emphasizing the socially and mentally impoverished life that Feener had led. He told the court, "My client had no motive when he killed this girl of high moral standards. Not sex. Not money. I say the hand that struck the blow was not ruled by the brain at all." The prosecutor agreed that Feener was socially disadvantaged, but added, "He is not an imbecile and he is not an idiot."

The jury returned with a verdict of guilty in only 15 minutes and the struggle to save Feener from hanging began. Latimer's letter to Solicitor-General W.J. Browne noted that psychiatrists had been rather uncertain about their diagnoses of Feener's behaviour. Two doctors from the North Bay Mental Hospital prepared reports for the prosecution prior to trial. Dr. Schwarzl had concluded, "...this man was in an epileptic twilight state at the time of his crime. An epileptic twilight state is a temporary insanity which clears up after some time but has a tendency to recur. My reasons for this diagnosis are...Mr. Feener has been an epileptic for many years, the dreamlike state of his mind...the explosive outburst of blind destructive aggressiveness, the loss of consciousness, and the consequent well circumscribed amnesia for a considerable part of the event.''

W. H. Weber agreed, writing, ''...this epileptic, after consuming considerable alcohol and while in company with a woman companion apparently developed a seizure and during this state assaulted his companion, resulting in her death. This examination did not reveal any premeditated intent, no evidence of sexual assault. Mr. Feener is showing remorse and apprehension regarding his situation and was most cooperative throughout.''

When in court, both doctors Schwarzl and Weber reversed their written diagnoses, apparently on the ground that they had been misled by Mickey Feener. It was — and is — difficult to reconcile their actions with their words. They were either duped by a 23-year-old ''moron'' with a Grade Three education or lacked confidence in their own ability to diagnose. In retrospect, some truth could probably be found in both of these explanations.

Latimer continued his fight for Feener's life, placing evidence of Feener's early childhood and institutional life before the government, and detailing the difficulties he had encountered in conducting a fully adequate defence without access to witnesses from Nova Scotia. He concluded his plea for clemency, ''My one concern in this matter is that an injustice should not be done to a young man, who through an accident of birth was not equipped, mentally and emotionally, to properly look after himself.''

One other piece of information that the government had before it concerned a missing person by the name of Dolly Woods. She was a 17-year-old waitress and her picture was among the eight taped to the dash of Feener's red sports car. She had disappeared from Kirkland Lake in April 1959.

The Cabinet met on June 8, 1961, to consider the possibility of a commutation. They were told of the circumstances of Kay Chouinor's murder and Cathie Essars' disappearance. They were told that Feener was a ''high level moron,'' but was not considered to be insane. And they were told that the

Kirkland Lake Chief of Police considered Feener to be guilty of the murder of Dolly Woods, a killing committed over a year before the deaths of Chouinor and Essars.

Some members of Cabinet said that the sentence should be commuted, that the behaviour of Feener was "that of an insane man...he should remain in an institution for the rest of his natural life." Others noted that the new capital murder legislation, just about to be passed into law, would not apply to Feener's case.[19] The Cabinet minutes note, "...it had not been planned and deliberate. He had killed Miss Chouinor because he became rattled after telling her of his earlier crime. The method of killing Miss Chouinor was also far from rational."

But the majority of the Diefenbaker Cabinet argued that Mickey Feener should be executed. They noted that the accused "had been sane enough to travel widely about eastern Canada and the United States and attract many young women." The murder of Miss Chouinor had involved a number of separate attacks and "he had also been sufficiently self-possessed to conceal the body."

On June 10, the Cabinet met again to consider the execution of Mickey Feener. The Governor-General, Georges Vanier, had been told of the Cabinet's decision to proceed with Feener's execution and he expressed concern. The Governor-General argued that the crime did not seem to be covered by the definition of capital murder proposed by the government given that it was not planned and deliberate. Further, he suggested, "it appeared that Feener was a moron and could hardly be regarded as normally responsible for his actions."

But the Governor-General's intervention did not move the majority of the Cabinet. They argued that the issues raised by Vanier had already been canvassed; the law would be allowed to take its course.

On June 12, 1961, Mickey Feener ordered a last supper in the Haileybury Jail. The menu was specifically prepared for his tastes — steak, French fries and ice cream — and he ate "every scrap." He had asked earlier in the evening that his eyes be given to an eye bank, saying, "I hope the poor devil who gets them trains himself to look at something besides skirts during the course of his life."

About an hour before he was to hang, Feener called Sheriff F.J. Donohue to his cell. He believed that he was going to "roast in Hell" and wanted to do so with a clear conscience. He confessed to the murder of Dolly Woods, back in April 1959, making the following statement: "I went out with Dolly Woods...while my wife was in hospital. We went driving, left Kirkland Lake at midnight and went down the highway to the Quebec border...I don't know the exact location of her body. It happened at daybreak and I got mad and choked her. I covered the body with brush."

A little after one a.m., Mickey Feener was hanged in the courtyard of the Haileybury Jail. When asked if he had any last words, he told those present that Nova Scotia men were not afraid to die. Feener left behind the eight photos on the dash of Cathie Essars' red sports car. Three were dead, but the story of the five other young women remains unanswered. According to one story, the photographs were not identified in any way, and in the days after Feener's arrest, police from across the country were unable to turn up any evidence of who these women were.

Superintendent Ken Stevens of the Timmins police force, an investigating officer in the case and the one who first pushed Chief Beacock to interview Feener, doesn't recall the five missing photos. He does remember, however, that Feener claimed, after his conviction, to have killed a number of other women in Toronto — pushing one off a viaduct, and strangling another. Police found it difficult to dissect truth from reality in these instances, unsure whether Feener was simply trying to delay his execution or actually helping police to clear missing persons cases. Some 27 years after the fact, Stevens figures that Feener probably did kill many more than three women, "but where and when, I don't know."[20]

And yet Mickey Feener's case is about more than the chillng reality of serial murder. It is included in this chapter, not because of the viciousness over a period of years that it reveals, but because of the many claims that Feener was either a "moron," "emotionally disturbed," or "insane."

Mickey Feener's intelligence quotient, calculated as falling between 60 and 70, placed him in a subnormal category, described in 1961 as the range of a "high-level moron." And yet Feener was neither incapable of making his way economically, nor incapable of attracting normal young women to his side, women who, in some instances, were willing to have sexual relations with him.

An intelligence quotient is a measure of certain verbal, mathematical and logical abilities. But it has little, if anything, to say about a person's social skills. There are those who believe that an I.Q. test is some kind of sensitive "probe," a tool possessing significant social utility.[21] But, for the most part, the social good that comes from such tests is very minimal and the reliability of the measurement is offset by the limited range of human experience that an I.Q. score can actually make sense of.

Mickey Feener had a kind of intelligence that I.Q. scores of 64 and 69 could not make sense of. Like Arthur Bannister — and most people who kill — he was raised in an environment that was both socially and economically impoverished. Was he "insane," or "emotionally disturbed"? As I have suggested earlier in this chapter, these are words that don't have much scientific or social value. We can be just as accurate, insofar as the dictates of science are concerned, in claiming that Mickey Feener was "strange," a young man with minimal verbal and mathematical skills, rejected by his parents and raised by the state.

The third man in this trilogy of Canadian murderers is John Murphy, now serving a life sentence for a killing in 1982.[22] Murphy was raised by his adoptive parents in Ontario and when he was about 10, he was told that he was not their natural son. He recalls the experience, "I think that was the start really, when I started really separating myself from my family in terms of not sharing things which I wanted to share, while I was reaching the age of puberty and whatnot."

He left high school and enrolled in a community college

course, but ultimately failed one term. He then travelled out west to a job with a civil engineering firm, doing work related to his education. It was the early Eighties and the recession was just beginning. Murphy recalls "...I learned that my job would probably end soon because there was a shortage of work. I was feeling guilty that I couldn't pay my parents back for college. And I was really down on myself...I quit work before they could lay me off..."

Murphy was alone in the city, without any money, and finally, without even a place to stay. He was sleeping in shelters for transients, experiencing both hunger and exhaustion. He was also becoming committed to Satan. "I'd made a conscious commitment to serve Satan about two or three weeks before the incident. And I changed my mind and then I went back and I decided that I wanted to serve him again...I wanted to do evil. That's basically it. I felt a lot of hatred towards society in general and I expended my hatred on this poor individual."

Murphy had been interested in Christianity when he was a teenager, "I finally asked Jesus in my life when I was 16 and that's the point where I actually knew there was a Satan, you know. I felt it. Once you know good, you can see evil...when I got rheumatoid arthritis, like I asked God and I prayed to God and Jesus, just to get rid of it. That didn't seem to happen, it seemed to get worse. So finally I came to the point where I said, I believe you can do it, God, but you don't want to, so I'm not going to follow you." The flip side of Murphy's Christianity was Satanism.

Three months after moving out west, Murphy committed his first and only crime. He broke into a house late at night, and "...before I went in, I was actually considering what if I met someone...I wasn't planning to kill anybody. I sort of said, that wouldn't be too bad, you know, 'cause I could do more evil if there was somebody in the house. That's kind of strange thinking, every time I look back."

Murphy walked into the bedroom of the house, armed with a knife, and found a husband and wife in bed. The woman started screaming, and Murphy told her to shut up, taking a step towards her, his knife out. The husband came after Murphy. "He was stabbed in his bedroom...I don't believe what the court said, it said about 15 times I think. But I think it was only eight.... My thinking was very...strong. It's like, it only took 20 seconds and it's lasted a lifetime, you know. I wasn't on any drugs, hadn't been smoking cigarettes. But I can still remember what happened in that 20 seconds fairly well. It's a vivid memory with me."

After a few nights of sleeping in shelters for transients, Murphy turned himself in to police. He was charged with and convicted of second degree murder; he will be eligible for parole just a couple of years before the turn of the century.

About a year after his conviction, Murphy renewed his relationship with God and Jesus: "By the way, I'm a Christian now. He came into my life about three years ago and I haven't been happier since. I was a Christian once and I turned my back on Him and I've been given a second chance and I know Jesus again. I love it. It gives me great peace of mind to know I've been forgiven for all my sins." His view of the future is similarly imbued, "If it's His will that I get out one day I'll accept that...and if it's not His will, if I'm to remain in prison for the rest of my natural life, that's fine with me. I feel a great sense of freedom."

What should we do about those who might be classified as "emotionally disturbed" or "insane" killers? Should we continue to draw a legal line between those who are "normal" and those who are not? We will probably always make social distinctions between a "normal" kind of murder and a very unusual murder — that is the point of this chapter. But should our law continue to convict some men as murderers and say that others are not responsible for their crime, by reason of insanity?

The best answer to this question is probably not. As real as emotional disturbance may be, the labels "sane" and "insane" do not offer us any greater understanding of killers and their killings. And by abandoning the notion of insanity we would not be abandoning our commitment to treat those who want or need psychiatric or psychological assistance. We would simply avoid our present difficulty of imposing different sentences for similar offences. Without a demonstrable reliability and validity, "insanity" remains as much of a theoretical construct in 1988 as it was in 1920. Unequal treatment, including a different release procedure for the sane and the insane, is difficult to justify.

I conclude this chapter and this book with the case of a woman who might be said to have been emotionally disturbed at the time that she killed. Women who are deprived of their liberty for murder are about three times more likely than men to be declared legally insane. The best empirical evidence available indicates that while about five per cent of all males charged with murder will be found not guilty by reason of insanity, about 15% of females who kill will be found insane.[23]

This differential treatment does not necessarily mean that women who kill are more likely to be "incapable of appreciating the nature and quality" of their violence, the decisions of Canadian courts notwithstanding. Rather, this differential treatment may suggest only that the violence of women is more likely to be understood, classified and controlled as a medical problem. Given the dictates of male chivalry — and condescension — the woman who kills is said to be more "sick" than evil, more in need of treatment than punishment.

Sally Bolton was not found legally insane, but was treated by psychiatrists for many years.[24] She grew up on the West Coast, and recalls her early years in a positive light, "My childhood was quite pleasant. I was very athletic and won sports awards, shooting medals and over 500 riding awards."

She married after graduating from high school. "[I] was happy for a time until I found out that my husband was a master at mental cruelty. I stuck it out for nine years, but the marriage was never happy enough to bring a child into. Then I left."

After a short stint in business, she enrolled in nursing school. "I was the top student in the class. Unfortunately, near the end of the first year I developed minor urological problems. I went in for a simple test called a cystoscopy...and the urologist then performed an unwanted and unnecessary operation, after which I almost bled to death over the next two days.''

Bolton recalls that blood transfusions and emergency surgery saved her life, but argues that she was never the same mentally. She managed to finish her first year of nursing school and went home for a month before second year began, "Then one day when I was out riding in the mountains, I saw a black blur which I took to be a bridge and I led my horse on to it. It turned out to be a railway trestle and my horse died there. I attempted suicide, after which my life became a horror of existence.''

Over the next five years, Bolton became immersed in programs of drug treatment, including antidepressants, tranquilizers, and sleeping pills. She wanted desperately to prove herself normal. "My only goal was to stay sane so the doctors couldn't put me in a mental hospital.''

She also wanted revenge on the urologist who had performed her original surgery, and decided to take him to court, a process that would ultimately take three years and lead nowhere. "Part of me wanted to kill him, but my conscience would never let me. Instead, I used to sit by my mare's grave and scream his name. The rest of the time I sat in my darkened room, staring at the wall, waiting for the hours to crawl past, till it was time to take my Tuinol and escape for eight hours in a dreamless sleep.''

About a year before she killed, she decided that she would take her own revenge on her urologist: "I had a crossbow and a pellet gun designed to paralyse him and blind him. To prevent him from ever operating again. Not to kill him.''

But ultimately she decided she couldn't go through with the crime and turned herself in to police. "I thought...if I just throw the weapons away I'll go and get them another day when I'm low. I've got to get rid of them...it seemed logical to take them to the police, right. It seems awful dumb to me now, but at the time...I mean, you must realize that my mind was not normal.''

She was taken to court and convicted of a weapons offence.

The judge gave her a discharge, with two conditions — that she stay away from the urologist and see a psychiatrist for a one-year period.

By early 1982 she was becoming increasingly worried about commitment to a mental hospital. She asked her psychiatrist for deep sleep therapy, in which "...every four hours you'd be given sleeping pills, so you were kept asleep the whole three days...I thought that if I could give my brain a total rest from all my thoughts and my anger and everything, that I could carry on a bit longer."

When she came out of the hospital after this experience, she received a letter from her lawyer. She didn't like what he had to say, called him and got no satisfaction. She decided that a threat of violence was the only way out. "I couldn't think of any way that I could get[my lawyer] to phone her [the opposing lawyer] and tell her he'd made a mistake. I couldn't think of any way to do that except at gunpoint."

She put on a couple of sweaters and three coats, loaded her father's rifle, and drove off to confront her advocate. "I walked into his office. I had the gun covered with a pair of coveralls and took the coveralls off. And he just looked at the gun and then he started, big smirk on his face, and he was just sitting back in his chair with his hands behind his head and his feet up on the desk, and he was just leering at me. And he said, 'Who do you think you are, coming in with that thing? Put that silly thing down and get out of here.'"

Bolton recalls that she was stunned, "...his secretary was in the room at the time and he told her to go out and get someone to get this — pointing at me — out of his office. So she brushed past me, went out into the other office and I started to feel panic...fear. And then he just sneered at me, and he said that he was going to phone the police. And he put his hand on the phone."

Bolton pulled the trigger. "There was a huge explosion and his chair spun around and he fell off and rolled into the corner. And I fired again. I later found out that first shot had hit him in the right chest and the second shot had bounced off into the back of his head. Anyway, I drove away very slowly."

The police found her in her car about 20 miles out of town and took her into custody. "Then they just left me alone and I slept for 15 hours, still under the influence of the drugs I had taken for these three days. And I'm a person that doesn't even get eight hours sleep, unless I take five Tuinols at once."

She was convicted of second degree murder and sentenced to life imprisonment, ineligible for parole for 20 years. She believes that her lawyers at trial "didn't do much for my case" and adds, "Who would take my case? Maybe the police were right, maybe nobody in B.C. would want to take my case. That's what the trouble is when you shoot a lawyer."

The B.C. Court of Appeal reduced the parole eligibility to 14 years, and Bolton was ultimately shipped to Kingston's Prison for Women to serve her time. She now feels sorry for her killing, "...and as my own life came back, as my own will to live came back, then I started feeling very guilty and bad about taking a life. But up until then it was just as if someone else had done it, as if it wasn't me because I was all drugged."

She is, however, not sure that she feels the same way about her urologist. "I must be honest here and say that if it had been the urologist I would never have felt any guilt, never ever in my life would I have felt any guilt."

Bolton argues that she should have been convicted of manslaughter, that she wasn't treated fairly by the courts. "I feel if I had a trial in a major city where they weren't so out for my blood, I could tell the whole story, right from 1977. Then I would have had a chance at justice. But I wasn't given that chance."

As 1988 unfolds at the Prison for Women, Sally Bolton argues that she has recovered, and that what she would really like to see is a separate form of housing for women serving life sentences. "Could we have animals, like cats or dogs, in this separate wing? You know, they wouldn't be allowed to wander all over the institution, just a separate wing. Because that's something we miss, like an emotional something towards another being. We're allowed to have fish now, but my God,

I can't get attached to fish, to tell you the truth. But I would love to have a kitten. I would love to have a kitten.''

1   See M. Schiffer, *Mental Disorder and the Criminal Trial Process,* Butterworths, Toronto, 1978, and M. Schiffer, *Psychiatry Behind Bars: A Legal Perspective,*Butterworths, Toronto, 1982.
2   See R.J. Menzies, ''Psychiatry, Dangerousness and Legal Control,'' in N. Boyd, *The Social Dimensions of Law,* Prentice-Hall, Scarborough, 1986, B. Ennis and T. Litwack, ''Psychiatry and the presumption of expertise: flipping coins in the courtroom,'' *62 California Law Review* 1974, 693-752.
3   T.S. Szasz, *The Myth of Mental Illness,* Harper and Row, New York, 1971.
4   See, for example, M.W. Jackson, ''Psychiatric Decision-Making for the Courts: Judges, Psychiatrists, Lay People?'', *9 International Journal of Law and Psychiatry* 507-520, 1986.
5   ''Donnie Armand'' is a pseudonym.
6   ''Vince Moro'' is a pseudonym.
7   In fairness, our criminal law acknowledges that the issue here is social, that psychiatrists have a contributory and not a decision-making role. See, for example, *R. v. Rabey* (1977) 37 C.C.C. (2d) 461, 79 D.L.R. (3d) 414 (Ontario Court of Appeal), affirmed 54 C.C.C. (2d) 1 [1980] 2 S.C.R. 513.
8   P. Reed, R. Gaucher et al., *Homicide in Canada: A Statistical Synopsis*, Statistics Canada, Ottawa, 1976, 132.
9   ''Dirk Rochester'' is a pseudonym.
10 *R. v. Rabey*, 54 Canadian Criminal Cases (2nd Series) 1, 1981.
11 ''Letter to the Commissioner, RCMP, F.P.S. #146606,'' *Valentine Schmidt, Capital Case Files,* RG 13 Series, National Archives, Ottawa, 1.
12 ''Memorandum for the Honourable The Acting Minister of Justice,'' Valentine Schmidt, *Capital Case Files*, note 10, *above*, August 17, 1927, 1.
13 Minutes of Cabinet, Capital Case: John Jacob Vollman, February 12, 13, 14, 1959, Privy Council Office, *Disclosed under the Canadian Access to Information Act*, 1987.
14 ''RCMP File 36 J 636-1,'' *Arthur Bannister, Capital Case Files*, RG 13 Series, National Archives, Ottawa, 1.
15 ''How Mounties Solved the Weird Doll-Baby Murder,'' *New York Sunday Mirror Magazine*, April 12, 1936, 3.

[16] "J.P.S. Cathcart, Interview with Owen Maxwell Feener, May 15, 1961," *Owen "Mickey" Feener, Capital Case Files*, RG 13 Series, National Archives, Ottawa, 6.

[17] "RCMP Division File 784911" in *Owen "Mickey" Feener, Capital Case Files*, note 16, above, 9.

[18] This interchange is described in Ruth Reynolds, "The Great Eastern Oil Justice Story," *The St. John's Evening Telegram*, St. John's, Newfoundland, May 3, 1963, 13.

[19] The Cabinet members in question were referring to the 1961 amendment to the *Criminal Code*, providing for both capital and non-capital murder. See Chapter 1, "Killings: Our History."

[20] Mackenzie "Ken" Stevens, personal communication, January 1988.

[21] See, for example, J.Q. Wilson and R. Herrnstein, *Crime and Human Nature*, Touchstone, New York, 1985. This book, promoted as "the definitive study of the causes of crime," proceeds to examine its subject matter without even the most cursory analysis of the process of criminal definition and treats intelligence as an invariably useful measure of human capabilities. See, particularly, Chapter 6, "Intelligence."

[22] "John Murphy" is a pseudonym.

[23] See note 8, *above*, 109.

[24] "Sally Bolton" is a pseudonym.